COMMODITY TRADER'S ALMANAC 2007

Editor: Scott W. Barrie

Consulting Editor: Jeffrey A. Hirsch

John Wiley & Sons, Inc.

Published by John Wiley & Sons, Inc., Hoboken, New Jersey
Published simultaneously in Canada

Editor Scott W. Barrie (www.commodityalmanac.com)
Data Consultant Lan H. Turner, Gecko Software (www.TRACKNTRADE.com)
Graphic Design Darlene Dion Design
Consulting Editor Jeffrey A. Hirsch, Hirsch Organization

ISBN-13 978-0-471-79219-2
ISBN-10 0-471-79219-5

FOREWORD

We are excited to introduce the inaugural edition of the ***Commodity Trader's Almanac***. Using the *Stock Trader's Almanac*, the Hirsch Organization's flagship product, as a template, we created the ***Commodity Trader's Almanac*** in the same mold and with the same mission statement: provide salient market information at a glance.

Our friend and colleague Scott Barrie was tapped to spearhead this project. Longtime *Stock Trader's Almanac* readers are familiar with Scott as he served as the Data Coordinator for the Almanac from 1998-2004. His background as a floor trader in the futures pits of Chicago and his knowledge of the inner workings of the Hirsch Organization and the Almanac made him an obvious choice.

The ***Commodity Trader's Almanac*** is based on the same tenet that has shaped the Hirsch Organization's research since the late 1960s: There is a cyclical pattern to free markets. There is a reason why sugar surges in the spring much the same way that there is a catalyst to coffee's crash in June. Weather, holidays, and human behavior — to name but a few influencing factors — shape the demand and supply, and therefore the price of a commodity.

In addition to recurring patterns, how commodities impact other markets tells the backstory of the economy. Whether you look at OPEC oil embargoes, the Hunt brothers' attempt to corner silver, or natural catastrophes, exogenous disruptions to the delicate balance of supply and demand — either man-made or *force majeure* — have a ripple effect that causes waves on Wall Street, Main Street, and Pennsylvania Avenue. Arming yourself with a basic understanding of the commodities markets can help you not only survive, but thrive in the futures market, stock market, bond market, or the supermarket in uncertain times.

We carefully crafted this publication to be a practical tool for investors of all categories. Understanding historical patterns will give the seasoned trader a leg up, and the more novice investors a solid foundation as they cut their teeth in the world of commodities. Utilizing Scott's vast experience as a commodities trader and analyst nonpareil, we feel that we have successfully integrated the elements of the *Stock Trader's Almanac* that have made it a perennial bestseller for forty years into a new product that will allow investors to see the commodities market in a new light.

A special thanks to J. Taylor Brown and Christopher Mistal, my trusted partners, for their Herculean efforts, savvy analysis, keen attention to detail, and rapier wit. None of this would be possible without the sturdy shoulders of our founder, mentor, enduring source of inspiration, and my father, Yale Hirsch, to stand on. Also, to our Editorial Director, Pamela van Giessen, your vision, tenacity, and knowledge of the financial market industry have been the guiding forces that brought the *Stock Trader's Almanac* to Wiley and made the ***Commodity Trader's Almanac*** a reality.

Jeffrey A. Hirsch, Hirsch Organization

USER'S GUIDE AND INTRODUCTION TO THE PREMIER EDITION OF THE *COMMODITY TRADER'S ALMANAC*

The ***Commodity Trader's Almanac*** is an annual organizer and databank of seasonal price data on twelve key commodities that update market knowledge by informing you of different market tendencies on a calendar basis.

During the 1990s, commodities were the "ugly, redheaded stepchild" of the stock bull market. Technology-driven gains fueled the economy, leaving basic building materials and the physical assets which drive the world economy in the backseat. However, booms in technology and other service-related industries do not preclude bull markets in commodities. Since 2000, commodity prices have generally risen or have been quite volatile. These conditions offer traders and investors both opportunities and dangers.

In 2005 and 2006, the mining and petroleum industries have proven to be two of the best performing sectors of the economy. It is no wonder. At their recent highs, Gold and Crude Oil futures prices have increased over 65% since 2004. No longer can the astute speculator ignore the building blocks of the modern economy.

The Almanac is intended to be used as a guide to the commodities markets throughout the year, based on data from specific commodities and delivery months. It is a monthly reminder and refresher course that alerts you to both seasonal opportunities and dangers, and furnishes an historical viewpoint by providing pertinent statistics on past market performance as well as the supply/demand trends which create them.

Knowledge of the natural production and consumption cycles of the physical commodities can provide traders, investors, hedgers, and speculators with insight into the fast-paced futures markets.

Each page in the Almanac is designed to either inform the speculator of a specific market opportunity which could be potentially beneficial, educate the trader on the finer points of a particular market, or to provide readers with insight into normal production/consumption cycles of the commodities covered.

All physical commodities have a "normal" supply or demand cycle. For example, Crude Oil consumption often increases during the summer months as a result of increased driving activity. But the astute trader understands that retail demand does not necessarily result in increased futures prices, as price increases often precede demand.

Speculation in the commodity futures markets — or elsewhere in life — is about drawing conclusions from an often incomplete set of previous facts to reach projections about the future.

The ***Commodity Trader's Almanac*** is designed to help traders understand not only the price behavior of the underlying futures but also the supply and demand cycles which create these pricing patterns. Inside the Almanac you will learn:

- How natural production and consumption cycles drive prices during specific times of the year.
- How the futures markets often factor in demand and supply concerns prior to the actual event.
- How similar, but different markets often react more strongly or weakly to the natural consumption/production cycle.
- That prices are often driven by regularly recurring patterns (or cycles) surrounding the calendar year and how often these patterns have continued or reversed.

The Almanac also provides a monthly overview of pertinent statistics and points out a particular futures market which may be poised for a dramatic move. Because futures traders can take either side (long or short) of the market, generally the Almanac highlights a market each month with the highest historical probability to rally or "break" with the best performance in the given direction. Daily performance statistics on each weekly calendar page show the percentage of time the 12 different commodity markets highlighted have rallied on specific trading days historically.

In total, the Almanac is designed to help point speculators, traders, and hedgers in the general direction of the normal natural supply/demand cycle of the market. The Almanac highlights specific strategies you may wish to employ, monthly overviews, and statistics to help hedgers with marketing or purchasing commodities.

The Almanac is intended to be used as a tool to assist market participants in making informed decisions. Within these pages, the historical statistics and studies can serve as a framework and guide when entering a new position (long or short) or deciding to either move a stop loss or add to a position. For hedgers, the Almanac provides a vast array of historical price data, daily probabilities, as well as longer-term studies and average price statistics.

KEY TO CODES & COMMODITY TERMINOLOGY

FND signifies 1st Notice Day for a futures contract in the 2007 Strategy Calendar on pages 10 and 11, or the date upon which all long (purchased) contracts are subject to delivery — as the seller (short) of a futures contract has the right to deliver the underlying commodity of a futures contract on this date. Though short (sold) position holders can maintain positions beyond this point, it is the belief of the author that all traders should look to exit positions in futures contracts on or before 1st Notice Day (FND) to avoid the associated drop in market liquidity normally seen.

OE signifies options expiration in the 2007 Strategy Calendar on pages 10 and 11. This is the date that options on commodity futures contracts expire, and will be converted into futures contracts (or cash in the event of non-delivery futures markets like Lean Hogs). Options traders should be aware that the exercise of a long option will result in a futures position. Futures positions have unlimited risk as well as reward potential — unlike the original long-option position in which the trader only has at risk the original premium paid for the option.

On each calendar page, the Almanac presents the Daily Probabilities for 12 commodity markets: **Crude Oil** (CL), **Natural Gas** (NG), **Gold** (GC), **Silver** (SI), **Soybeans** (S), **CBOT Wheat** (W), **Corn** (C), **Live Cattle** (LC), **Lean Hogs** (LH), **Coffee** (KC), **Sugar** (SB), and **Cocoa** (CC). The numbers represent the percentage of time between January 1987 and December 2005 (or January 1991 and December 2005 in the case of Natural Gas), that the nearby widely traded contract settled the trading day in question higher than the previous day. For complete Daily Probability Calendars, specific contracts used, monthly commodity data, ticker and contract terminology, refer to pages 120 to 183.

Throughout the Almanac, certain other terms are used. "**Basis**" in the futures markets can refer to the difference between cash and futures prices. But "basis" is used throughout the Almanac to indicate a specific contract month. For example, "December weakness basis March Cocoa" means that the March Cocoa contract is the specific delivery month that is weak in December.

"**Rally**" refers to a period of price increases. A "**break**" is the opposite. Breaks refer to periods of price decreases, or corrections.

It has been both a joy and an undertaking to begin to relate my observations of the inner workings and patterns of the commodity futures markets. This inaugural edition, and future editions, can by no means cover all there is to know about commodities. But it is our intention to make it an evolving tool that responds to users' needs. We are constantly searching for new insights and nuances about the commodities market and welcome any suggestions from our readers.

Have a healthy and prosperous 2007!

Scott W. Barrie

2007 COMMODITY OUTLOOK

Opportunities for traders in 2007 should, at the very least, be interesting. Three significant macroeconomic forces will continue to drive commodity prices: global demand, decreased political stability in key producing countries, and dwindling supplies.

Increased demand for commodities comes from developing nations, especially China. China has become the world's largest consumer — and in some cases, the largest producer as well — of steel, cement, and other commodities. With robust economic growth at a double digit pace, China's appetite for raw materials spanning the commodity spectrum will remain strong and support prices generally across the board.

India — the most densely populated country — is also another force on consumption. Per capita income is rising, and with the increase in income comes an increased appetite not only for goods and foods, but also industrial commodities (metals and petroleum). Indians value gold and other precious metals in the form of jewelry not only as a means of adornment, but also as a store of wealth and a currency in many regions of this highly populated country.

Strong demand from China and India is a trend that is expected to continue in 2007. Generally, commodity prices are kept in check by increasing productivity. Producers tend to be efficient, generating supply increases above normal growth in demand. However, several commodities may not benefit from this trend in the coming years for political reasons. The Iraq war, tension over Iran's nuclear ambitions, and terrorism are destabilizing access to the world's oil reserves in the Middle East.

South America is nationalizing efficient global multinational producers, potentially interfering with petroleum and transportation from this region, while Russia is looking more and more unstable. Several countries (Iran, Venezuela, and Bolivia) are looking to price their exports in Euros (€) as opposed to U.S. Dollars ($), a move which could also add increased volatility to world trade. Consumers may well be forced to pay more for secure supplies as future supply from these regions could be subject to short-term interruptions which can tip the supply-to-demand balance violently — forcing the marketplace to put "risk premiums" on prices above levels usually dictated by normal supply and demand trends.

The combination of strong global demand coupled with political uncertainty has impacted the commodities markets most dramatically the past several years. Gold prices reached their highest levels in over two decades in 2006, while petroleum markets are in uncharted territory. Metals and petroleum markets are struggling with limited supply. Inventory levels have fallen well below those of years past. Such a situation makes pricing even more vulnerable to spikes, as consumers have little inventory to draw upon in times of supply interruptions. The efficiency of the marketplace is not to be doubted.

The Law of Demand dictates that as prices rise, consumption will fall as end users either abstain or find alternatives. For example, with record-high petroleum prices, the automobile industry is selling more hybrid cars, and the use of alternative fuels (like ethanol) is increasing. Such substitution could be a boon for commodities like sugar and corn, as they are used more for the production of petroleum substitutes. Silver may benefit from increased jewelry demand, as price-conscious consumers switch to jewelry made from this cheaper metal. Producers in other commodities are already reacting to higher petroleum prices by planting crops which are less fuel-intensive (like soybeans versus corn). High petroleum prices of 2006 may be beneficial to substitute commodities like corn and sugar in 2007; gold at elevated levels may be a boon to silver or possibly copper in 2007 due to substitution as well.

Trading in 2007 will definitely be interesting! Though global macroeconomic factors are lining up for a continuation of the trend to higher commodity prices, traders need to be aware of the natural supply and demand factors which have affected prices year in and year out for decades. The increasing likelihood of supply interruptions will be multiplied during times when future supply is at risk, or during times when usage tends to be strong. However, during periods when future supply is known, or demand tends to be weak (stable), such exogenous forces may not have as strong an influence. Almanac readers should be well-prepared to face 2007 and all of the wild cards it will throw at traders (political unrest, weather, plight, and pestilence) as they are armed with a historical reference to put these events into perspective and make rational speculative decisions.

THE 2007 COMMODITY TRADER'S ALMANAC

CONTENTS

2007 STRATEGY CALENDAR

	MONDAY	TUESDAY	WEDNESDAY	THURSDAY	FRIDAY	SATURDAY	SUNDAY
JANUARY	1 JANUARY New Year's Day	2	3	4	5	6	7
	8	9	10	11	12	13	14
	15 Martin Luther King Day	16	17 OE:CL(G)	18	19	20	21
	22 FND: CL(G)	23	24	25 OE: GC(G)	26 OE: NG(G)	27	28
	29 FND: NG(G)	30	31 FND: GC(G)	1 FEBRUARY	2 OE: LC(G), CC(H)	3	4
FEBRUARY	5 FND: LC(G)	6	7	8	9 OE: KC(H)	10	11
	12	13	14♥ FND: LH(G)	15	16	17	18
	19 Presidents' Day	20 FND: CL(H, KC(H))	21 Ash Wednesday	22 OE: SI(H, SB(H)	23 OE: NG(H), S(H), C(H), W(H)	24	25
	26 FND: NG(H)	27 FND: S(H), C(H), W(H)	28 FND: SI(H), SB(H)	1 MARCH	2	3	4
MARCH	5	6	7	8	9 OE: KC(K)	10	11 Daylight Saving Time Begins
	12	13	14	15 OE: CL(J)	16	17 ♣ St. Patrick's Day	18
	19	20 FND: CL(J)	21	22	23	24	25
	26	27 OE: NG(J), GC(J)	28 FND: NG(J)	29	30	31	1 APRIL
APRIL	2	3 Passover	4	5 OE: LC(J), CC(K)	6 Good Friday	7	8 Easter
	9 FND: LC(J)	10	11	12	13	14	15
	16 FND: LH(J) OE: LH(J)	17 FND: CC(K) OE: CL(K)	18	19	20 FND: CL(K), KC(K) OE: S(K), W(K), C(K)	21	22
	23	24	25 OE: NG(K), SI(K) OE: SB(K)	26 FND: NG(K)	27 FND: S(K), W(K), C(K)	28	29
	30 FND: GC(J), SI(K), SB(K)	1 MAY	2	3	4	5	6
MAY	7	8	9	10	11	12	13 Mother's Day
	14	15	16	17 OE: CL(M)	18	19	20
	21	22 FND: CL(M)	23	24 OE:GC(M)	25 OE: NG(M)	26	27
	28 Memorial Day	29 FND: NG(K)	30	31	1 JUNE OE: LC(M), CC(N)	2	3
JUNE	4 FND: LC(M)	5	6	7	8 OE: KC(N)	9	10
	11	12	13	14 FND: LH(M)	15 OE:CL(N)	16	17 Father's Day
	18 FND: CC(N)	19	20 FND: CL(N)	21 FND: KC(N)	22 OE: S(N), W(N), C(N)	23	24
	25	26 OE: NG(N), SI(N), SB(N)	27 FND: NG(N)	28 FND: S(N), W(N), C(N)	29 FND: GC(M), SI(N), SB(N)	30	1 JULY

Market closed on shaded weekdays; closes early when half-shaded.

2007 STRATEGY CALENDAR

MONDAY	TUESDAY	WEDNESDAY	THURSDAY	FRIDAY	SATURDAY	SUNDAY	
2	3	4 Independence Day	5	6	7	8	
9	10	11	12	13	14	15	JULY
16 FND: LH(N)	17 OE: CL(Q)	18	19	20 FND: CL(Q)	21	22	
23	24 OE: S(Q)	25	26 OE: NG(Q), GC(Q)	27 FND: NG(Q)	28	29	
30 FND: S(Q)	31 FND: GC(Q)	1 AUGUST	2	3 OE: LC(Q), CC(U)	4	5	
6 FND: LC(Q)	7	8	9	10 OE: KC(U)	11	12	
13	14 FND: LH(Q) OE: LH(Q)	15	16 OE: CL(U)	17	18	19	AUGUST
20 FND: LC(U)	21 FND: CL(U)	22	23 FND: KC(U)	24 OE: S(U), W(U), C(U)	25	26	
27	28 OE: NG(U), SI(U), SB(V)	29 FND: NG(U)	30 FND: S(U), W(U), C(U)	31 FND: SI(U)	1 SEPTEMBER	2	
3 Labor Day	4	5	6	7 OE: LC(U)	8	9	
10 FND: LH(U)	11	12	13 Rosh Hashanah	14	15	16	SEPTEMBER
17 FND: CL(V)	18	19	20 FND: LC(V)	21	22 Yom Kippur	23	
24	25 OE: NG(V), GC(V)	26 FND: NG(V)	27	28 FND: GC(V) SB(V)	29	30 FND: SB(V)	
1 OCTOBER	2	3	4	5 OE: LC(V)	6	7	
8 Columbus Day FND: LC(V)	9	10	11	12 FND: LH(V) OE: LH(V)	13	14	OCTOBER
15	16	17 OE: CL(X)	18	19	20	21	
22 FND: CL(X)	23	24	25	26 OE: NG(X), S(X)	27	28	
29 FND: NG(X)	30 FND: S(X)	31	1 NOVEMBER	2 OE: CC(Z)	3	4 Daylight Saving Time Ends	
5	6 Election Day	7	8	9 OE: KC(Z)	10	11 Veterans' Day	
12	13 OE: CL(Z)	14	15 FND: CC(Z)	16 FND: CL(Z)	17	18	NOVEMBER
19	20 FND: KC(Z)	21	22 Thanksgiving	23 OE: W(Z), C(Z)	24	25	
26	27 OE: NG(Z), GC(Z), SI(Z)	28 FND: NG(Z)	29 FND: W(Z), C(Z)	30 FND: GC(Z), SI(Z)	1 DECEMBER	2	
3	4	5 Chanukah	6	7 OE: LC(Z)	8	9	
10 FND: LC(Z)	11	12	13	14 FND: LH(Z) OE: LH(Z)	15	16	DECEMBER
17	18	19	20	21	22	23	
24	25 Christmas	26	27	28	29	30	
31	1 JANUARY New Year's Day	2	3	4	5	6	

JANUARY ALMANAC

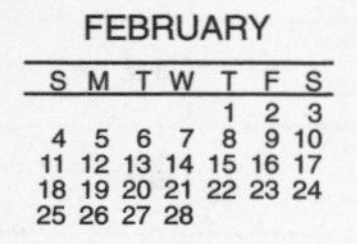

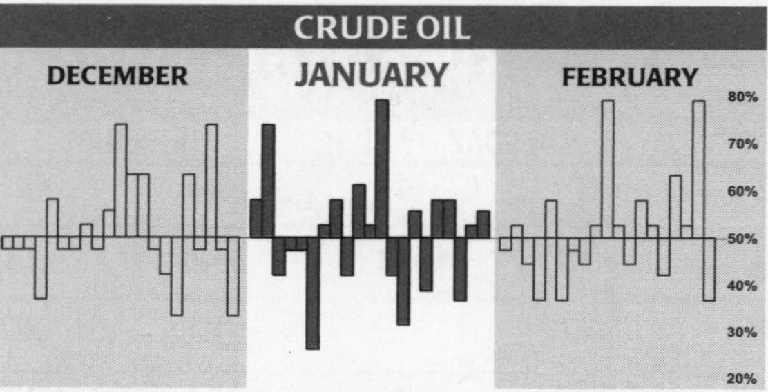

Market Probability Chart above is a graphic representation of Crude Oil futures taken from the Market Probability Calendar on page 124

PETROLEUM FUTURES: End of previous year Crude Oil weakness commonly reversed in January ◆ Breaks in March Crude Oil of -$1.00/bbl or more during December have seen March Crude Oil settle above these levels in January on 12 of last 14 occurrences ◆ Worst month on record for Natural Gas futures ◆ June Natural Gas futures reversed January weakness on 8 of 10 last occurrences.

METALS FUTURES: Worst month on record for Gold since 1987 ◆ April Gold down an average of -$3.85/ounce during January as jewelry demand wanes post-holidays ◆ Platinum futures gain relative to Gold in 1st quarter — see page 18.

GRAIN FUTURES: January is worst month for Soybeans ◆ March Soybeans up 5 / down 14 ◆ All but one January rally basis March CBOT Wheat has been reversed in February (see page 16) ◆ May Corn is the only grain to post a gain in January/February period on average.

LIVESTOCK FUTURES: Live Cattle futures begin year strong up 15 of last 19, gaining an average of +0.67 cents/lb ◆ December's monthly high exceeded in January 16 of 19 in Cattle ◆ 2nd-strongest month on record for Hog futures ◆ January's monthly direction predicts April hogs February direction (13 of 19).

SOFTS FUTURES: January breaks in Sugar tend to be continued in February (7 of 10) ◆ March Sugar down in January 10 / up 9 ◆ December weakness basis March Cocoa continues in January (9 of 11) ◆ March Cocoa down in January 13 of 19 ◆ Though down usually, March Cocoa has had two major rallies in January (in 2003 & 2001) due to political unrest on the Ivory Coast.

COMMODITY SPOTLIGHT CRUDE OIL

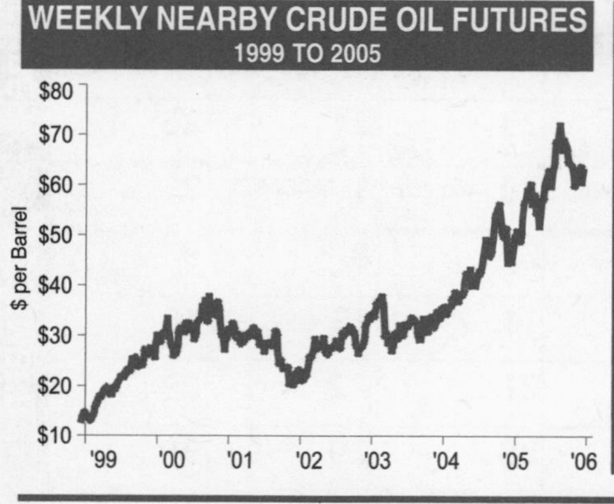

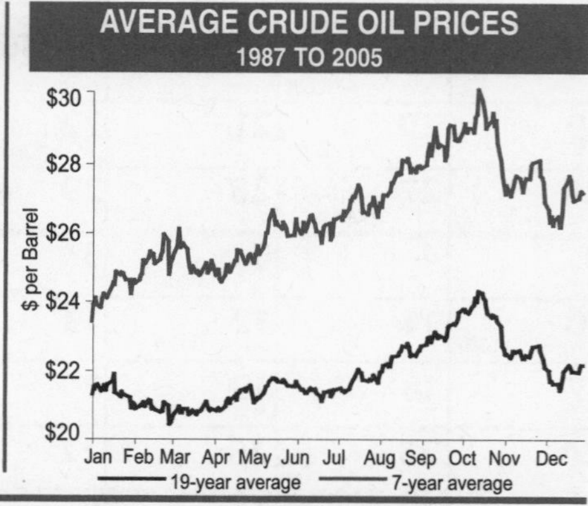

Petroleum prices are demand-driven primarily, with prices often rising in anticipation of the driving and heating seasons. But the petroleum markets also tend to be an excellent barometer of world tensions, rising in times of political uncertainty — especially in producing nations.

JANUARY 2007

New Year's Day (Market Closed)

MONDAY
1

In the stock market those who expect history to repeat itself exactly are doomed to failure. — Yale Hirsch

TUESDAY
2

CL	57.9	**NG**	47.4	**GC**	78.9	**SI**	63.2
S	73.7	**W**	52.6	**C**	55.6	**LC**	52.6
LH	47.4	**KC**	42.1	**CC**	44.4	**SB**	73.7

There is no tool to change human nature…people are prone to recurring bouts of optimism and pessimism that manifest themselves from time to time in the buildup or cessation of speculative excesses.
— Alan Greenspan (Fed Chairman, July 18, 2001, monetary policy report to Congress)

WEDNESDAY
3

CL	72.2	**NG**	42.1	**GC**	26.3	**SI**	36.8
S	42.1	**W**	63.2	**C**	38.9	**LC**	38.9
LH	66.7	**KC**	66.7	**CC**	52.6	**SB**	47.4

Human beings, who are almost unique in having the ability to learn from the experience of others, are also remarkable for their apparent disinclination to do so. — Douglas Adams

THURSDAY
4

CL	47.4	**NG**	52.6	**GC**	31.6	**SI**	42.1
S	68.4	**W**	63.2	**C**	57.9	**LC**	38.9
LH	63.2	**KC**	61.1	**CC**	42.1	**SB**	31.6

Every great advance in natural knowledge has involved the absolute rejection of authority.
— Thomas H. Huxley (British scientist and humanist, defender of Darwinism, 1825–1895)

FRIDAY
5

CL	47.4	**NG**	55.6	**GC**	42.1	**SI**	63.2
S	57.9	**W**	66.7	**C**	89.5	**LC**	55.6
LH	66.7	**KC**	63.2	**CC**	61.1	**SB**	68.4

In a bear market everyone loses. And the winner is the one who loses the least. — Richard Russell (*Dow Theory Letters*)

SATURDAY
6

SUNDAY
7

NEW YEAR WEAKNESS CREATES BARGAINS IN CRUDE OIL

January tends to be a strong month for Crude Oil futures. March Crude Oil futures gained 13 times during January in the last 19 years. However, breaks in January are not uncommon, though they tend to be extremely short-lived.

Since 1988, March Crude Oil futures have broken -$1.90/bbl on average below their December closes to their lows during the first two weeks of January. Fourteen times these early-January breaks have exceeded -$1.00/bbl, with the worst break of -$4.39/bbl occurring in 2003. However, following these breaks in excess of -$1.00/bbl, March Crude Oil futures have finished the month of January above these levels 12 times (85.7%) during the aforementioned period.

MARCH CRUDE OIL FUTURES DOLLARS PER BARREL CHANGES

Rally	December-January Rally			January Break		January 1st 2 wks Low-Close		
	Prev Dec Close	Jan High	Dec Close-Jan high	Jan Low 1st 2 wks	Dec Close Jan Low	Jan Close	1st 2 wks Low-Jan Close	Jan Change
1988	$16.59	$18.55	$1.96	$14.70	– $1.89	$16.94	$2.24	$0.35
1989	16.69	16.75	0.06	14.83	– 1.86	17.03	2.20	0.34
1990	21.49	21.65	0.16	19.38	– 2.11	22.68	3.30	1.19
1991	27.80	29.10	1.30	24.00	– 3.80	21.54	– 2.46	– 6.26
1992	19.12	21.07	1.95	18.40	– 0.72	18.90	0.50	– 0.22
1993	19.71	20.15	0.44	18.86	– 0.85	20.26	1.40	0.55
1994	14.50	15.98	1.48	14.32	– 0.18	15.19	0.87	0.69
1995	17.71	18.05	0.34	16.57	– 1.14	18.39	1.82	0.68
1996	19.06	19.08	0.02	17.79	– 1.27	17.74	– 0.05	– 1.32
1997	24.67	25.12	0.45	22.20	– 2.47	24.15	1.95	– 0.52
1998	17.83	19.34	1.51	17.70	– 0.13	17.21	– 0.49	– 0.62
1999	12.19	13.15	0.96	11.10	– 1.09	12.75	1.65	0.56
2000	24.79	25.99	1.20	22.80	– 1.99	27.64	4.84	2.85
2001	25.98	32.30	6.32	25.14	– 0.84	28.66	3.52	2.68
2002	20.11	21.60	1.49	18.45	– 1.66	19.48	1.03	– 0.63
2003	30.59	32.80	2.21	26.20	– 4.39	33.51	7.31	2.92
2004	32.28	33.40	1.12	29.20	– 3.08	33.05	3.85	0.77
2005	43.63	49.18	5.55	41.00	– 2.63	48.20	7.20	4.57
2006	61.90	63.45	1.55	57.95	– 3.95	67.92	9.97	6.02
Averages			**$1.58**		**– $1.90**	**$2.67**	**$0.77**	
			# Jan Breaks < -$1.00		**14**	**< -$1.00 Break Avg**	**$3.20**	
						# Up	**16**	**13**
						# Down	**3**	**6**

Since January 1988, only 5 years have not seen a break in the first 2 weeks of January of -$1.00/bbl or more below the December close: 1992, 1993, 1994, 1998, and 2001. Following the 14 -$1.00/bbl breaks in January, March Crude Oil futures have finished higher 12 times for an average gain of +$3.20/bbl.

Waiting for a $1 break in early January is an excellent opportunity to establish positions for a January low-to-close rally.

JANUARY

MONDAY
8

CL 44.4	**NG** 47.4	**GC** 63.2	**SI** 68.4
S 55.6	**W** 68.4	**C** 61.1	**LC** 68.4
LH 47.4	**KC** 57.9	**CC** 42.1	**SB** 83.3

Education is a progressive discovery of our own ignorance. — Will Durant

TUESDAY
9

CL 33.3	**NG** 66.7	**GC** 47.4	**SI** 47.4
S 47.4	**W** 61.1	**C** 47.4	**LC** 55.6
LH 72.2	**KC** 52.6	**CC** 36.8	**SB** 42.1

Big money is made in the stock market by being on the right side of major moves. I don't believe in swimming against the tide. — Martin Zweig

WEDNESDAY
10

CL 47.4	**NG** 47.4	**GC** 57.9	**SI** 55.6
S 52.6	**W** 33.3	**C** 47.4	**LC** 73.7
LH 47.4	**KC** 63.2	**CC** 42.1	**SB** 47.4

The heights by great men reached and kept, were not attained by sudden flight, but they, while their companions slept, were toiling upward in the night. — Henry Wadsworth Longfellow

THURSDAY
11

CL 47.4	**NG** 38.9	**GC** 42.1	**SI** 31.6
S 36.8	**W** 52.6	**C** 38.9	**LC** 63.2
LH 57.9	**KC** 42.1	**CC** 57.9	**SB** 52.6

The worst trades are generally when people freeze and start to pray and hope rather than take some action. — Robert Mnuchin (Goldman, Sachs)

FRIDAY
12

CL 31.6	**NG** 42.1	**GC** 57.9	**SI** 42.1
S 47.4	**W** 57.9	**C** 47.4	**LC** 42.1
LH 47.4	**KC** 47.4	**CC** 57.9	**SB** 36.8

The facts are unimportant! It's what they are perceived to be that determines the course of events. — R. Earl Hadady

SATURDAY
13

SUNDAY
14

FADE JANUARY RALLIES IN MARCH CBOT WHEAT

A combination of increased crop marketing and transportation problems tends to weigh on Chicago Board of Trade (CBOT) Wheat futures at the beginning of the year.

At the end of the calendar year, producers limit crop marketing because if they postpone sales into the New Year, the associated tax burden can be pushed forward into the following tax year. As such, sales at the end of December tend to be light, and increase in January and especially February. These increased sales are difficult to move by barge during the winter, hence supplies tend to build up in the interior of the nation, pressuring prices.

This dynamic can readily be seen by the fact that since 1988 all but one (2006) of the January rallies in the March CBOT Wheat futures have reversed in February. March CBOT Wheat futures have also declined in 15 of the last 19 years during February under these pressures. Wheat traders should be very skeptical of strength at the beginning of the year, anticipating a February break, especially after a January rally.

MARCH CBOT WHEAT FUTURES CENTS PER BUSHEL CHANGES

Date	Prev Dec Close	Jan Close	Jan Change	Feb High	Feb Low	February Break Jan Close-Feb Low	Feb Close	Feb Change
1988	310 3/4	326	15 1/4	339	309 1/2	– 16 1/2	315 1/2	– 10 1/2
1989	440	440 1/2	1/2	439 1/2	419 1/2	– 21	436 1/4	– 4 1/4
1990	409 1/4	375 3/4	– 33 1/2	398 1/4	373 1/4	– 2 1/2	393 1/4	17 1/2
1991	260 1/2	263	2 1/2	263 1/2	248	– 15	259 3/4	– 3 1/4
1992	404 3/4	440 1/4	35 1/2	463 1/4	401	– 39 1/4	401 1/2	– 38 3/4
1993	353 3/4	380	26 1/4	380 1/2	356 1/4	– 23 3/4	372 1/4	– 7 3/4
1994	378 1/4	371 3/4	– 6 1/2	378 1/2	340	– 31 3/4	342 1/2	– 29 1/4
1995	401 1/2	373 1/2	– 28	378	349	– 24 1/2	349 3/4	– 23 3/4
1996	512 1/4	519 1/2	7 1/4	533	495	– 24 1/2	512 1/2	– 7
1997	381 1/4	359 3/4	– 21 1/2	380	351	– 8 3/4	373	13 1/4
1998	325 3/4	337 1/4	11 1/2	347	316	– 21 1/4	327 1/2	– 9 3/4
1999	276 1/4	275 1/2	– 3/4	274 1/2	236 1/2	– 39	237 1/4	– 38 1/4
2000	248 1/2	256 1/4	7 3/4	273 1/2	244	– 12 1/4	247	– 9 1/4
2001	279 1/2	273	– 6 1/2	273	256 1/4	– 16 3/4	265	– 8
2002	289	286	– 3	288 1/4	266 1/4	– 19 3/4	267 1/4	– 18 3/4
2003	325	320 1/2	– 4 1/2	338	308 1/2	– 12	312 1/2	– 8
2004	377	389	12	395	364	– 25	380 3/4	– 8 1/4
2005	307 1/2	291	– 16 1/2	337 1/2	287	– 4	337 1/4	46 1/4
2006	339 1/4	343 1/4	4	378	337 1/2	– 5 3/4	370 1/4	27
	Averages		**0**			**– 19**		**– 6 1/4**
	# Up		**10**		**Subseq Avg Break**	**– 20 1/2**		**– 7 1/4**
						# Up Feb After Up Jan		**1**
						# Down Feb After Up Jan		**9**

JANUARY

Martin Luther King Jr. Day (Market Closed)

MONDAY
15

Genius is one percent inspiration and ninety-nine percent perspiration.
— Thomas Alva Edison (American inventor, 1093 patents, 1847–1931)

TUESDAY
16

CL	44.4	**NG**	47.4	**GC**	42.1	**SI**	47.4
S	47.4	**W**	57.9	**C**	61.1	**LC**	61.1
LH	38.9	**KC**	52.6	**CC**	47.4	**SB**	22.2

I never buy at the bottom and I always sell too soon. — Baron Nathan Rothchild's success formula (London financier, 1777–1836)

WEDNESDAY
17

CL	52.6	**NG**	73.7	**GC**	27.8	**SI**	66.7
S	61.1	**W**	36.8	**C**	68.4	**LC**	47.4
LH	47.4	**KC**	38.9	**CC**	42.1	**SB**	66.7

I am glad that I paid so little attention to good advice; had I abided by it I might have been saved from my most valuable mistakes.
— Gene Fowler (Journalist, screenwriter, film director, biographer, 1890–1960)

THURSDAY
18

CL	66.7	**NG**	55.6	**GC**	68.4	**SI**	72.2
S	57.9	**W**	47.4	**C**	52.6	**LC**	44.4
LH	66.7	**KC**	57.9	**CC**	63.2	**SB**	36.8

If the world were a logical place, men would ride sidesaddle. — Rita Mae Brown

FRIDAY
19

CL	31.6	**NG**	42.1	**GC**	57.9	**SI**	42.1
S	47.4	**W**	57.9	**C**	47.4	**LC**	42.1
LH	47.4	**KC**	47.4	**CC**	57.9	**SB**	36.8

Under capitalism, the seller chases after the buyer, and that makes both of them work better; under socialism, the buyer chases the seller, and neither has time to work. — Andrei Sakharov's Uncle Ivan

SATURDAY
20

SUNDAY
21

A TALE OF TWO DEMAND STRUCTURES: PLATINUM VS. GOLD IN THE 1ST QUARTER

Platinum is used primarily by the automotive industry in the production of catalytic converters, and in jewelry and electronics as well. The lion's share of the demand for Gold comes from the jewelry industry.

The demand for Gold tends to wane in the first quarter, after the holiday shopping season is over. At the same time, the demand for Platinum tends to increase, as the automotive industry begins gearing up production for the release of new model year cars. As such, Platinum prices tend towards strength in the 1st quarter, while Gold prices tend to languish.

During the 19-year period from January 1988 to March 2006, April Platinum futures have gained relative to April Gold futures in 17 years (89.5%). On average, April Platinum has gained $29.6/oz relative to April Gold.

In the world of commodity trading, a position entailing buying (long) one commodity and selling (short) a similar but different commodity is known as an "Intercommodity" spread (see page 26) position — like long April Platinum and short April Gold. Such positions benefit when the long (purchased) contract gains in value relative to the short (sold) contract, as April Platinum has done relative to April Gold futures in 17 of the last 19 years from the beginning of January through the end of March.

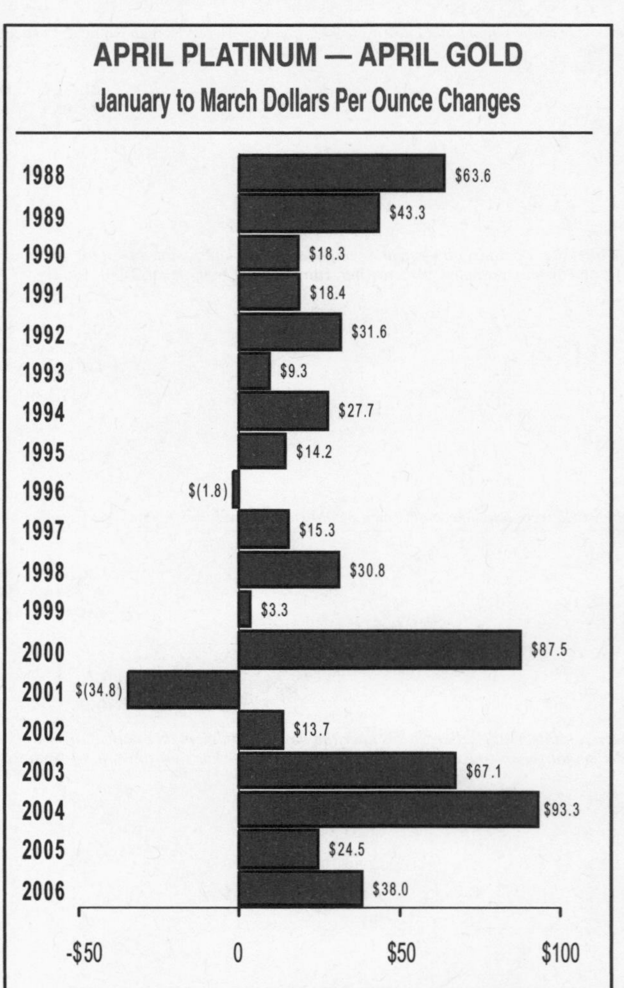

In order to take advantage of this "Inter-Market" spread properly, traders have to even out the contract sizes. Platinum futures represent 50 ounces of Platinum, while Gold futures represent 100 ounces of Gold. As such, traders must purchase 2 contracts of Platinum, and sell 1 contract of Gold, so each futures position represents 100 ounces.

Long 2 Platinum versus short 1 Gold futures contract is an exchange-recognized spread position and as such may be subject to lower margin requirements, though not necessarily, as margins are subject to change without notice.

MONDAY **22**

CL 52.6	NG 36.8	GC 57.9	SI 52.6
S 57.9	W 66.7	C 44.4	LC 26.3
LH 36.8	KC 44.4	CC 63.2	SB 61.1

As investors, we are only the limited product of our own experiences and therefore vulnerable unless we read and assimilate the accumulated wisdom of the great ones. And financial history definitely tends to repeat itself. — Barton Biggs

TUESDAY **23**

CL 36.8	NG 36.8	GC 63.2	SI 52.6
S 52.6	W 36.8	C 31.6	LC 38.9
LH 36.8	KC 55.6	CC 52.6	SB 42.1

There are no secrets to success. Don't waste your time looking for them. Success is the result of perfection, hard work, learning from failure, loyalty to those for whom you work, and persistence. — General Colin Powell

WEDNESDAY **24**

CL 52.6	NG 47.4	GC 36.8	SI 68.4
S 38.9	W 42.1	C 61.1	LC 47.4
LH 63.2	KC 57.9	CC 44.4	SB 55.6

The men who can manage men manage the men who manage only things, and the men who can manage money manage all. — Will Durant

THURSDAY **25**

CL 57.9	NG 47.4	GC 57.9	SI 57.9
S 68.4	W 55.6	C 66.7	LC 63.2
LH 57.9	KC 31.6	CC 42.1	SB 47.4

With enough inside information and a million dollars, you can go broke in a year. — Warren Buffett

FRIDAY **26**

CL 55.6	NG 52.6	GC 61.1	SI 63.2
S 36.8	W 44.4	C 55.6	LC 47.4
LH 47.4	KC 61.1	CC 55.6	SB 31.6

When a country lives on borrowed time, borrowed money, and borrowed energy, it is just begging the markets to discipline it in their own way at their own time. Usually the markets do it in an orderly way — except when they don't.
— Thomas L. Friedman (Op-ed columnist, *New York Times,* February 24, 2005)

SATURDAY **27**

SUNDAY **28**

FEBRUARY ALMANAC

FEBRUARY

S	M	T	W	T	F	S
				1	2	3
4	5	6	7	8	9	10
11	12	13	14	15	16	17
18	19	20	21	22	23	24
25	26	27	28			

MARCH

S	M	T	W	T	F	S
				1	2	3
4	5	6	7	8	9	10
11	12	13	14	15	16	17
18	19	20	21	22	23	24
25	26	27	28	29	30	31

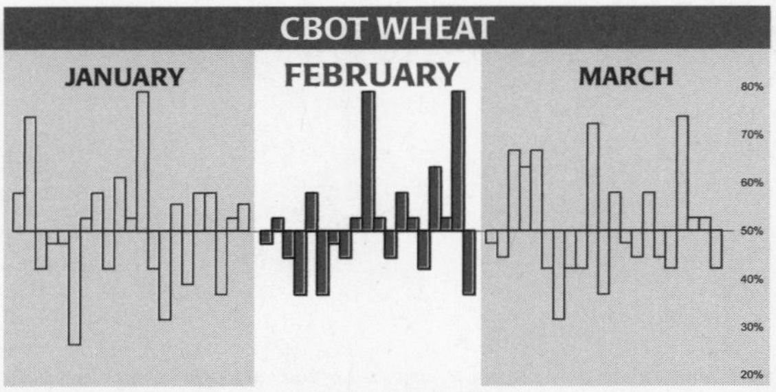

Market Probability Chart above is a graphic representation of CBOT Wheat futures taken from the Market Probability Calendar on page 149

PETROLEUM FUTURES: Crude Oil futures mixed in February (up 9 / down 10) ◆ February breaks reversed in March (7 of 8) basis June Crude ◆ Best Februarys in Natural Gas follow strong Januarys ◆ June Natural Gas rallies in February continue in March (8 of 10).

METALS FUTURES: 1st quarter gold demand is usually weak ◆ Platinum and Silver tend to gain relative to Gold ◆ April Gold down 12 / up 7 in last 19 years ◆ May Silver up 8 / down 11 ◆ Despite poor batting averages, May Silver gained an average of 4.2 cents/ounce in February since 1987 ◆ Worst Februarys have followed January weakness.

GRAIN FUTURES: March CBOT Wheat down 15 of last 19 ◆ Worst Februarys have followed January strength in Wheat ◆ 9 of 11 March CBOT Wheat rallies in January have been reversed in February ◆ Soybeans tend towards strength as southern hemisphere producers (Brazil/Argentina) begin harvest ◆ 9 of last 12 February rallies have continued through March basis May Soybeans.

LIVESTOCK FUTURES: Generally a strong month for Live Cattle (up +9.575 cents/lb) ◆ 10 of 15 January rallies have continued through February basis April Live Cattle ◆ Mixed month for Hog futures (up 8 / down 11) ◆ Watch for breaks following January strength in April Hogs ◆ 7 of 11 February rallies have continued through March basis June Hogs.

SOFTS FUTURES: January weakness continues in February (7 of 10) basis May Sugar ◆ February weakness is often reversed in March (7 of 10) basis May Sugar ◆ Ivory Coast main crop harvest finale causes February weakness in May Cocoa to continue through March (6 of 8).

COMMODITY SPOTLIGHT CBOT WHEAT

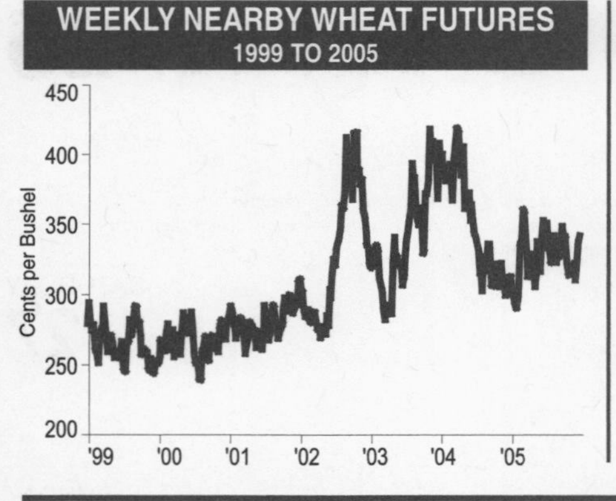

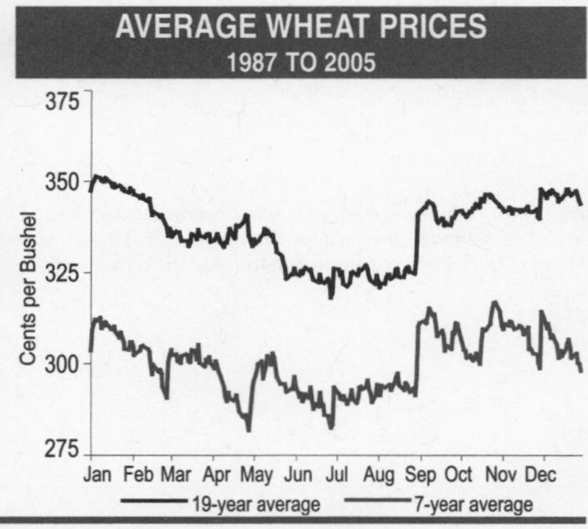

The combination of dwindling winter risk coupled with increased wheat sales to meet tax and lease obligations pressures CBOT Wheat futures in February (down 15 of last 19).

JANUARY/FEBRUARY

MONDAY **29**

CL 47.4	NG 47.4	GC 36.8	SI 38.9
S 47.4	W 47.4	C 44.4	LC 47.4
LH 47.4	KC 31.6	CC 36.8	SB 44.4

Chance favors the informed mind. — Louis Pasteur (French chemist, founder of microbiology, 1822–1895)

TUESDAY **30**

CL 66.7	NG 52.6	GC 33.3	SI 44.4
S 36.8	W 44.4	C 38.9	LC 36.8
LH 44.4	KC 42.1	CC 57.9	SB 33.3

In investing, the return you want should depend on whether you want to eat well or sleep well. — J. Kenfield Morley

WEDNESDAY **31**

CL 44.4	NG 44.4	GC 31.6	SI 36.8
S 31.6	W 52.6	C 33.3	LC 42.1
LH 47.4	KC 36.8	CC 21.1	SB 47.4

Good judgment comes from experience, and often experience comes from bad judgment. — Rita Mae Brown

THURSDAY **1**

CL 44.4	NG 44.4	GC 31.6	SI 36.8
S 47.4	W 72.2	C 33.3	LC 55.6
LH 52.6	KC 36.8	CC 21.1	SB 47.4

When the market goes against you, you hope that every day will be the last day — and you lose more than you should had you not listened to hope. And when the market goes your way, you become fearful that the next day will take away your profit and you get out — too soon. The successful trader has to fight these two deep-seated instincts. — Jesse Livermore

FRIDAY **2**

CL 47.4	NG 55.6	GC 66.7	SI 57.9
S 38.9	W 68.4	C 55.6	LC 44.4
LH 52.6	KC 57.9	CC 47.4	SB 26.3

Science (or "speculation") is a wonderful thing if one does not have to earn one's living at it.
— Albert Einstein (German/American physicist, 1921 Nobel Prize, 1879–1955)

SATURDAY **3**

SUNDAY **4**

THE FABLED FEBRUARY BREAK IN WINTER WHEAT

Winter Wheat, the type represented by the Chicago Board of Trade (CBOT) Wheat futures, is planted in October/November and harvested during the summer. Typically, near year-end, farmers tend to postpone marketing (sales) of their crops for tax abatement purposes into the New Year — effectively postponing tax payments on sales into the following tax year.

However, as the New Year rolls forward, cash-flow management forces many producers to sell. Typically in March and April, lease payments and taxes are due. Transportation difficulties along the major waterways cause supply excesses near production centers, adding to price pressures in February.

These pressures on prices can be seen by the fact that March CBOT Wheat futures have declined in February 15 times (78.9%) during the 19-year period from 1988 to 2006. Since 1988, March CBOT Wheat futures have lost a total of -120 3/4 cents/bu (average -6 1/4) for the whole month February and fell a total of -690 cents/bu (average -36 1/4) for the Janaury high to the February low.

Traders should note that the worst February CBOT Wheat breaks have followed January rallies — see page 16 — proving that the "Trend Is Not Always Your Friend" in the commodity futures markets.

MARCH CBOT WHEAT FUTURES CENTS PER BUSHEL CHANGES

						February Breaks		
Date	Jan High	Jan Low	Jan Close	Feb High	Feb Low	Jan High-Feb Low	Feb Close	Feb Change
1988	336 1/2	311 1/4	326	339	309 1/2	– 27	315 1/2	– 10 1/2
1989	449	428 1/2	440 1/2	439 1/2	419 1/2	– 29 1/2	436 1/4	– 4 1/4
1990	412	371 1/2	375 3/4	398 1/4	373 1/4	– 38 3/4	393 1/4	17 1/2
1991	264	244 1/2	263	263 1/2	248	– 16	259 3/4	– 3 1/4
1992	442 3/4	392 1/2	440 1/4	463 1/4	401	– 41 3/4	401 1/2	– 38 3/4
1993	393	353	380	380 1/2	356 1/4	– 36 3/4	372 1/4	– 7 3/4
1994	394 1/2	361	371 3/4	378 1/2	340	– 54 1/2	342 1/2	– 29 1/4
1995	402 3/4	363 1/4	373 1/2	378	349	– 53 3/4	349 3/4	– 23 3/4
1996	527 1/2	473	519 1/2	533	495	– 32 1/2	512 1/2	– 7
1997	399 3/4	357	359 3/4	380	351	– 48 3/4	373	13 1/4
1998	348	319 1/4	337 1/4	347	316	– 32	327 1/2	– 9 3/4
1999	294	263	275 1/2	274 1/2	236 1/2	– 57 1/2	237 1/4	– 38 1/4
2000	269	241	256 1/4	273 1/2	244	– 25	247	– 9 1/4
2001	294 1/2	268	273	273	256 1/4	– 38 1/4	265	– 8
2002	313 1/4	283 1/2	286	288 1/4	266 1/4	– 47	267 1/4	– 18 3/4
2003	339	307 1/2	320 1/2	338	308 1/2	– 30 1/2	312 1/2	– 8
2004	407	373	389	395	364	– 43	380 3/4	– 8 1/4
2005	312	287 1/2	291	337 1/2	287	– 25	337 1/4	46 1/4
2006	350	321 1/2	343 1/4	378	337 1/2	– 12 1/2	370 1/4	27
					Totals	– 690		– 120 3/4
					Averages	– 36 1/4		– 6 1/4
							# Up	4
							# Down	15

FEBRUARY

MONDAY
5

CL	47.4	**NG**	61.1	**GC**	52.6	**SI**	52.6
S	57.9	**W**	61.1	**C**	57.9	**LC**	52.6
LH	31.6	**KC**	47.4	**CC**	61.1	**SB**	55.6

Brilliant men are often strikingly ineffectual; they fail to realize that the brilliant insight is not by itself achievement. They never have learned that insights become effectiveness only through hard systematic work.
— Peter Drucker (Management consultant, "The man who invented the corporate society," born in Austria 1909)

TUESDAY
6

CL	52.6	**NG**	36.8	**GC**	42.1	**SI**	57.9
S	44.4	**W**	42.1	**C**	31.6	**LC**	66.7
LH	52.6	**KC**	42.1	**CC**	44.4	**SB**	47.4

Most of the important things in the world have been accomplished by people who have kept on trying when there seemed to be no hope at all. — Dale Carnegie

WEDNESDAY
7

CL	42.1	**NG**	73.7	**GC**	36.8	**SI**	47.4
S	47.4	**W**	42.1	**C**	52.6	**LC**	44.4
LH	42.1	**KC**	57.9	**CC**	47.4	**SB**	55.6

Education is when you read the fine print. Experience is what you get if you don't. — Pete Seeger

THURSDAY
8

CL	47.4	**NG**	52.6	**GC**	21.1	**SI**	26.3
S	42.1	**W**	57.9	**C**	55.6	**LC**	47.4
LH	61.1	**KC**	52.6	**CC**	42.1	**SB**	31.6

An educated person is one who has learned that information almost always turns out to be, at best, incomplete and very often false, misleading, fictitious, mendacious — just dead wrong. — Russell Baker

FRIDAY
9

CL	52.6	**NG**	47.4	**GC**	72.2	**SI**	68.4
S	61.1	**W**	66.7	**C**	72.2	**LC**	72.2
LH	57.9	**KC**	47.4	**CC**	57.9	**SB**	44.4

I am opposed to millionaires, but it would be dangerous to offer me the position.
— Mark Twain (American novelist and satirist, pen name of Samuel Longhorne Clemens, 1835–1910)

SATURDAY
10

SUNDAY
11

WINTER KILL CAUSES KCBT WHEAT GAINS RELATIVE TO CBOT WHEAT

Kansas City Board of Trade (KCBT) Wheat tends to be the strongest class of Wheat as the marketplace begins to brace for the winter wheat harvest. In most years, KCBT Hard Red Winter Wheat commands a premium over CBOT Soft Red Winter Wheat, due to its higher protein content. At the end of January, May KCBT Wheat traded at a premium to the May CBOT Wheat +10 3/4 cents/bushel on average from 1988 through 2006. KCBT Wheat traded at a discount to CBOT Wheat in only 5 of the 19 years.

The relative performance of KCBT Wheat over CBOT Wheat may be due to the fact that KCBT Hard Red Winter Wheat is grown in more northern climates, with greater temperature fluctuations. The crop is more susceptible to damage, especially from heaving (thawing and refreezing of the ground) which causes soil to expand and contract, potentially damaging the wheat crop. Because CBOT Soft Red Winter Wheat is grown in more southern climates, this type of damage is less prevalent.

Since 1988, May KCBT Wheat futures gained relative to May CBOT Wheat futures in 15 of the 19 years (78.9%) from February through April for an average gain differential of +9 1/4 cents/bushel.

Traders can take advantage of the gain in KCBT Wheat relative to CBOT Wheat by establishing an "Intermarket" spread position (see page 26). This involves buying one futures contract on one exchange (like May KCBT Wheat) and simultaneously selling the same commodity and contract month on a different exchange (like May CBOT Wheat). The position will be profitable if the purchased (long) contract either gains in value more than, or decreases in value less than, the sold (short) contract.

MAY KCBT WHEAT VS. CBOT WHEAT FUTURES
JANUARY TO APRIL CENTS PER BUSHEL DIFFERENCES

	May KCBT Wheat			May CBOT Wheat			KCBT – CBOT		
Date	January Close	April Close	Feb - Apr Change	January Close	April Close	Feb - Apr Change	January Close	April Close	Feb - Apr Change
1988	312 3/4	305 1/4	– 7 1/2	327	304 1/2	– 22 1/2	– 14 1/4	3/4	15
1989	429	428 3/4	– 1/4	435	417 1/2	– 17 1/2	– 6	11 1/4	17 1/4
1990	369 1/2	374 1/4	4 3/4	362 3/4	374 1/4	11 1/2	6 3/4	0	– 6 3/4
1991	273	282 1/4	9 1/4	271 1/4	272 3/4	1 1/2	1 3/4	9 1/2	7 3/4
1992	420 3/4	358	– 62 3/4	421 1/2	372 1/4	– 49 1/4	– 3/4	– 14 1/4	– 13 1/2
1993	339 1/4	323	– 16 1/4	352 3/4	348	– 4 3/4	– 13 1/2	– 25	– 11 1/2
1994	350	346 1/2	– 3 1/2	353 3/4	326 1/2	– 27 1/4	– 3 3/4	20	23 3/4
1995	360	356 1/4	– 3 3/4	358 3/4	350 1/2	– 8 1/4	1 1/4	5 3/4	4 1/2
1996	491	672	181	485 1/2	641 1/2	156	5 1/2	30 1/2	25
1997	366 1/2	457	90 1/2	348 1/2	423	74 1/2	18	34	16
1998	357 1/2	315 1/2	– 42	347 1/4	289 3/4	– 57 1/2	10 1/4	25 3/4	15 1/2
1999	318	278	– 40	285 1/2	259	– 26 1/2	32 1/2	19	– 13 1/2
2000	294	271	– 23	268	242 1/4	– 25 3/4	26	28 3/4	2 3/4
2001	328 3/4	331	2 1/4	285	272 3/4	– 12 1/4	43 3/4	58 1/4	14 1/2
2002	291 1/2	274	– 17 1/2	289 3/4	261 3/4	– 28	1 3/4	12 1/4	10 1/2
2003	340 1/2	321 1/2	– 19	313	279 1/2	– 33 1/2	27 1/2	42	14 1/2
2004	395 1/2	394	– 1 1/2	395	381 1/2	– 13 1/2	1/2	12 1/2	12
2005	317	341	24	298 3/4	318	19 1/4	18 1/4	23	4 3/4
2006	401	429 3/4	28 3/4	354 1/2	346 1/4	– 8 1/4	46 1/2	83 1/2	37
		Totals	**103 1/2**			**– 72**	**202**		**175 1/2**
		Averages	**5 1/2**			**– 3 3/4**	**10 3/4**		**9 1/4**
		# Up	**7**			**5**	**14**		**15**
		# Down	**12**			**14**	**5**		**4**

FEBRUARY

MONDAY 12

CL	52.6	NG	68.4	GC	42.1	SI	36.8
S	63.2	W	57.9	C	66.7	LC	42.1
LH	22.2	KC	57.9	CC	52.6	SB	66.7

When you argue with reality (or the market), you lose — but only 100% of the time. — Byron Katie

TUESDAY 13

CL	42.1	NG	38.9	GC	47.4	SI	47.4
S	55.6	W	57.9	C	61.1	LC	47.4
LH	57.9	KC	55.6	CC	52.6	SB	63.2

There are three principal means of acquiring knowledge...observation of nature, reflection, and experimentation. Observation collects facts; reflection combines them; experimentation verifies the result of that combination.
— Denis Diderot (French editor, philosopher. He edited the first modern encyclopedia in 1745, 1713–1784)

Valentine's Day ♥

WEDNESDAY 14

CL	83.3	NG	66.7	GC	21.1	SI	57.9
S	31.6	W	38.9	C	36.8	LC	33.3
LH	36.8	KC	68.4	CC	36.8	SB	33.3

The heights by great men reached and kept were not attained by sudden flight;
but they, while their companions slept, were toiling upward in the night. — Henry Wadsworth Longfellow

THURSDAY 15

CL	42.1	NG	38.9	GC	47.4	SI	47.4
S	55.6	W	57.9	C	61.1	LC	47.4
LH	57.9	KC	55.6	CC	52.6	SB	63.2

Don't confuse brains with a bull market. — Humphrey Neill

FRIDAY 16

CL	52.6	NG	68.4	GC	42.1	SI	36.8
S	63.2	W	57.9	C	66.7	LC	42.1
LH	22.2	KC	57.9	CC	52.6	SB	66.7

While markets often make double bottoms, three pushes to a high is the most common topping pattern. — John Bollinger (Bollinger Capital Management, created Bollinger Bands, *Capital Growth Letter, Bollinger on Bollinger Bands*)

SATURDAY 17

SUNDAY 18

WIN, PLACE, OR SHOW
COMMODITY SPECULATING USING SPREADS

Futures markets provide a variety of trading opportunities. In addition to trading futures contracts and options on futures contracts, there is an opportunity to profit from the relationship between different contracts — or Spreads. A Spread refers to the simultaneous purchase and sale of two or more different futures contracts.

There are three basic types of spreads: Interdelivery, Intermarket, and Intercommodity. The main reasons for trading spreads are two-fold: lower risk and attractive margin rates.

The most common spread type traded is the **Interdelivery Spread**. An Interdelivery Spread position attempts to take advantage of the price difference between two delivery months of a single futures market when the trader perceives the difference to be abnormal.

Intermarket Spreads try to exploit price anomalies of the same commodity and delivery month on two different exchanges. Intermarket Spreads are basically limited to the Wheat market for most traders, trading either Chicago Wheat versus Kansas City or Minneapolis, or Kansas City versus Minneapolis Wheat.

COMMON SPREAD DEFINITIONS

Interdelivery Spread: Simultaneous purchase of one delivery month and the sale of another delivery month of the same commodity on the same exchange. AKA Intramarket or Calendar Spread. See Lean Hog Spread on page 104.

Intermarket Spread: Simultaneous purchase of a given commodity and delivery month on one exchange and the sale of the same commodity and delivery month on a different exchange. AKA Interexchange Spread. See KCBT Wheat/CBOT Wheat Spread on page 24.

Intercommodity Spread: Simultaneous purchase of one commodity and delivery month and the sale of another different but related commodity with the same (or similar) delivery month. See Platinum/Gold and Heating Oil/Unleaded Gasoline Spreads on pages 18, 40 and 66.

The last general category for spreads is the **Intercommodity Spread**, or trading one commodity against another. These spreads are commonly done, and can theoretically include any commodity against any other commodity. However, only a few of the combinations of Intercommodity Spreads are exchange-recognized, and receive a break in margins, as margins for spreads are usually lower (but subject to change without notice by the exchange).

Because of their hedged nature, spreads are generally less risky than outright futures positions. Since the prices of two different futures contracts (on the same commodity or different but related commodities) exhibit a strong tendency to move up or down together, spread trading offers protection against losses that arise from unexpected or extreme price volatility. Spreads offer "protection" because losses on one side of the spread are often offset by gains from the other side of the spread.

Due to the partially hedged nature of spread positions, margin requirements tend to be lower than outright futures positions. This is not always the case, but as a general rule of thumb, one can expect spread margins to be lower than outright futures positions for exchange-recognized spread positions. Like any other margin requirement, spread margins are subject to change, without notice, by either your brokerage house or the exchange.

Like anything else in the futures market, margin levels for spreads can be used as a rough guide for the level of risk involved in that particular market. Generally, the higher the margin rate, the higher the risk involved in trading that particular market, as well as the higher the potential reward. Spread traders usually choose this avenue because of the lower perceived risks, and are willing to sacrifice the tremendous upside potential of trading straight futures positions in return for the lower risk of trading spreads.

Spread trading is still considered much too complicated or esoteric for most, leaving many of the market anomalies or opportunities for the astute trader willing to venture off the traditional path. However, spread trading has its own unique set of risks, and in some cases may actually entail more risk than an outright futures position. Traders should fully understand the potential risks and rewards involved in spread trading before initiating any position.

Presidents' Day (Market Closed)

MONDAY
19

Selling a soybean contract short is worth two years at the Harvard Business School.
— Robert Stovall (Managing director, Wood Asset Management)

TUESDAY
20

CL 57.9	**NG** 61.1	**GC** 38.9	**SI** 42.1
S 55.6	**W** 44.4	**C** 44.4	**LC** 47.4
LH 55.6	**KC** 52.6	**CC** 38.9	**SB** 55.6

Bull markets are born on pessimism, grow on skepticism, mature on optimism, and die on euphoria.
— Sir John Templeton (Founder Templeton Funds, philanthropist, 1994)

Ash Wednesday

WEDNESDAY
21

CL 47.4	**NG** 36.8	**GC** 55.6	**SI** 47.4
S 47.4	**W** 57.9	**C** 52.6	**LC** 66.7
LH 22.2	**KC** 78.9	**CC** 52.6	**SB** 61.1

The usual bull market successfully weathers a number of tests until it is considered invulnerable, whereupon it is ripe for a bust.
— George Soros (1987, Financier, philanthropist, political activist, author and philosopher, b. 1930)

THURSDAY
22

CL 31.6	**NG** 44.4	**GC** 55.6	**SI** 42.1
S 73.7	**W** 52.6	**C** 44.4	**LC** 61.1
LH 63.2	**KC** 47.4	**CC** 55.6	**SB** 31.6

One machine can do the work of fifty ordinary men. No machine can do the work of one extraordinary man.
— Elbert Hubbard (American author, *A Message To Garcia,* 1856–1915)

FRIDAY
23

CL 63.2	**NG** 47.4	**GC** 38.9	**SI** 42.1
S 36.8	**W** 47.4	**C** 47.4	**LC** 52.6
LH 61.1	**KC** 36.8	**CC** 47.4	**SB** 33.3

The generally accepted view is that markets are always right — that is, market prices tend to discount future developments accurately even when it is unclear what those developments are. I start with the opposite point of view. I believe that market prices are always wrong in the sense that they present a biased view of the future.
— George Soros (1987, Financier, philanthropist, political activist, author and philosopher, b. 1930)

SATURDAY
24

SUNDAY
25

MARCH ALMANAC

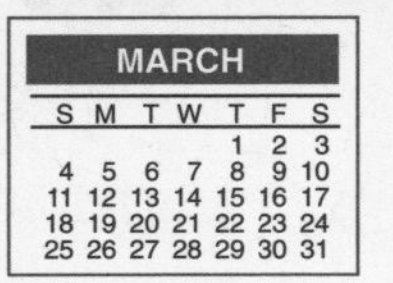

APRIL

S	M	T	W	T	F	S
1	2	3	4	5	6	7
8	9	10	11	12	13	14
15	16	17	18	19	20	21
22	23	24	25	26	27	28
29	30					

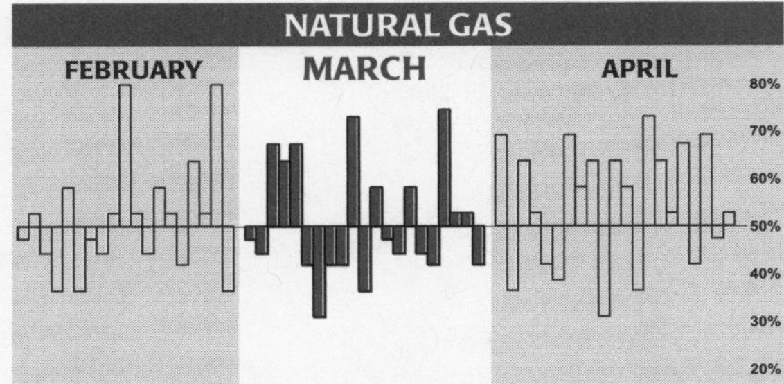

Market Probability Chart above is a graphic representation of Natural Gas taken from the Market Probability Calendar on page 129

PETROLEUM FUTURES: June Natural Gas up 11 of last 14 Marches, average gain of 0.189 cents/BTU ◆ 8 of last 10 February rallies have continued through March ◆ June Crude up 13 of 19 in March, average March gain of $0.84/bbl ◆ Best March performance follows February weakness.

METALS FUTURES: March mixed for June Gold (up 8 / down 11) ◆ Gold weakness in March continues through April (7 of 11) ◆ Gold begins to gain strength against industrial metals (Platinum and Silver) ◆ May Silver up 9 / down 10 ◆ March 2nd-strongest month on average for Silver ◆ May Silver up 212 cents/ounce between 1987 and 2005.

GRAIN FUTURES: July Soybeans up 12 / Down 7 ◆ Best March performance in Soybeans follows February rallies (up 9 of 12) ◆ February weakness continues in March basis May Wheat (8 of 12) ◆ Corn up 12 / down 7 in March ◆ March weakness basis July Corn has continued through April on each of last 7 occurrences.

LIVESTOCK FUTURES: Mixed month for Live Cattle ◆ June Live Cattle up 9 / down 10 ◆ 7 of 10 last March breaks have continued in April basis June Cattle ◆ Tends towards strength in Lean Hogs (up 12 / down 7).

SOFTS FUTURES: 3rd-worst month on record for Coffee Down 11 / up 8 ◆ February strength reversed in March basis May Coffee ◆ May Sugar breaks in February reversed in March (7 of 10) ◆ May Sugar up 12 / down 7 ◆ Cocoa down 11 / up 8 ◆ 6 of 8 last February breaks continued through March.

COMMODITY SPOTLIGHT NATURAL GAS

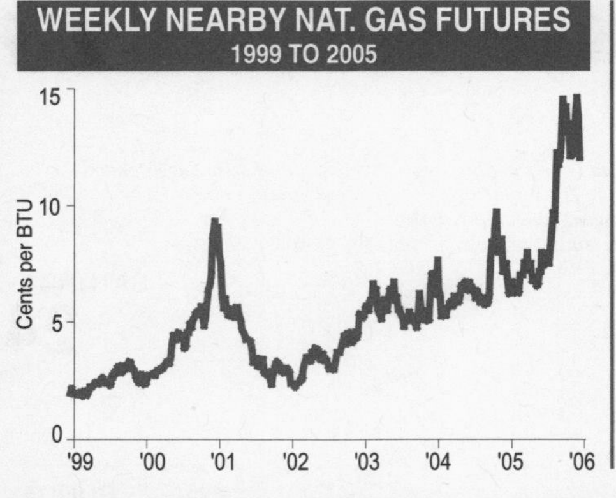

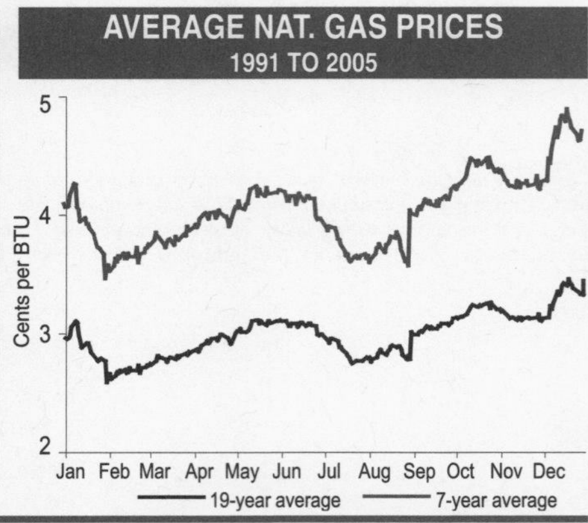

Like other Petroleum Products, Natural Gas tends to anticipate cooling and heating needs ahead of retail demand. Price truly does precede demand in the Petroleum markets.

FEBRUARY/MARCH

MONDAY **26**

CL 47.4	**NG** 55.6	**GC** 42.1	**SI** 42.1
S 47.4	**W** 61.1	**C** 66.7	**LC** 61.1
LH 42.1	**KC** 47.4	**CC** 68.4	**SB** 47.4

Don't be scared to take big steps—you can't cross a chasm in two small jumps.
— David Lloyd George (British Prime Minister, 1916–1922)

TUESDAY **27**

CL 73.7	**NG** 57.9	**GC** 44.4	**SI** 26.3
S 42.1	**W** 31.6	**C** 33.3	**LC** 36.8
LH 57.9	**KC** 47.4	**CC** 63.2	**SB** 36.8

I've never been poor, only broke. Being poor is a frame of mind. Being broke is only a temporary situation.
— Mike Todd (Movie producer, 1903–1958)

WEDNESDAY **28**

CL 36.8	**NG** 55.6	**GC** 57.9	**SI** 47.4
S 57.9	**W** 44.4	**C** 47.4	**LC** 42.1
LH 52.6	**KC** 36.8	**CC** 38.9	**SB** 52.6

The commodity futures game is a money game — not a game involving the supply-demand of the actual commodity as commonly depicted. — R. Earl Hadady

THURSDAY **1**

CL 47.4	**NG** 55.6	**GC** 63.2	**SI** 78.9
S 73.7	**W** 44.4	**C** 68.4	**LC** 44.4
LH 66.7	**KC** 47.4	**CC** 33.3	**SB** 66.7

Ignorance is not knowing something; stupidity is not admitting your ignorance. — Daniel Turov (*Turov on Timing*)

FRIDAY **2**

CL 52.6	**NG** 47.4	**GC** 31.6	**SI** 42.1
S 63.2	**W** 61.1	**C** 72.2	**LC** 61.1
LH 61.1	**KC** 47.4	**CC** 42.1	**SB** 66.7

I don't wait for moods. You accomplish nothing if you do that. Your mind must know it has got to get down to work.
— Pearl S. Buck

SATURDAY **3**

SUNDAY **4**

ARRIVAL OF SPRING LIFTS NATURAL GAS IN MARCH

Natural Gas is used to both heat and cool homes. Natural Gas can be used to run residential air conditioners — which are growing in popularity — but the major impetus for demand during the summer months comes from electricity generation needed to run air conditioners. During the cooler winter months, residential Natural Gas heating drives the market.

Though the strongest period for Natural Gas is August/September, March exhibits the most consistent gains in Natural Gas prices. The August/September period is a transitional period from the cooling season to the heating season and Natural Gas plays a larger role in heating homes than cooling them. However, the transition from heating to cooling is also significant, as late cold snaps and builds-of-inventory can translate into higher prices.

June Natural Gas futures have risen 12 times since 1991 during March's transitional price increase and fallen thrice. In 1991, when the futures began trading, June Natural Gas settled unchanged during March.

February strength has continued in March 8 of 10 times. However, February weakness in June Natural Gas has proved fleeting. Four of the last 5 down Februarys have reversed in March. June Natural Gas February weakness can provide a trading opportunity ahead of March's usual strength.

JUNE NATURAL GAS DOLLARS PER MMBTU CHANGES

Date	Feb High	Feb Low	Feb Close	Feb Change	Mar High	Mar Low	Mar Close	Mar Change	Rally Feb Close - Mar High
1991	1.450	1.390	1.430	−0.010	1.430	1.390	1.430	NC	0.000
1992	1.250	1.140	1.180	−0.050	1.350	1.170	1.330	0.150	0.170
1993	1.800	1.630	1.770	0.140	2.000	1.730	1.980	0.210	0.230
1994	2.210	2.050	2.150	−0.010	2.180	2.040	2.090	−0.060	0.030
1995	1.590	1.480	1.550	0.070	1.780	1.500	1.750	0.200	0.230
1996	2.070	1.890	2.010	0.060	2.340	1.950	2.260	0.250	0.330
1997	2.130	1.880	1.900	−0.140	2.100	1.870	1.970	0.070	0.200
1998	2.420	2.240	2.350	0.040	2.560	2.160	2.560	0.210	0.210
1999	1.940	1.690	1.700	−0.170	2.090	1.720	2.040	0.340	0.390
2000	2.780	2.470	2.780	0.220	3.020	2.720	2.950	0.170	0.240
2001	5.860	5.120	5.330	0.150	5.780	4.980	5.080	−0.250	0.450
2002	2.610	2.260	2.480	0.150	3.600	2.470	3.310	0.830	1.120
2003	6.600	4.850	5.770	0.870	6.070	5.030	5.100	−0.670	0.300
2004	5.520	5.030	5.490	0.450	6.000	5.350	5.990	0.500	0.510
2005	6.940	6.110	6.870	0.440	7.840	6.710	7.760	0.890	0.970
2006	10.050	6.950	7.075	−2.975	7.790	6.870	7.420	0.345	0.715
			Totals	**−0.765**				**3.185**	**6.095**
			Averages	**−0.048**				**0.212**	**0.381**
			# Up	**10**				**12**	**15**
			# Down	**6**				**3**	**0**

MARCH

MONDAY

5

CL	68.4	**NG**	57.9	**GC**	38.9	**SI**	44.4
S	61.1	**W**	36.8	**C**	38.9	**LC**	44.4
LH	42.1	**KC**	63.2	**CC**	47.4	**SB**	36.8

Whatever games are played with us, we must play no games with ourselves.
— Ralph Waldo Emerson (American author, poet, and philosopher, 1803–1882)

TUESDAY

6

CL	52.6	**NG**	47.4	**GC**	38.9	**SI**	31.6
S	36.8	**W**	16.7	**C**	44.4	**LC**	61.1
LH	47.4	**KC**	57.9	**CC**	36.8	**SB**	44.4

If the winds of fortune are temporarily blowing against you, remember that you can harness them and make them carry you toward your definite purpose, through the use of your imagination. — Napoleon Hill (Author, *Think and Grow Rich,* 1883–1970)

WEDNESDAY

7

CL	66.7	**NG**	63.2	**GC**	47.4	**SI**	66.7
S	63.2	**W**	78.9	**C**	55.6	**LC**	42.1
LH	63.2	**KC**	63.2	**CC**	52.6	**SB**	33.3

I always keep these seasonal patterns in the back of my mind. My antennae start to purr at certain times of the year. — Kenneth Ward

THURSDAY

8

CL	42.1	**NG**	52.6	**GC**	55.6	**SI**	63.2
S	55.6	**W**	52.6	**C**	44.4	**LC**	73.7
LH	78.9	**KC**	52.6	**CC**	57.9	**SB**	63.2

An expert is a person who has made all the mistakes that can be made in a very narrow field.
— Niels Bohr (Danish physicist, 1922 Nobel Prize, 1885–1962)

FRIDAY

9

CL	42.1	**NG**	57.9	**GC**	36.8	**SI**	55.6
S	55.6	**W**	52.6	**C**	68.4	**LC**	55.6
LH	52.6	**KC**	47.4	**CC**	57.9	**SB**	47.4

Small volume is usually accompanied by a fall in price; large volume by a rise in price. — Charles C. Ying (Computer study)

SATURDAY

10

Daylight Saving Time Begins

SUNDAY

11

MARCH BEEF BAROMETER: MARCH'S CATTLE TREND CONTINUES IN APRIL

March is a critical month for Live Cattle futures. March marks the beginning of the slaughter season, coming off the low point and usually tight beef supplies. Spring also marks the time when the meat industry is gearing up for the summer barbeque season.

At first glance, the importance of March is not readily seen. With its up 10, down 9 batting average since 1987, the month is not that impressive. However, March acts as a great barometer for the performance of June Live Cattle futures in April. Prices have continued their March trend in April 14 of 19 times since 1987 (73.6%). Following the last 10 March rallies, June Live Cattle futures have posted an average gain of +0.725 cents/lb during April, posting gains 7 times. Following the last 9 April declines, June Live Cattle futures have continued lower in April 7 times — registering an average decline of -0.745 cents/lb during April.

When the March trend continues in April, June Live Cattle futures have averaged a trend continuation Rally or Break of 2.798 cents/lb, twenty-three times greater than the average 0.122 cents/lb when the trend reversed.

JUNE LIVE CATTLE CENTS PER POUND CHANGES

Date	Feb Close	Mar Close	Mar Change	Apr High	Apr Low	Apr Close	Apr Change	Trend	Rally Mar Close-Apr High	Break Mar Close-Apr Low
1987	62.400	63.425	1.025	67.250	62.750	67.200	3.775	Continuation	3.825	−0.675
1988	68.400	70.875	2.475	72.375	68.600	70.900	0.025	Continuation	1.500	−2.275
1989	75.050	73.025	−2.025	73.375	70.100	71.450	−1.575	Continuation	0.150	−2.925
1990	70.950	72.925	1.975	74.200	72.400	72.975	0.050	Continuation	0.025	−0.525
1991	77.025	77.125	0.100	78.375	75.525	76.100	−1.025	*Reversal*	0.150	−1.600
1992	73.775	74.775	1.000	74.850	72.500	73.100	−1.675	*Reversal*	−0.150	−2.275
1993	74.325	76.250	1.925	77.025	74.775	76.775	0.525	Continuation	−0.175	−1.475
1994	74.975	74.275	−0.700	74.950	70.550	71.300	−2.975	Continuation	0.125	−3.725
1995	67.400	61.700	−5.700	64.725	61.050	62.950	1.250	*Reversal*	0.150	−0.650
1996	63.175	62.475	−0.700	63.850	54.000	57.350	−5.125	Continuation	0.225	−8.475
1997	65.500	65.075	−0.425	65.650	63.000	64.750	−0.325	Continuation	−0.125	−2.075
1998	66.575	65.775	−0.800	69.600	65.625	69.500	3.725	*Reversal*	−0.125	−0.150
1999	65.600	63.600	−2.000	65.500	62.400	62.825	−0.775	Continuation	−0.075	−1.200
2000	68.650	68.975	0.325	70.200	68.225	69.275	0.300	Continuation	0.075	−0.750
2001	73.950	72.675	−1.275	73.825	71.025	71.650	−1.025	Continuation	1.150	−1.025
2002	69.625	65.800	−3.825	67.100	59.325	63.625	−2.175	Continuation	1.300	−6.475
2003	70.400	70.375	−0.025	72.300	70.200	71.925	1.550	*Reversal*	1.925	−0.175
2004	72.925	76.225	3.300	82.150	74.750	80.400	4.175	Continuation	5.925	−1.475
2005	82.350	85.250	2.900	87.350	83.050	85.625	0.375	Continuation	2.100	−2.200
	Totals		**−2.450**				**−0.925**		**17.975**	**−40.125**
	Averages		**−0.129**				**−0.049**		**0.946**	**−2.112**
	# Up		**9**				**10**	**Cont Avg**	**1.896**	**−3.700**
	# Down		**10**				**9**	**Rev Avg**	**NC**	**−0.244**

MONDAY **12**

CL 42.1	NG 52.6	GC 73.7	SI 68.4
S 63.2	W 33.3	C 42.1	LC 33.3
LH 21.1	KC 52.6	CC 27.8	SB 78.9

A cynic is a man who knows the price of everything and the value of nothing. — Oscar Wilde (Irish-born writer and wit)

TUESDAY **13**

CL 42.1	NG 57.9	GC 55.6	SI 47.4
S 42.1	W 42.1	C 47.4	LC 36.8
LH 68.4	KC 52.6	CC 42.1	SB 36.8

If people think that nature (or "the market") is their friend, then they sure don't need an enemy. — Kurt Vonnegut

WEDNESDAY **14**

CL 66.7	NG 38.9	GC 55.6	SI 73.7
S 57.9	W 47.4	C 61.1	LC 57.9
LH 57.9	KC 42.1	CC 73.7	SB 61.1

There is nothing like a ticker tape except a woman — nothing that promises, hour after hour, day after day, such sudden developments; nothing that disappoints so often or occasionally fulfils with such unbelievable, passionate magnificence.
— Walter K. Gutman (Financial analyst, described as the "Proust of Wall Street" by *New Yorker*, *You Only Have to Get Rich Once*, 1961, *The Gutman Letter*, 1903–1986)

THURSDAY **15**

CL 31.6	NG 38.9	GC 36.8	SI 38.9
S 52.6	W 52.6	C 36.8	LC 31.6
LH 52.6	KC 36.8	CC 52.6	SB 61.1

Follow the course opposite to custom and you will almost always do well. — Jean Jacques Rousseau

FRIDAY **16**

CL 57.9	NG 52.6	GC 47.4	SI 47.4
S 38.9	W 44.4	C 44.4	LC 42.1
LH 63.2	KC 52.6	CC 47.4	SB 55.6

Statements by high officials are practically always misleading when they are designed to bolster a falling market.
— Gerald M. Loeb

St. Patrick's Day 

SATURDAY **17**

SUNDAY **18**

DON'T BUY CORN IN MARCH
PLANTING PREMIUMS ARE OFTEN OVERDONE

Corn futures generally run up ahead of the spring planting season. This "planting premium" is a legacy of years past when the fate of crops was more at the mercy of Mother Nature.

Modern agriculture is an amazing thing. Despite the trials and tribulations of weather and blight during the planting effort, the United States still managed to produce an average of 8.76 billion bushels of Corn from 1987 to 2005. Due to the pervasiveness of state-of-the-art agronomics — with drought- and pestilence-resisting seed strains as well as genetic modifications — once a crop is planted, future supply is almost totally guaranteed. After planting season is underway, Corn prices tend to break.

Since 1987, July Corn futures have declined 16 times in April. But traders can get a jump on the April Corn break by watching for March rallies. Following the last 12 March rallies in July Corn, prices have fallen 9 times, or 75% of the time, in April. The average April break, from the March close to the April low, has been -10 3/4 cents/bushel. But after the 9 March rallies of +10 cents/bushel or more, July Corn has broken 8 times for an average of -11 1/2 cents/bushel at the April low.

If you miss selling the March rally, fear not, the 7 down Marches were all followed by down Aprils. Thanks to bio-engineering, U.S. corn crops are rarely at risk.

JULY CORN CENTS PER BUSHEL CHANGES

Date	Feb Close	Mar High	Rally Feb Close - Mar High	Mar Low	Mar Close	Mar Change	Apr High	Apr Low	Apr Close	Break Mar Close - Apr Low	Apr Change
1987	157 1/4	167 3/4	10 1/2	155	165 3/4	8 1/2	184 1/2	160 1/2	184 1/4	-5 1/4	18 1/2
1988	213 1/2	217 3/4	4 1/4	205 3/4	215 3/4	2 1/4	219 1/4	207	211 1/4	-8 3/4	-4 1/2
1989	281 3/4	288 1/2	6 3/4	266	271	-10 3/4	283	261	270 1/2	-10	- 1/2
1990	257 3/4	265 1/2	7 3/4	252	263 3/4	6	285	265	283	1 1/4	19 1/4
1991	258 3/4	267 1/4	8 1/2	253 1/2	259 1/2	3/4	268 1/2	253 3/4	254	-5 3/4	-5 1/2
1992	279 1/4	285	5 3/4	269	269 1/4	-10	270	249 1/4	249 1/2	-20	-19 3/4
1993	225 3/4	237 3/4	12	225 1/2	235 3/4	10	239 1/2	227 3/4	232 1/2	-8	-3 1/4
1994	296 1/2	297 3/4	1 1/4	279 1/2	279 3/4	-16 3/4	282	257 3/4	272	-22	-7 3/4
1995	248 1/4	258 1/2	10 1/4	245 1/2	255 3/4	7 1/2	260	249	255 1/4	-6 3/4	- 1/2
1996	382	395	13	370	394	12	484	394 1/2	452	1/2	58
1997	294	311 1/2	17 1/2	291 1/2	310 1/4	16 1/4	320 3/4	290	293 1/4	-20 1/4	-17
1998	276 3/4	289	12 1/4	265 1/4	265 3/4	-11	268	251 1/4	252 1/4	-14 1/2	-13 1/2
1999	216	240 1/4	24 1/4	216 1/2	231 1/2	15 1/2	231 1/2	217 1/2	218 3/4	-14	-12 3/4
2000	232 1/4	249 1/2	17 1/4	230 1/4	244 1/2	12 1/4	248	231 1/2	232	-13	-12 1/2
2001	230 1/2	233 3/4	3 1/4	211	212	-18 1/2	222 3/4	201 1/2	207 1/2	-10 1/2	-4 1/2
2002	214 1/4	219 1/2	5 1/4	208 1/2	209	-5 1/4	211 1/4	199 1/2	200 1/2	-9 1/2	-8 1/2
2003	235 1/2	242 3/4	7 1/4	227 1/4	237	1 1/2	246 1/2	229 1/2	231 1/4	-7 1/2	-5 3/4
2004	305 3/4	327 1/2	21 3/4	294 3/4	325 1/2	19 3/4	342	303	320 1/4	-22 1/2	-5 1/4
2005	229 3/4	238	8 1/4	217	221	-8 3/4	223 3/4	211 1/4	213 1/2	-9 3/4	-7 1/2
		Averages	**10 1/4**			**1 3/4**				**-10 3/4**	**-1 3/4**
		# Rallies > 10 cents				**9**		**Subsequent Avg Break**		**-11 1/2**	**1 1/4**
					# Up	**12**		**Subsequent Avg Break**		**-9 1/4**	**2 1/2**
					# Down	**7**		**Subsequent Avg Break**		**-13 3/4**	**-8 3/4**

MARCH

MONDAY
19

CL	52.6	NG	55.6	GC	27.8	SI	21.1
S	66.7	W	52.6	C	47.4	LC	47.4
LH	47.4	KC	44.4	CC	63.2	SB	63.2

I have learned as a composer chiefly through my mistakes and pursuits of false assumptions, not by my exposure to founts of wisdom and knowledge. — Igor Stravinsky (Russian composer)

TUESDAY
20

CL	47.4	NG	52.6	GC	57.9	SI	63.2
S	68.4	W	73.7	C	77.8	LC	63.2
LH	47.4	KC	38.9	CC	26.3	SB	42.1

Good judgment is usually the result of experience and experience frequently is the result of bad judgment.
— Robert Lovell (Quoted by Robert Sobel, *Panic on Wall Street*)

WEDNESDAY
21

CL	55.6	NG	27.8	GC	55.6	SI	57.9
S	55.6	W	52.6	C	42.1	LC	57.9
LH	68.4	KC	42.1	CC	52.6	SB	47.4

In this age of instant information, investors can experience both fear and greed at the exact same moment.
— Sam Stovall (Chief Investment Strategist, Standard & Poor's, October 2003)

THURSDAY
22

CL	55.6	NG	63.2	GC	63.2	SI	47.4
S	61.1	W	52.6	C	47.4	LC	52.6
LH	52.6	KC	52.6	CC	33.3	SB	57.9

The less a man knows about the past and the present, the more insecure must be his judgment of the future. — Sigmund Freud

FRIDAY
23

CL	42.1	NG	57.9	GC	68.4	SI	68.4
S	42.1	W	55.6	C	44.4	LC	63.2
LH	44.4	KC	55.6	CC	57.9	SB	42.1

Fanaticism consists of redoubling your effort when you have forgotten your aim.
— George Santayana (American philosopher, poet, 1863–1952)

SATURDAY
24

SUNDAY
25

APRIL ALMANAC

MAY						
S	M	T	W	T	F	S
		1	2	3	4	5
6	7	8	9	10	11	12
13	14	15	16	17	18	19
20	21	22	23	24	25	26
27	28	29	30	31		

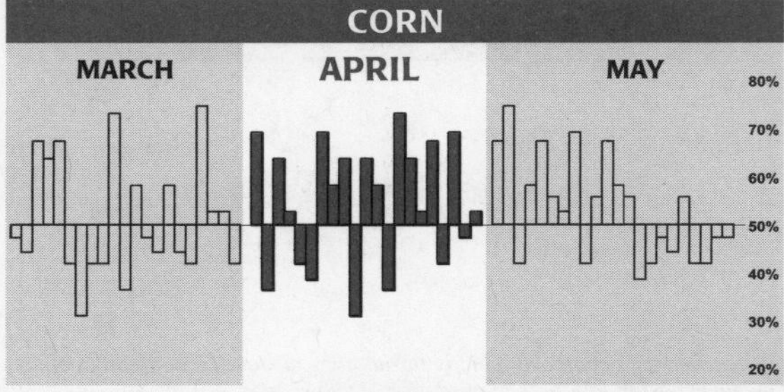

Market Probability Chart above is a graphic representation of Corn futures taken from the Market Probability Calendar on page 154

PETROLEUM FUTURES: June Natural Gas mixed in April, up 7 / down 8 ◆ April high/low exceeded in trend direction (11 of 15) ◆ June Crude Oil up 12 / down 7 ◆ April's trend follows March's (16 of 19), however April trends are usually reversed in May (14 of 19).

METALS FUTURES: March weakness in June Gold continues in April (7 of 11) ◆ June Gold up 8 / down 11 in April ◆ July Silver up 7 / down 12 ◆ July Silver breaks in April often reversed in May (8 of 12).

GRAIN FUTURES: July Soybeans down 10 / up 9 ◆ April rallies reversed in May (6 of 9) ◆ Best Aprils follow March strength ◆ July CBOT Wheat down 10 / up 9 in April ◆ April is a weak month for July Corn (16 of 19) ◆ Worst Aprils follow March weakness ◆ Expect lower monthly lows in May following April weakness (14 of 16).

LIVESTOCK FUTURES: Mixed month for April Live Cattle (up 10 / down 9) ◆ April rallies reversed in May (7 of 10) ◆ April follows March's trend (14 of 19).

SOFTS FUTURES: 2nd-worst month for Cocoa ◆ Down 11 / up 8, losing -$750/ton since 1987 ◆ Mixed month for July Sugar (up 9 / down 10) ◆ April weakness reversed in May (7 of 10).

COMMODITY SPOTLIGHT CORN

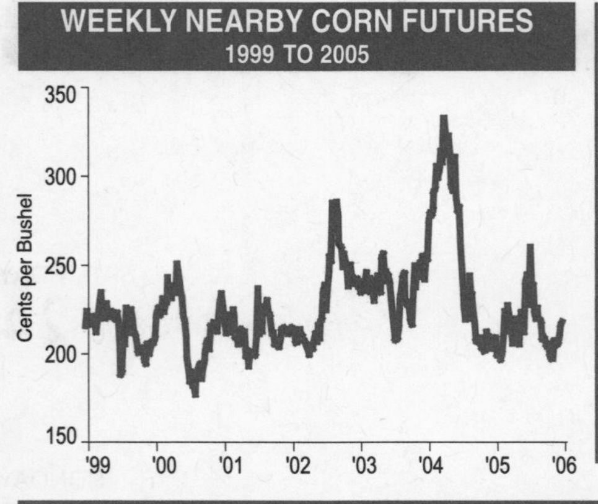

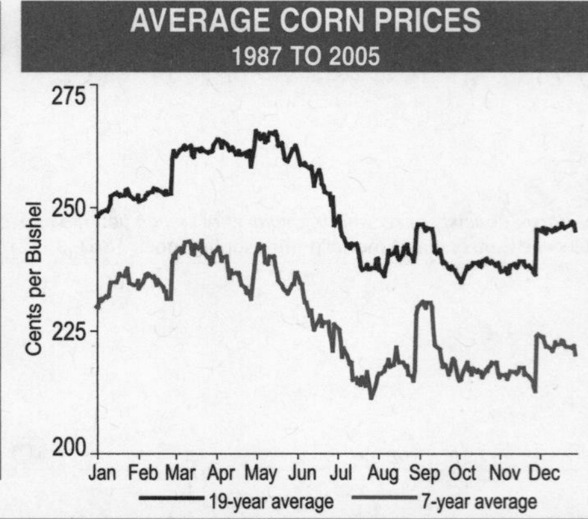

Planting, Pollination, and Harvest are the three key stages of production. The market anticipates problems during these stages and rallies. Corn breaks after progress is made.

MARCH/APRIL

MONDAY **26**

CL 47.4	NG 57.9	GC 42.1	SI 63.2
S 52.6	W 22.2	C 38.9	LC 38.9
LH 63.2	KC 63.2	CC 52.6	SB 47.4

People with a sense of fulfillment think the world is good, while the frustrated blame the world for their failure.
— Eric Hoffer (*The True Believer*, 1951)

TUESDAY **27**

CL 73.7	NG 52.6	GC 63.2	SI 47.4
S 33.3	W 52.6	C 33.3	LC 38.9
LH 63.2	KC 44.4	CC 47.4	SB 47.4

There's nothing wrong with cash. It gives you time to think. — Robert Prechter, Jr. (*Elliott Wave Theorist*)

WEDNESDAY **28**

CL 52.6	NG 47.4	GC 21.1	SI 42.1
S 47.4	W 47.4	C 63.2	LC 47.4
LH 68.4	KC 31.6	CC 31.6	SB 66.7

Wall Street's graveyards are filled with men who were right too soon. — William Hamilton

THURSDAY **29**

CL 55.6	NG 57.9	GC 42.1	SI 52.6
S 42.1	W 52.6	C 47.4	LC 57.9
LH 47.4	KC 47.4	CC 47.4	SB 42.1

There are only two families in the world, the Haves and the Have-nots.
— Miguel de Cervantes (Spanish writer, *Don Quixote*, 1547–1616)

FRIDAY **30**

CL 47.4	NG 44.4	GC 38.9	SI 47.4
S 33.3	W 66.7	C 38.9	LC 52.6
LH 31.6	KC 38.9	CC 57.9	SB 52.6

I was determined to know beans. — Henry David Thoreau

SATURDAY **31**

SUNDAY **1**

APRIL CORN BREAKS

The planting season for Corn in the Top 5 producing states (IA, IL, NE, MN, IN) begins during the 3rd week of April and extends to the beginning of June. Once the crop is planted (sown) — thanks in large part to modern technology and the ability of American farmers — production will follow in some form by the end of the November harvest.

As April progresses, future supply becomes more and more certain. Commodity markets tend to build a premium going into times of uncertainty and remove that uncertainty as time progresses. Case in point, the behavior of July Corn futures during April.

With planting well under way, the market begins to anticipate future supply by reducing prices in the vast majority of years. During the 19-year period from 1987 to 2005, July Corn futures have declined 16 times dropping a total of -33 1/4 cents/bu during the aforementioned period.

Traders should beware, however, that upon the rare occasion of an April rally they have been powerful: 1996 up +58 cents/bu on a settlement basis and up +90 cents/bu from the March settlement to the April high; 1990 up +19 1/4 cents/bu on a settlement basis and up +21 1/4 cents/bu above the March settlement; and 1987 up +18 3/4 cents/bu on a settlement basis and up +18 3/4 cents/bu to the April highs.

However, April breaks have been fairly dynamic as well. In 2004, July Corn futures declined by -22 1/2 cents/bu below their March settlement value during April to finally settle down -5 1/4 cents/bu. 1997, 1994, and 1992 also saw breaks in excess of -20 cents/bu from the March settlement to the April lows, showing that April breaks can be powerful as well.

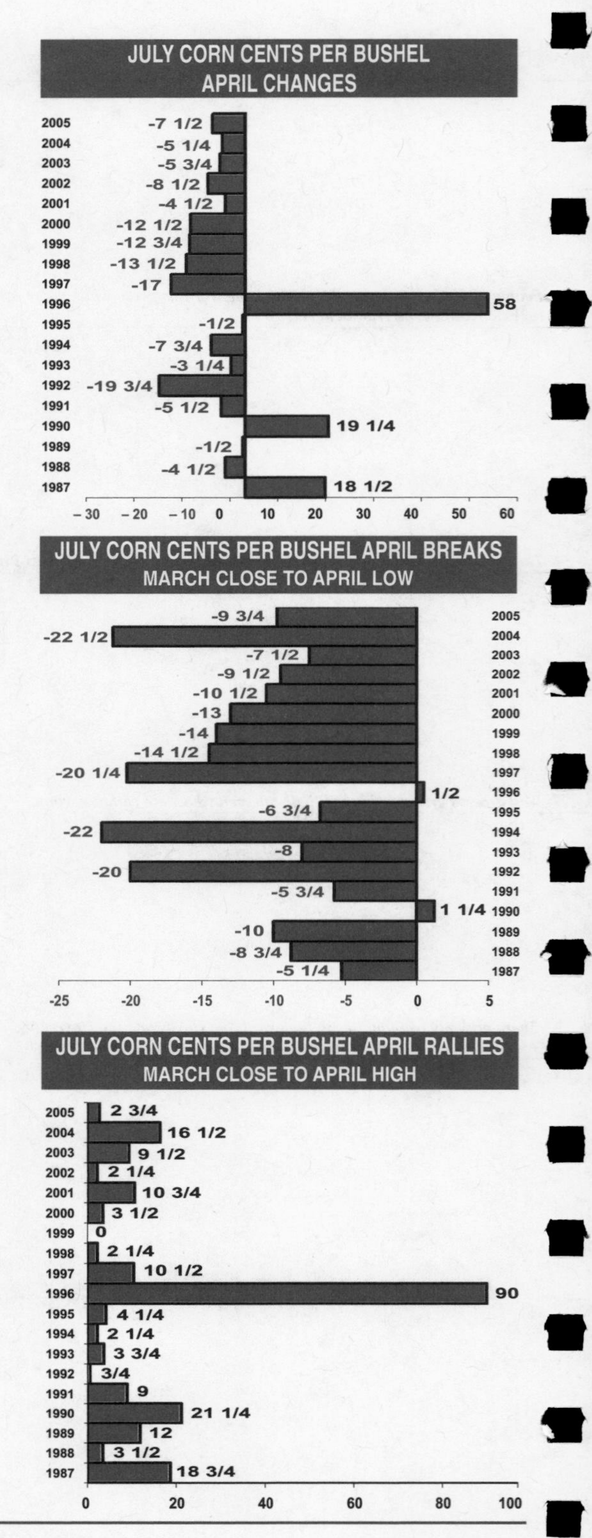

APRIL

MONDAY
2

CL	63.2	**NG**	55.6	**GC**	63.2	**SI**	52.6
S	57.9	**W**	31.6	**C**	47.4	**LC**	47.4
LH	44.4	**KC**	72.2	**CC**	68.4	**SB**	57.9

Every truth passes through three stages before it is recognized. In the first it is ridiculed; in the second it is opposed; in the third it is regarded as self-evident. — Arthur Schopenhauer (German philosopher, 1788–1860)

Passover

TUESDAY
3

CL	44.4	**NG**	47.4	**GC**	52.6	**SI**	57.9
S	57.9	**W**	52.6	**C**	68.4	**LC**	66.7
LH	63.2	**KC**	31.6	**CC**	21.1	**SB**	36.8

Getting ahead in a difficult profession requires avid faith in yourself. That is why some people with mediocre talent, but with great inner drive, go much further than people with vastly superior talent. — Sophia Loren

WEDNESDAY
4

CL	57.9	**NG**	61.1	**GC**	44.4	**SI**	52.6
S	47.4	**W**	66.7	**C**	72.2	**LC**	57.9
LH	47.4	**KC**	55.6	**CC**	55.6	**SB**	72.2

There is nothing more important than your emotional balance. — Jesse Livermore

THURSDAY
5

CL	61.1	**NG**	57.9	**GC**	52.6	**SI**	47.4
S	47.4	**W**	57.9	**C**	38.9	**LC**	66.7
LH	52.6	**KC**	52.6	**CC**	52.6	**SB**	52.6

'Tis better to be silent and be thought a fool, than to speak and remove all doubt.
— Abraham Lincoln (16th U.S. President, 1809–1865)

Good Friday (Market Closed)

FRIDAY
6

When speculation has done its worst, two and two still make four. — Samuel Johnson (English essayist, 1709–1784)

SATURDAY
7

Easter

SUNDAY
8

UNLEADED GASOLINE GAINS IN 2ND HALF OF APRIL BOTH ABSOLUTELY AND RELATIVELY

The summer driving season begins in earnest starting with the long Memorial Day weekend (the last weekend in May). In preparation for this onslaught of demand, Gasoline prices have tended to rise both on an absolute as well as on a relative basis in the latter half of April.

During the 19-year period from 1988 to 2006, June Unleaded Gasoline futures have gained during the last two weeks of April 17 times (89.4%), posting an average gain during this period of +4.51 cents/gallon.

At the same time, June Unleaded futures have gained relative to June Heating Oil futures 14 times (73.6%), with an average increase relative to Heating Oil of +1.62 cents/gallon.

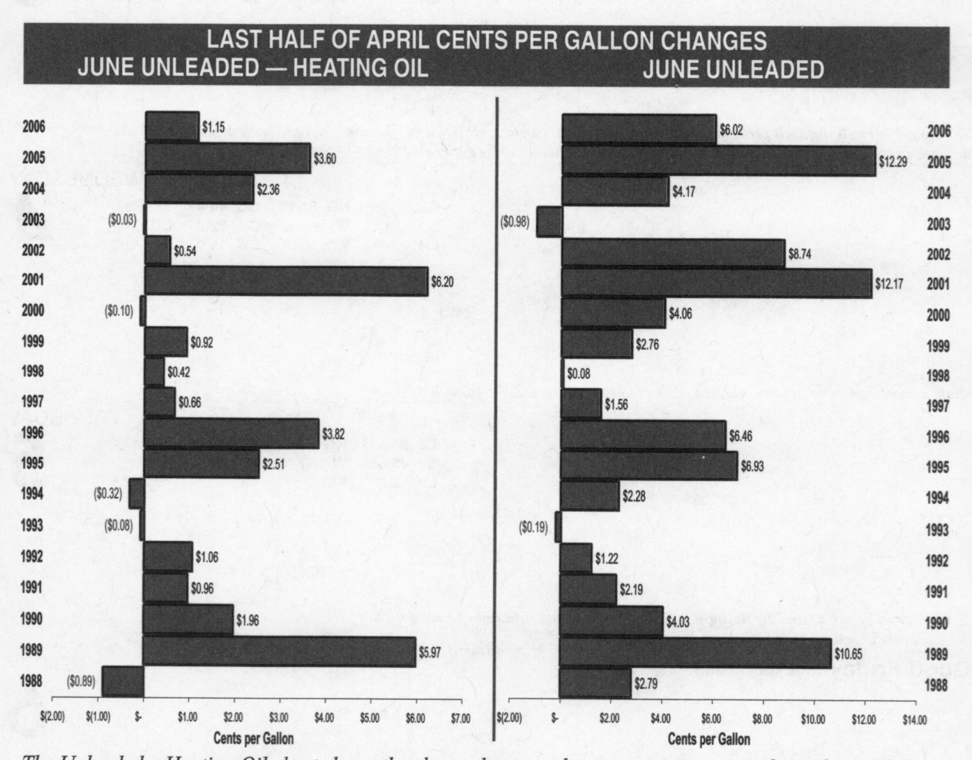

The Unleaded – Heating Oil chart shows the change between the two contracts on a relative basis while the Unleaded Chart simply shows the absolute change in June Unleaded futures from the 2nd week of April through to the 4th week.

Unleaded Gasoline futures tend to rise during the last two weeks in April due to inventory building ahead of the summer driving season.

June Unleaded Gasoline also tends to gain ground relative to June Heating Oil, as the industry concentrates on building Gasoline inventories. Traders can take advantage of this market by establishing long June Unleaded, short June Heating Oil positions. The normal margin requirement for this Intercommodity Spread (see page 26) is 75% less than the combined positions — subject to change without notice. As such, traders may find the spread to be a less volatile and more affordable way to participate in the Petroleum markets at this time of year.

APRIL

MONDAY
9

CL 47.4	NG 55.6	GC 44.4	SI 52.6
S 42.1	W 47.4	C 55.6	LC 31.6
LH 42.1	KC 47.4	CC 42.1	SB 36.8

A gold mine is a hole in the ground with a liar on top.
— Mark Twain (1835–1910, pen name of Samuel Longhorne Clemens, American novelist and satirist)

TUESDAY
10

CL 33.3	NG 57.9	GC 63.2	SI 47.4
S 68.4	W 47.4	C 55.6	LC 52.6
LH 31.6	KC 52.6	CC 26.3	SB 42.1

The two most abundant elements in the universe are Hydrogen and Stupidity. — Harlan Ellison (Science fiction writer, b. 1934)

WEDNESDAY
11

CL 68.4	NG 68.4	GC 44.4	SI 47.4
S 42.1	W 42.1	C 57.9	LC 31.6
LH 66.7	KC 52.6	CC 52.6	SB 31.6

Ideas are easy; it's execution that's hard. — Jeff Bezos (Amazon.com)

THURSDAY
12

CL 52.6	NG 55.6	GC 47.4	SI 57.9
S 42.1	W 38.9	C 47.4	LC 61.1
LH 61.1	KC 31.6	CC 47.4	SB 57.9

The time to buy is when blood is running in the streets. — Baron Nathan Rothschild (London financier, 1777–1836)

FRIDAY
13

CL 57.9	NG 47.4	GC 57.9	SI 61.1
S 47.4	W 47.4	C 47.4	LC 44.4
LH 42.1	KC 44.4	CC 52.6	SB 47.4

Life is not a spectacle or a feast; it is a predicament. — George Santayana (American philosopher, poet, 1863–1952)

SATURDAY
14

SUNDAY
15

COMMODITY SEASONALITY PERCENTAGE PLAYS

Ecclesiastes 3:1-8 says that for everything there is a season. Though the commodity markets are far removed from the world Ecclesiastes "the preacher" was describing, his sentiment is very applicable.

Most physical commodities have either a season of production or consumption — planting, harvest, or peak demand periods. Throughout the Almanac we describe these times and the markets' corresponding tendencies. The following table shows the best 24 seasonal tendencies from 1987 through 2005 for the 12 commodity futures markets covered: Crude Oil, Natural Gas, Gold, Silver, Soybeans, CBOT Wheat, Corn, Live Cattle, Lean Hogs, Coffee, Sugar, and Cocoa.

24 BEST COMMODITY SEASONALITIES

Commodity	Symbol	Position	Entry Date	Exit Date	# Win	# Loss	Average P&L	Average Loss
April Live Cattle	LCJ7	Long	01/02	03/05	16	3	$880.11	($1,346.67)
April Gold	GCJ7	Short	01/23	03/06	16	3	$778.95	($716.67)
March Soybeans	SF8	Short	01/24	02/08	16	3	$413.16	($575.00)
March CBOT Wheat	WH7	Short	01/31	02/27	16	3	$469.08	($987.50)
May Corn	CK7	Long	02/26	03/16	15	4	$201.32	($353.13)
June Natural Gas	NGM7	Long	03/01	04/11	12	2	$2,745.71	($2,135.00)
May Sugar	SBK7	Short	03/21	04/17	16	3	$539.37	($798.93)
July Cocoa	CCN8	Short	04/05	06/12	17	2	$818.42	($1,225.00)
October Crude Oil	CLV7	Long	04/13	05/07	16	3	$683.16	($266.67)
July Soybeans	SN7	Long	04/16	05/09	16	3	$913.82	($895.83)
September Coffee	KCU7	Short	06/05	06/25	16	3	$3,592.70	($1,368.75)
July Silver	SIN7	Short	06/07	06/28	16	3	$763.16	($678.33)
September Natural Gas	NGU7	Short	06/26	07/20	12	2	$3,125.71	($2,480.00)
August Live Cattle	LCQ7	Long	06/27	07/31	16	3	$644.84	($956.00)
December CBOT Wheat	WZ7	Long	08/06	08/24	16	3	$238.16	($550.00)
December Corn	CZ7	Short	08/27	09/27	16	3	$445.39	($712.50)
October Lean Hogs	LHV7	Long	08/30	09/28	16	3	$1,098.95	($1,098.67)
December Coffee	KCZ7	Short	09/10	10/01	16	3	$2,282.37	($1,706.25)
January Silver	SIF8	Long	09/10	09/25	15	4	$426.84	($1,107.50)
December Gold	GCZ7	Long	09/18	09/26	15	4	$617.89	($570.00)
March Cocoa	CCH8	Short	09/27	11/02	16	3	$600.00	($900.00)
March Crude Oil	CLH8	Short	10/15	11/08	16	3	$896.32	($400.00)
March Sugar	SBH8	Long	10/26	12/03	17	2	$417.94	($722.40)
April Lean Hogs	LHJ8	Long	12/20	01/26	16	3	$800.63	($1,236.67)

Average P&L refers to $ value of average move across all dates during time frame studied on a closing basis.
Average loss refers to the average closing value of all losses during the aforementioned time frame.

Of course, these trading ideas should not be followed blindly. Cycles change in the futures markets rapidly and traders should be on guard that the abovementioned time frames may not result in the expected move, as nothing in the world of futures speculation is for sure. However, traders should pay attention to these time frames, as they have been the strongest (or weakest) periods for the abovementioned commodity futures during the 1987 through 2005 period.

APRIL

MONDAY 16

CL 33.3	NG 57.9	GC 52.6	SI 47.4
S 52.6	W 57.9	C 47.4	LC 52.6
LH 47.4	KC 63.2	CC 63.2	SB 44.4

Not only is the universe (and "marketplace") stranger than we imagine, it is stranger than we can imagine.
— Arthur Eddington

TUESDAY 17

CL 63.2	NG 63.2	GC 38.9	SI 63.2
S 55.6	W 57.9	C 52.6	LC 44.4
LH 52.6	KC 47.4	CC 42.1	SB 31.6

You cannot dream yourself into a character; you must hammer and forge yourself one. — James A. Foude

WEDNESDAY 18

CL 63.2	NG 44.4	GC 47.4	SI 47.4
S 36.8	W 38.9	C 31.6	LC 47.4
LH 66.7	KC 36.8	CC 42.1	SB 78.9

There are sadistic scientists who hurry to hunt down errors instead of establishing the truth.
— Marie Curie (Polish chemist, 1st female Nobel laureate, 1903 Physics & 1911 Chemistry, 1867–1934)

THURSDAY 19

CL 68.4	NG 52.6	GC 47.4	SI 31.6
S 57.9	W 68.4	C 63.2	LC 55.6
LH 61.1	KC 77.8	CC 57.9	SB 47.4

If you're not confused, you're not paying attention. — Tom Peters (*In Search Of Excellence*)

FRIDAY 20

CL 68.4	NG 77.8	GC 57.9	SI 57.9
S 33.3	W 42.1	C 31.6	LC 47.4
LH 47.4	KC 36.8	CC 57.9	SB 52.6

No amount of experimentation can ever prove me right; a single experiment can prove me wrong.
— Abraham Lincoln (16th U.S. President, 1809–1865)

SATURDAY 21

SUNDAY 22

MONEY MAKES THE WORLD GO ROUND AS WELL AS THE COMMODITY MARKETS

Prior to establishing the first Standardized Futures contracts, commodities were traded between parties — one buyer and one seller. All aspects of the transaction were negotiated, including the amount of the commodity, as well as time of delivery and quality. This style of negotiation worked well for centuries but was rife with risk, as one side of the contract could renege, but with the establishment of the Chicago Board of Trade (CBOT), futures became standardized and the only thing left up to negotiation became price.

In 1848, 48 merchants started the CBOT. Contract sizes were set (and sometimes adjusted), and the exchange became the middleman for every transaction. With standardized futures, no longer did one side have to hope the other side would fulfill the contract, as the Exchange became the buyer for every seller and seller for every buyer — the counter party. With counterparty risk eliminated, futures rapidly became the most widely accepted vehicle for transferring risk from those who did not wish to bear it (hedgers) to those who did (speculators).

At the cornerstone of the exchanges' involvement is a performance bond — or margin requirements. In order to initiate a futures position (either long or short), the market participant must have an initial amount of funds — known as Initial Margin. Initial margin is the amount of money one must have in a trading account prior to establishing a futures position.

SAMPLE MARGIN REQUIREMENTS
(in $'s per contract)

Commodity	Initial Margin	Maintenance Margin
METALS		
COMEX GOLD	1350	1000
COMEX SILVER	2025	1500
GRAINS		
WHEAT	506	375
CORN	506	375
SOYBEANS	1080	800
SOFTS		
COCOA	980	700
COFFEE	3080	2200
SUGAR	700	500
MEATS		
LIVE CATTLE	1080	800
LEAN HOGS	1080	800
ENERGIES		
CRUDE OIL	9112	6750
NAT. GAS	21600	16000

Exchanges may change margin requirements without notice to reflect current market conditions.

To make sure the performance bond is upheld, the futures exchanges require that funds on deposit with a registered exchange broker must exceed the maintenance margin level. If available funds on deposit with a brokerage slip below the maintenance margin level, traders are forced to either liquidate their positions or deposit more funds in a very timely fashion (before the close of trading).

For example, assume a trader with a $1,000 account initiates a position in Corn futures. The current initial margin for Corn is $500, with maintenance of $400. If the trader bought Corn and prices dip by 12 cents/bushel, the trader will receive a margin call from his/her broker and have to either liquidate the position, or deposit sufficient funds to bring the account back above the initial margin requirement. Any account which slips below the maintenance margin level must be brought above the initial margin level, effectively ensuring the exchange that the trader has the financial wherewithal to participate in the market.

Margin requirements are at the cornerstone of futures trading. The margin (performance bond) system ensures that traders have adequate capital to cover their obligation in general. Of course, due to the margin and resulting financial leverage involved in commodity trading, it is possible to lose more than your initial invenstment. But even when this happens, the trader's brokerage makes good on the investment and seeks remedy from the individual trader privately.

APRIL

MONDAY
23

CL 52.6	NG 57.9	GC 57.9	SI 73.7
S 57.9	W 31.6	C 42.1	LC 47.4
LH 44.4	KC 63.2	CC 52.6	SB 63.2

Charts not only tell what was, they tell what is; and a trend from was to is (projected linearly into the "will be") contains better percentages than clumsy guessing. — R. A. Levy

TUESDAY
24

CL 72.2	NG 44.4	GC 36.8	SI 47.4
S 72.2	W 36.8	C 61.1	LC 47.4
LH 77.8	KC 78.9	CC 55.6	SB 57.9

To accomplish great things we must not only act, but also dream, not only plan, but also believe.
— Anatole France (French author, 1844–1924)

WEDNESDAY
25

CL 44.4	NG 42.1	GC 42.1	SI 31.6
S 36.8	W 36.8	C 31.6	LC 57.9
LH 72.2	KC 47.4	CC 47.4	SB 63.2

Give me a lever long enough and a fulcrum on which to place it, and I shall move the world.
— Archimedes (Sicilian-born Greek mathematician, physicist, engineer, astronomer, and philosopher, 287–212 B.C.)

THURSDAY
26

CL 73.7	NG 38.9	GC 36.8	SI 52.6
S 47.4	W 66.7	C 52.6	LC 52.6
LH 44.4	KC 31.6	CC 47.4	SB 38.9

One moment of patience may ward off great disaster. One moment of impatience may ruin a whole life. — Chinese proverb

FRIDAY
27

CL 47.4	NG 44.4	GC 47.4	SI 36.8
S 47.4	W 36.8	C 61.1	LC 72.2
LH 72.2	KC 33.3	CC 27.8	SB 21.1

In times of change, learners inherit the Earth, while the learned find themselves beautifully equipped to deal with a world that no longer exists. — Eric Hoffer (*The True Believer*, 1951)

SATURDAY
28

SUNDAY
29

MAY ALMANAC

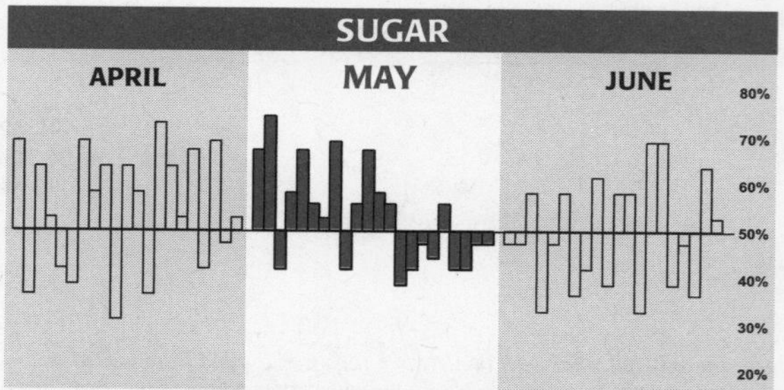

Market Probability Chart above is a graphic representation of Sugar futures taken from the Market Probability Calendar on page 174

PETROLEUM FUTURES: April strength in Crude tends to reverse in May, however new monthly highs are usually made (10 of 13) and the May break is not very hard ◆ September Crude up 9 / down 10 in May ◆ October Natural Gas up 8 / down 7 in May ◆ Best Mays have followed April strength.

METALS FUTURES: August Gold up 9 / down 10 ◆ May rallies reversed in June (7 of 9) ◆ Best Mays basis July Silver have followed April weakness ◆ 8 of last 11 April breaks have been reversed in May in July Silver ◆ May Silver rallies, however, are fleeting ◆ 8 of last 11 May Silver rallies basis July futures have been reversed in June.

GRAIN FUTURES: 12 of last 19 years have seen July Soybeans move in the opposite direction of their April trend ◆ 6 of 9 April rallies reversed, 6 of 10 April breaks continued in May, basis July Soybeans ◆ Harvest pressures weigh on CBOT wheat ◆ July Wheat up 8 / down 11 ◆ 7 of 10 May rallies in July Corn have reversed in June.

LIVESTOCK FUTURES: April strength in June Live Cattle reversed in May (7 of 10) ◆ 4th-weakest month for Live Hogs ◆ Best Mays follow strong April ◆ August Lean Hogs up 8 / down 11 in April.

SOFTS FUTURES: Coffee futures down 10 of 19 ◆ 8 of 9 May rallies reversed in June and 8 of 10 May breaks continued in June, basis July Coffee ◆ April breaks in July Sugar reversed 7 of 10 ◆ July Sugar up 13 of 19 ◆ 9 of 11 May rallies continued in June and 4 of 8 May breaks continued ◆ July Cocoa up 7 / down 12.

COMMODITY SPOTLIGHT SUGAR

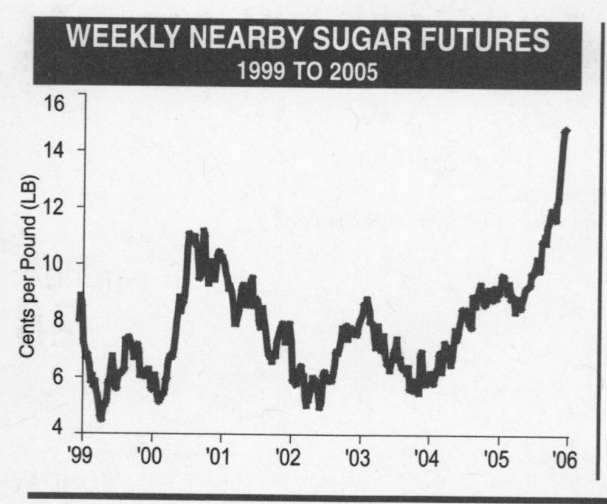

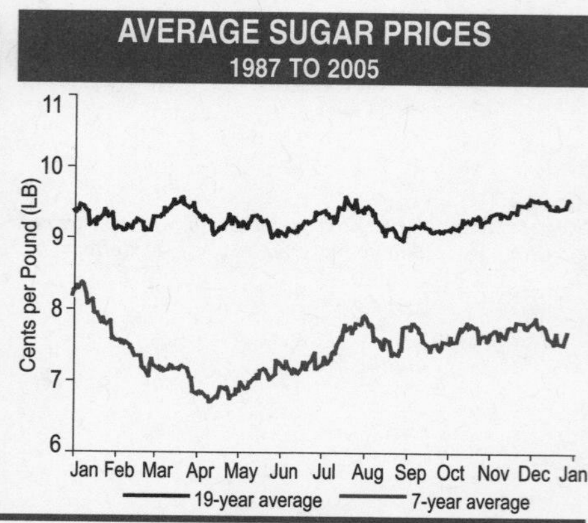

Sugar is not only important in fueling the body and sweet tooth, but it is becoming more strategic as a Petroleum additive… case in point Brazil, which has used Sugar to curtail foreign petroleum imports.

APRIL/MAY

MONDAY
30

CL 52.6	NG 42.1	GC 55.6	SI 63.2
S 36.8	W 33.3	C 47.4	LC 47.4
LH 47.4	KC 42.1	CC 52.6	SB 57.9

Give me six hours to chop down a tree and I will spend the first four sharpening the axe.
— Abraham Lincoln (16th U.S. President, 1809–1865)

TUESDAY
1

CL 57.9	NG 47.4	GC 55.6	SI 72.2
S 78.9	W 72.2	C 63.2	LC 61.1
LH 52.6	KC 52.6	CC 55.6	SB 22.2

I don't believe in intuition. When you get sudden flashes of perception, it is just the brain working faster than usual.
— Katherine Anne Porter (American author, 1890–1980)

WEDNESDAY
2

CL 72.2	NG 47.4	GC 63.2	SI 52.6
S 63.2	W 52.6	C 68.4	LC 55.6
LH 68.4	KC 47.4	CC 47.4	SB 38.9

True individual freedom cannot exist without economic security and independence.
— Franklin D. Roosevelt (32nd U.S. President, 1882–1945)

THURSDAY
3

CL 38.9	NG 61.1	GC 47.4	SI 52.6
S 47.4	W 52.6	C 57.9	LC 63.2
LH 55.6	KC 47.4	CC 61.1	SB 52.6

Towering genius disdains a beaten path. It scorns to tread in the footsteps of any predecessor, however illustrious. It thirsts for distinction. — Abraham Lincoln (16th U.S. President, 1809–1865)

FRIDAY
4

CL 63.2	NG 47.4	GC 63.2	SI 66.7
S 52.6	W 57.9	C 47.4	LC 27.8
LH 55.6	KC 57.9	CC 55.6	SB 47.4

In nature there are no rewards or punishments; there are consequences. — Horace Annesley Vachell (*The Force of Clay*)

SATURDAY
5

SUNDAY
6

SUGAR MAY BE SWEET FOLLOWING APRIL BREAKS

Two of the three largest producers of Sugar worldwide (Brazil and India) usually finish harvesting their cane/beet crops in March. The 3rd-largest producer (China) begins planting in April. As such, the marketplace is usually flush with supply in April and concerned about future supply as well. Thus, April has been the 2nd-worst month for Sugar prices — basis the nearby active contract.

But as the old saying goes... "it is usually darkest before the dawn." Following the last 10 April breaks in July futures during the 1987 to 2005 period, July Sugar futures have bounced back in May, posting positive monthly changes 7 times (70%).

On average during the aforementioned period, July Sugar futures have declined in April by -0.18 cents/lb. Following these April breaks, July Sugar has posted an average gain of +0.24 cents/lb in May. The average rally in May has been +0.75 cents/lb. The average May break is -0.35 cents/lb.

Remembering that the "trend is not always your friend," traders may well be served by looking to buy (long) July Sugar following April weakness. After all, prices have rebounded in May 70% of the time during the 1987 to 2005 period, with the average rally being more than twice as strong as the average break. As the following table shows, Sugar may be sweet after an April break. (See page 52 for an additional May related Sugar strategy.)

JULY SUGAR CENTS PER POUND CHANGES

Date	Mar Close	Apr Low	April Break Mar Close to Apr Low	Apr Close	Apr Change	May Rally Apr Close to May High	May Break Apr Close to May Low	May Change
1987	6.87	6.54	-0.33	7.31	0.44	0.07	-0.78	-0.59
1988	8.80	8.31	-0.49	8.51	-0.29	1.18	-0.41	0.96
1989	12.69	11.51	-1.18	11.54	-1.15	1.30	-0.69	-0.68
1990	15.71	15.17	-0.54	16.02	0.31	0.25	-2.49	-2.34
1991	8.68	7.63	-1.05	7.73	-0.95	0.50	-0.18	0.32
1992	8.64	8.59	-0.05	9.36	0.72	0.68	-0.21	0.67
1993	12.53	10.85	-1.68	12.82	0.29	0.44	-2.30	-2.06
1994	12.22	10.75	-1.47	11.67	-0.55	0.68	-0.32	0.37
1995	13.14	11.32	-1.82	11.56	-1.58	0.49	-0.50	0.16
1996	10.96	10.15	-0.81	10.39	-0.57	1.20	-0.08	0.82
1997	10.58	10.58	0.00	10.96	0.38	0.29	-0.31	0.21
1998	9.75	8.31	-1.44	8.46	-1.29	0.99	-0.31	-0.18
1999	5.67	3.93	-1.74	4.33	-1.34	0.72	0.03	0.67
2000	5.78	5.65	-0.13	6.64	0.86	1.40	-0.32	0.91
2001	7.42	7.55	0.13	8.50	1.08	0.85	-0.10	0.05
2002	5.25	4.83	-0.42	5.36	0.11	0.68	-0.29	0.54
2003	7.27	6.84	-0.43	7.20	-0.07	0.27	-0.55	-0.12
2004	6.58	6.32	-0.26	6.95	0.37	0.12	-0.70	0.11
2005	8.90	8.13	-0.77	8.66	-0.24	0.15	-0.45	0.10
Averages			**-0.76**		**-0.18**	**0.65**	**-0.58**	**-0.00**
# Down			**17**		**10**		**18**	**6**
April Breaks					**-0.35**			
Averages following April Break						**0.75**	**-0.35**	**0.24**

April weakness as defined by a lower April settlement than March are highlighted in Purple.

MAY

MONDAY 7

CL	57.9	**NG**	38.9	**GC**	42.1	**SI**	42.1
S	42.1	**W**	63.2	**C**	47.4	**LC**	47.4
LH	68.4	**KC**	31.6	**CC**	44.4	**SB**	78.9

You try to be greedy when others are fearful, and fearful when others are greedy. — Warren Buffett

TUESDAY 8

CL	61.1	**NG**	47.4	**GC**	42.1	**SI**	47.4
S	63.2	**W**	61.1	**C**	55.6	**LC**	44.4
LH	55.6	**KC**	47.4	**CC**	42.1	**SB**	36.8

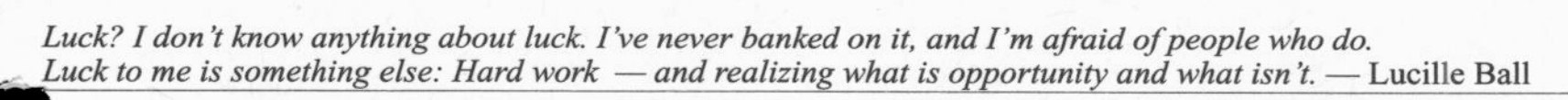

Luck? I don't know anything about luck. I've never banked on it, and I'm afraid of people who do. Luck to me is something else: Hard work — and realizing what is opportunity and what isn't. — Lucille Ball

WEDNESDAY 9

CL	57.9	**NG**	57.9	**GC**	31.6	**SI**	52.6
S	42.1	**W**	42.1	**C**	26.3	**LC**	36.8
LH	31.6	**KC**	73.7	**CC**	52.6	**SB**	73.7

A man is not idle because he is absorbed in thought. There is a visible labor and there is an invisible labor.
— Victor Hugo (French novelist, playwright, *Hunchback of Notre Dame* and *Les Misérables*, 1802–1885)

THURSDAY 10

CL	63.2	**NG**	63.2	**GC**	78.9	**SI**	52.6
S	68.4	**W**	55.6	**C**	66.7	**LC**	52.6
LH	52.6	**KC**	72.2	**CC**	36.8	**SB**	57.9

Throughout all my years of investing I've found that the big money was never made in the buying or the selling. The big money was made in the waiting. — Jesse Livermore

FRIDAY 11

CL	42.1	**NG**	57.9	**GC**	42.1	**SI**	36.8
S	26.3	**W**	47.4	**C**	47.4	**LC**	47.4
LH	47.4	**KC**	42.1	**CC**	61.1	**SB**	72.2

Stock prices tend to discount what has been unanimously reported by the mass media.
— Louis Ehrenkrantz (Ehrenkrantz, Lyons & Ross)

SATURDAY 12

Mother's Day

SUNDAY 13

HARVEST BREAKS IN WHEAT CONTINUE

The price of a commodity is set by buyers and sellers. This balance between buying and selling usually sets a fair price. However, especially in annually produced commodities like Wheat, one side usually tips its hand with aggressive action, especially around harvest. Case in point: September Chicago Board of Trade (CBOT) Wheat futures in May.

During the 19-year period beginning in 1987, September CBOT Wheat futures have advanced in May 8 times and declined 11 times. Rallies in May were punctuated by aggressive buying or a lack of producer selling based on perceptions regarding supply and demand. During breaks, the psychology of the market is one of producer panic and consumer caution equating to aggressive selling and mild buying.

Eight of the last 11 (72.7%) years which have seen September CBOT Wheat futures finish the month of May lower have experienced continued weakness through July. On average, September CBOT Wheat has experienced a June/July Break of -38 3/4 cents/bushel following May weakness. The average Jun/Jul Rally following May weakness has averaged only +16 1/2 cents/bushel. In other words, May weakness in September CBOT Wheat futures tends to foreshadow above average weakness in the coming months as harvest approaches.

SEPTEMBER CBOT WHEAT CENTS PER BUSHEL CHANGES

Date	May Close	May Change	Jun/Jul High	Jun/Jul Rally	Jun/Jul Low	Jun/Jul Break	Jul Close	Jun/Jul Change
1987	278 3/4	2 1/4	284	5 1/4	254 3/4	-24	261 1/4	-17 2/4
1988	361 2/4	37 3/4	421	59 2/4	351 2/4	-10	368 1/4	6 3/4
1989	393 1/4	-19 2/4	415 1/4	22	384	-9 1/4	384 2/4	-8 3/4
1990	339 3/4	-12	343 1/4	3 2/4	287 2/4	-52 1/4	288 1/4	-51 2/4
1991	294	1 2/4	310	16	258 2/4	-35 2/4	294	0
1992	354 1/4	-3 1/4	380	25 3/4	317	-37 1/4	317 1/4	-37
1993	291 1/4	-12 2/4	325	33 3/4	282 1/4	-9	304	12 3/4
1994	333 3/4	-2/4	351	17 1/4	312	-21 3/4	330 2/4	-3 1/4
1995	379	22 2/4	480 2/4	101 2/4	375	-4	464 1/4	85 1/4
1996	531 3/4	-26 1/4	527	-4 3/4	428	-103 3/4	440	-91 3/4
1997	367 2/4	-71 1/4	379 2/4	12	321 2/4	-46	362	-5 2/4
1998	294 2/4	-16 3/4	306 2/4	12	251 1/4	-43 1/4	252 2/4	-42
1999	262 2/4	-15 1/4	276 2/4	14	240 3/4	-21 3/4	263 3/4	1 1/4
2000	286 3/4	20 1/4	291 2/4	4 3/4	239	-47 3/4	246 1/4	-40 2/4
2001	277	-16 2/4	295	18	254	-23	278 2/4	1 2/4
2002	288 2/4	13	343	54 2/4	281	-7 2/4	334	45 2/4
2003	330	41 3/4	355 2/4	25 2/4	303 2/4	-26 2/4	348 2/4	18 2/4
2004	370 1/4	-25 2/4	399	28 3/4	310	-60 1/4	312 1/4	-58
2005	342 1/4	7 3/4	356	13 3/4	320 2/4	-21 3/4	327 3/4	-14 2/4
Averages		**-3 3/4**		**24 1/4**		**-31 3/4**		**-10 2/4**
# Down		**11**		**1**		**19**		**12**
Average Down May		**-20**						
Subsequent Averages				**16 2/4**		**-38 3/4**		**-25 3/4**
# Up				**10**		**0**		**3**
# Down				**1**		**11**		**8**

May weakness as defined by a lower May settlement than April are highlighted in Purple.

MAY

MONDAY **14**

CL 52.6	**NG** 63.2	**GC** 52.6	**SI** 36.8
S 52.6	**W** 63.2	**C** 55.6	**LC** 68.4
LH 52.6	**KC** 21.1	**CC** 42.1	**SB** 55.6

The test of success is not what you do when you are on top. Success is how high you bounce when you hit bottom.
— General George S. Patton, Jr. (1885–1945)

TUESDAY **15**

CL 61.1	**NG** 52.6	**GC** 52.6	**SI** 63.2
S 31.6	**W** 27.8	**C** 47.4	**LC** 52.6
LH 44.4	**KC** 47.4	**CC** 63.2	**SB** 63.2

The market is a voting machine, whereon countless individuals register choices which are the product partly of reason and partly of emotion. — Graham & Dodd

WEDNESDAY **16**

CL 57.9	**NG** 55.6	**GC** 68.4	**SI** 55.6
S 47.4	**W** 36.8	**C** 52.6	**LC** 36.8
LH 52.6	**KC** 68.4	**CC** 42.1	**SB** 42.1

Press on. Nothing in the world can take the place of persistence. Talent will not: nothing is more common than unrewarded talent. Education alone will not: the world is full of educated failures. Persistence alone is omnipotent. — Calvin Coolidge

THURSDAY **17**

CL 52.6	**NG** 63.2	**GC** 52.6	**SI** 36.8
S 52.6	**W** 63.2	**C** 55.6	**LC** 68.4
LH 52.6	**KC** 21.1	**CC** 42.1	**SB** 55.6

It's not the strongest of the species (think "traders") that survive, nor the most intelligent, but the one most responsive to change. — Charles Darwin

FRIDAY **18**

CL 36.8	**NG** 42.1	**GC** 47.4	**SI** 44.4
S 63.2	**W** 31.6	**C** 47.4	**LC** 52.6
LH 38.9	**KC** 63.2	**CC** 55.6	**SB** 63.2

Learning from experience is a faculty almost never practiced. — Barbara Tuchman

SATURDAY **19**

SUNDAY **20**

SUGAR'S MAY TREND CONTINUES THROUGH JUNE

As mentioned earlier (page 48), the April/May period is critical for Sugar. Harvests are completing in Brazil and India and planting in China is starting. These factors set the tone for the supply side, often driving prices higher or lower.

In years when May is strong, the price strength in May tends to continue through June on the July futures. Following the last 13 May rallies, July Sugar futures have continued higher through June 11 times (84.6%) during the 1987 to 2005 period. Following the 6 occurrences of May weakness during the same time period, July Sugar futures have continued their decline in June 4 times (66.6%).

May's monthly trend has continued through June 15 of the 19 years studied (78.9%) — basis July futures. The average trend continuation has seen a June rally of +1.21 cents/lb and a June break of -0.47 cents/lb. Following strong Mays, July Sugar has continued higher in June 11 times (84.6%) with an average rally of +1.38 cents/lb and a break of -0.47 cents/lb during June. Following May weakness, July Sugar futures have continued lower 4 times (66.6%), with an average break of -0.90 cents/lb and a rally of +0.82 cents/lb during June.

Entering into the critical crop time of April/May, traders may do well to buy after April weakness, and hold positions through June if by the end of May the trend has reversed. Otherwise, Sugar market participants should follow May's trend.

JULY SUGAR CENTS PER POUND CHANGES

Date	Apr Close	May Close	May Change	Jun Close	Jun Change	Comment	Jun Rally May Close to Jun High	Jun Break May Close to Jun Low
1987	7.31	6.72	-0.59	6.66	-0.06	Continuation	0.23	-0.36
1988	8.51	9.47	0.96	13.33	3.86	Continuation	4.23	0.11
1989	11.54	10.86	-0.68	14.33	3.47	Reversal	3.49	0.08
1990	16.02	13.68	-2.34	12.99	-0.69	Continuation	0.02	-1.53
1991	7.73	8.05	0.32	10.70	2.65	Continuation	3.35	-0.05
1992	9.36	10.03	0.67	10.55	0.52	Continuation	1.19	-0.39
1993	12.82	10.76	-2.06	9.95	-0.81	Continuation	0.49	-1.51
1994	11.67	12.04	0.37	11.49	-0.55	Reversal	0.56	-0.64
1995	11.56	11.72	0.16	12.03	0.31	Continuation	1.18	-0.43
1996	10.39	11.21	0.82	12.43	1.22	Continuation	1.64	-0.06
1997	10.96	11.17	0.21	11.00	-0.17	Reversal	0.41	-0.29
1998	8.46	8.28	-0.18	8.46	0.18	Reversal	0.69	-1.08
1999	4.33	5.00	0.67	5.60	0.60	Continuation	1.17	0.02
2000	6.64	7.55	0.91	8.50	0.95	Continuation	1.95	0.02
2001	8.50	8.55	0.05	9.59	1.04	Continuation	1.15	-0.16
2002	5.36	5.90	0.54	5.91	0.01	Continuation	0.10	-0.93
2003	7.20	7.08	-0.12	6.33	-0.75	Continuation	0.02	-1.01
2004	6.95	7.06	0.11	7.24	0.18	Continuation	0.37	-0.49
2005	8.66	8.76	0.10	9.34	0.58	Continuation	0.66	-0.17
	# Up		13		13		19	4
					Averages			Averages
	# Continued				0.66	15	1.21	-0.47
	# Up May Continued				0.86	11	1.38	-0.47
	# Down May Continued				0.22	4	0.82	-0.90

Continuation is defined as a June monthly change in the same direction as that of May and are labeled in Purple.

MAY

MONDAY 21

CL 63.2	NG 38.9	GC 42.1	SI 47.4
S 31.6	W 42.1	C 33.3	LC 52.6
LH 55.6	KC 47.4	CC 61.1	SB 36.8

It's not that I am so smart; it's just that I stay with problems longer.
— Albert Einstein (German/American physicist, 1921 Nobel Prize, 1879–1955)

TUESDAY 22

CL 47.4	NG 47.4	GC 68.4	SI 61.1
S 47.4	W 47.4	C 44.4	LC 31.6
LH 36.8	KC 52.6	CC 57.9	SB 55.6

The true mystery of the world is the visible, not the invisible. — Oscar Wilde (Irish-born writer and wit)

WEDNESDAY 23

CL 42.1	NG 31.6	GC 47.4	SI 57.9
S 42.1	W 47.4	C 42.1	LC 66.7
LH 38.9	KC 36.8	CC 42.1	SB 63.2

Every action is a speculation, i.e., guided by a definite opinion concerning the uncertain conditions of the future.
— Ludwig von Mises

THURSDAY 24

CL 47.4	NG 47.4	GC 36.8	SI 38.9
S 47.4	W 36.8	C 44.4	LC 57.9
LH 42.1	KC 31.6	CC 57.9	SB 47.4

I measure what's going on, and I adapt to it. I try to get my ego out of the way. The market is smarter than I am so I bend.
— Martin Zweig

FRIDAY 25

CL 52.6	NG 47.4	GC 52.6	SI 47.4
S 47.4	W 44.4	C 36.8	LC 38.9
LH 31.6	KC 36.8	CC 21.1	SB 31.6

Good people (or "traders") are good because they've come to wisdom through failure.
We get very little wisdom from success, you know. — William Saroyan

SATURDAY 26

SUNDAY 27

JUNE ALMANAC

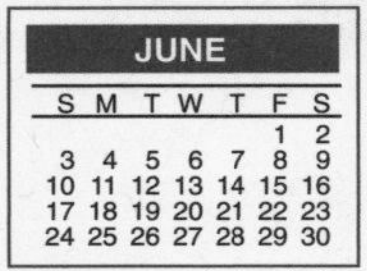

S	M	T	W	T	F	S
					1	2
3	4	5	6	7	8	9
10	11	12	13	14	15	16
17	18	19	20	21	22	23
24	25	26	27	28	29	30

JULY

S	M	T	W	T	F	S
1	2	3	4	5	6	7
8	9	10	11	12	13	14
15	16	17	18	19	20	21
22	23	24	25	26	27	28
29	30	31				

Market Probability Chart above is a graphic representation of Coffee futures taken from the Market Probability Calendar on page 169

PETROLEUM FUTURES: Best Junes have followed May strength, worst May weakness ◆ September Crude Oil up 9 / down 10 in June ◆ June / July worst period on record for Natural Gas ◆ October Natural Gas down -0.061 cents/BTU on average during June.

METALS FUTURES: October Gold tends toward weakness in June (down 12 / up 7) ◆ Worst Junes have followed May rallies (down 7 of 9) ◆ 4th-worst month on record for Gold ◆ Following May rallies, September Silver has declined 8 of 11 ◆ June down 12 of 19 basis September futures.

GRAIN FUTURES: November Soybeans up 7 / down 12 ◆ 6 of last 9 May rallies have resulted in June losses ◆ 8 of 12 June breaks have continued through July basis November Soybeans ◆ September CBOT Wheat down 14 of 19 on harvest pressures ◆ Worst Junes have followed May weakness basis September CBOT Wheat (9 of 11) ◆ September Corn down 13 of 19.

LIVESTOCK FUTURES: August Live Cattle up 8 / down 11 ◆ Worst Junes in Cattle have followed May rallies ◆ Every June rally from 1987 through 2005 has continued in June (9 of 9) ◆ 6 of last 10 June breaks have reversed in July ◆ Hogs tend towards weakness (up 8 / down 11) especially after May weakness.

SOFTS FUTURES: Coffee down 16 of 19 basis September futures ◆ Worst June Coffee breaks have followed May rallies (down 8 of 9, average decline of -12.48 cents) ◆ Sugar up 13 of 19 ◆ Best Junes follow May strength (9 of 11, average +0.61 cents/lb) ◆ Mid-crop harvest pressures Cocoa (down 10 / up 9) ◆ Best Junes have followed weak Mays (7 of 11).

COMMODITY SPOTLIGHT COFFEE

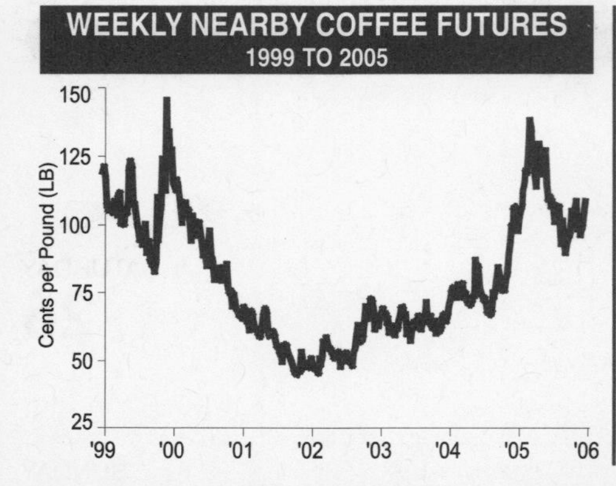

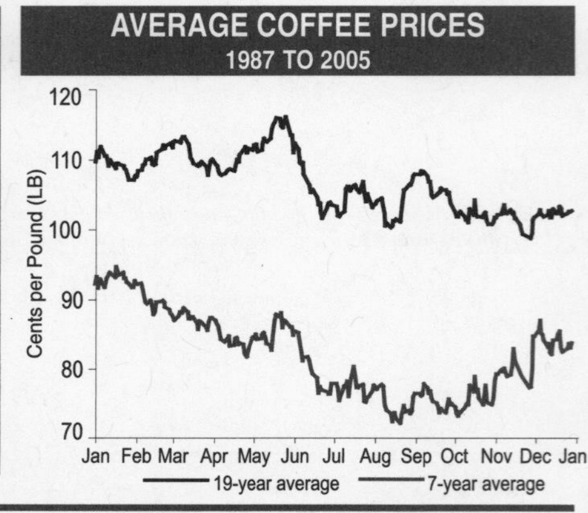

Coffee is the ultimate weather commodity! It builds massive risk premiums ahead of harvest and breaks violently unless there is a major frost.

MAY / JUNE

Memorial Day (Market Closed)

MONDAY
28

Things should be made as simple as possible, but not any simpler.
— Albert Einstein (German/American physicist, 1921 Nobel Prize, 1879–1955)

TUESDAY
29

CL	44.4	**NG**	57.9	**GC**	33.3	**SI**	26.3
S	31.6	**W**	42.1	**C**	42.1	**LC**	55.6
LH	57.9	**KC**	42.1	**CC**	47.4	**SB**	44.4

I don't know where speculation got such a bad name, since I know of no forward leap which was not fathered by speculation.
— John Steinbeck

WEDNESDAY
30

CL	42.1	**NG**	63.2	**GC**	57.9	**SI**	44.4
S	47.4	**W**	22.2	**C**	33.3	**LC**	15.8
LH	27.8	**KC**	44.4	**CC**	47.4	**SB**	16.7

It is a thousand times better to have common sense without education than to have education without common sense.
— Robert Green Ingersoll

THURSDAY
31

CL	52.6	**NG**	57.9	**GC**	26.3	**SI**	47.4
S	77.8	**W**	63.2	**C**	77.8	**LC**	42.1
LH	73.7	**KC**	31.6	**CC**	57.9	**SB**	63.2

The word "crisis" in Chinese is composed of two characters: the first, the symbol of danger; the second, opportunity. — Anonymous

FRIDAY
1

CL	52.6	**NG**	57.9	**GC**	26.3	**SI**	47.4
S	77.8	**W**	63.2	**C**	77.8	**LC**	42.1
LH	73.7	**KC**	31.6	**CC**	57.9	**SB**	63.2

What the superior man seeks, is in himself. What the inferior man seeks, is in others. — Confucius

SATURDAY
2

SUNDAY
3

COFFEE CRASHES IN JUNE

During the summer months, Coffee is dealt a double shock — southern hemisphere harvest pressures and lower consumption rates in the northern hemisphere.

Latin America is the major coffee-producing region of the world, accounting for over 60% of the world's production. Brazil is by far the largest producer in the region, with the Minas Gerais region alone producing as much coffee as Colombia and Costa Rica combined.

The Brazilian Coffee harvest usually begins in June, as the southern hemisphere begins winter. As harvest begins, supply on the world market becomes more available. This influx of supply comes at a time when major consuming countries in the northern hemisphere are going into summer — a time when coffee consumption tends to decrease.

This dynamic of increasing available supply and slowing demand in most years is readily apparent by the fact that September Coffee futures have declined 16 times (84.2%) in June during the 1987 to 2005 period. On average, September Coffee futures have declined by -8.41 cents/lb. They have surpassed the May lows 16 times (84.2%) as well, and have fallen from the May settlement to the June lows by an average of –14.90 cents/lb. Coffee prices have exceeded their May highs in June only twice, but remember 1994 when prices soared by +58.20 cents/lb above their May highs due to inclement weather.

Coffee traders should note that following the last 9 strong Mays, September Coffee has continued lower through July 8 times (88.8%) during the aforementioned 19-year period.

SEPTEMBER COFFEE CENTS PER POUND CHANGES

Date	May High	May Low	May Close	June Rally May Close to Jun High	June Break May Close to Jun Low	Jun Change	
1987	126.90	115.50	120.15	-1.40	-17.45	-14.40	
1988	138.40	132.15	134.92	8.23	-4.57	-3.49	May high exceeded in June
1989	130.00	120.10	124.50	1.90	-21.80	-16.44	
1990	99.95	91.75	96.05	1.20	-10.80	-10.45	
1991	93.00	88.20	88.80	2.00	-3.30	-2.90	
1992	67.80	61.00	65.30	0.60	-8.50	-7.20	
1993	68.00	58.00	65.35	-0.50	-6.45	-4.00	
1994	141.80	89.50	123.85	76.15	-7.35	67.75	May high exceeded in June
1995	180.00	152.00	156.80	7.10	-26.80	-26.50	
1996	128.50	115.10	115.35	7.65	-4.25	6.10	
1997	277.00	188.00	238.30	-2.30	-73.30	-65.90	
1998	135.25	122.00	129.60	-0.85	-21.10	-19.40	
1999	128.00	102.75	123.20	2.20	-24.10	-21.80	
2000	107.40	95.50	96.20	4.30	-9.70	-8.75	
2001	72.50	60.10	60.20	4.05	-3.10	-1.70	
2002	55.85	51.25	54.35	0.10	-5.85	-5.50	
2003	72.30	60.30	60.50	3.15	-2.60	0.60	
2004	88.75	71.40	87.60	0.30	-15.10	-12.30	
2005	131.50	119.05	121.55	8.45	-17.05	-13.50	
			Averages	6.44	-14.90	-8.41	
			# Up	15	0	3	
			# Down	4	19	16	

Continuation is defined as a June monthly change in the same direction as that of May and are labeled in Purple.

JUNE

MONDAY
4

CL 42.1	**NG** 57.9	**GC** 52.6	**SI** 47.4
S 47.4	**W** 47.4	**C** 44.4	**LC** 73.7
LH 63.2	**KC** 31.6	**CC** 31.6	**SB** 57.9

During the first period of a man's life, the greatest danger is: not to take the risk. — Søren Kierkegaard

TUESDAY
5

CL 52.6	**NG** 33.3	**GC** 47.4	**SI** 63.2
S 47.4	**W** 63.2	**C** 68.4	**LC** 55.6
LH 52.6	**KC** 77.8	**CC** 47.4	**SB** 42.1

The symbol of all relationships among...men, the moral symbol of respect for human beings, is the trader.
— Ayn Rand (Russian-born American novelist and philosopher, from Galt's Speech, *Atlas Shrugged*, 1957, 1905–1982)

WEDNESDAY
6

CL 31.6	**NG** 47.4	**GC** 42.1	**SI** 42.1
S 44.4	**W** 61.1	**C** 36.8	**LC** 61.1
LH 47.4	**KC** 47.4	**CC** 36.8	**SB** 36.8

Individualism, private property, the law of accumulation of wealth and the law of competition...
are the highest result of human experience, the soil in which, so far, has produced the best fruit.
— Andrew Carnegie (Scottish-born U.S. industrialist, philanthropist, *The Gospel Of Wealth*, 1835–1919)

THURSDAY
7

CL 52.6	**NG** 38.9	**GC** 61.1	**SI** 66.7
S 57.9	**W** 57.9	**C** 52.6	**LC** 63.2
LH 61.1	**KC** 36.8	**CC** 36.8	**SB** 52.6

We all live with the objective of being happy; our lives are all different and yet the same. — Anne Frank

FRIDAY
8

CL 52.6	**NG** 52.6	**GC** 47.4	**SI** 57.9
S 63.2	**W** 52.6	**C** 57.9	**LC** 47.4
LH 63.2	**KC** 52.6	**CC** 26.3	**SB** 61.1

Learn from the mistakes of others; you can't live long enough to make them all yourself.
— Eleanor Roosevelt (First Lady, 1884–1962)

SATURDAY
9

SUNDAY
10

JUNE BREAKS IN CRUDE OIL CREATE BARGAINS

Crude Oil is the raw material for all petroleum products, ranging from gasoline to lubricants. A typical 42-gallon barrel of Crude Oil produces 19.5 gallons of gasoline, 9.2 gallons of distillate fuels (such as Heating Oil), and 4.1 gallons of jet fuel; and 2.3 gallons is used in the production of residual fuels like kerosene. The remainder is primarily for chemical production and lubricants.

Crude Oil demand runs high during the summer months, as driving conditions are good and air conditioners are running, decreasing mileage per gallon, taxing available supply. Even in years when supply is somewhat plentiful, refineries must buy Crude Oil to begin building stocks of heating oil for the winter, on top of keeping up with demand for gasoline. As such, refineries tend to run at full capacity.

Futures prices bear this out. September Crude Oil futures have increased in value in July 15 times (78.9%) during the 19-year period from 1987 to 2005. September Crude Oil futures have gained an average of $0.77/bbl during July. However, traders may get a leg up on the July rally in Crude Oil by buying following June weakness in Crude Oil.

Since 1987, September Crude Oil futures have declined in June a total 10 times. Following these 10 June breaks, September Crude Oil futures have posted gains in July 8 times (80%), for an average gain of $1.12/bbl. Traders may get a leg up on the July rally by buying September Crude Oil following a June break, picking up this black gold at bargain prices before demand picks up.

SEPTEMBER CRUDE OIL DOLLARS PER BARREL CHANGES

Date	Jun Close	Jun Change	Jun High	July Rally Jun Close to Jul High	July Break Jun Close to Jul Low	Jul Close	Jul Change
1987	20.09	1.09	21.91	1.82	-0.09	21.37	1.28
1988	15.32	-2.49	16.50	1.18	-0.79	16.31	0.99
1989	19.50	1.11	20.12	0.62	-1.63	18.31	-1.19
1990	17.72	-0.91	20.92	3.20	-0.82	20.69	2.97
1991	20.54	-0.77	22.20	1.66	-0.08	21.68	1.14
1992	21.57	-0.47	22.17	0.60	-0.50	21.87	0.30
1993	19.11	-1.20	19.09	-0.02	-2.05	17.88	-1.23
1994	18.83	1.06	20.44	1.61	-0.30	20.30	1.47
1995	17.25	-1.45	17.72	0.47	-0.65	17.56	0.31
1996	20.10	1.44	21.85	1.75	-0.12	20.42	0.32
1997	19.84	-1.17	20.40	0.56	-0.74	20.14	0.30
1998	14.67	-1.41	15.20	0.53	-1.12	14.21	-0.46
1999	19.30	2.54	21.12	1.82	-0.08	20.53	1.23
2000	31.13	3.24	31.02	-0.11	-3.78	27.43	-3.70
2001	26.09	-2.34	27.75	1.66	-1.45	26.35	0.26
2002	26.71	1.47	28.18	1.47	-1.02	27.02	0.31
2003	29.73	1.98	31.37	1.64	-0.56	30.54	0.81
2004	37.14	-2.21	43.85	6.71	-0.34	43.80	6.66
2005	57.64	4.61	62.89	5.25	-1.14	60.57	2.93
Average		**0.22**		**1.71**	**-0.91**		**0.77**
# Up		**9**		**17**	**0**		**15**
Averages Following Down Junes				**1.66**	**-0.85**		**1.12**
# Up							**8**

JUNE

MONDAY **11**

CL 42.1	NG 44.4	GC 47.4	SI 31.6
S 26.3	W 42.1	C 27.8	LC 47.4
LH 22.2	KC 63.2	CC 57.9	SB 38.9

Those heroes of finance are like beads on a string, when one slips off, the rest follow. — Henrik Ibsen

TUESDAY **12**

CL 42.1	NG 44.4	GC 36.8	SI 38.9
S 63.2	W 57.9	C 52.6	LC 68.4
LH 57.9	KC 42.1	CC 36.8	SB 42.1

The average man does not want to be free. He simply wants to be safe. — H.L. Mencken (Newspaperman, editor, critic, 1880–1956)

WEDNESDAY **13**

CL 55.6	NG 47.4	GC 44.4	SI 55.6
S 31.6	W 57.9	C 44.4	LC 38.9
LH 44.4	KC 44.4	CC 47.4	SB 47.4

It is a miracle that curiosity survives formal education.
— Albert Einstein (German/American physicist, 1921 Nobel Prize, 1879–1955)

THURSDAY **14**

CL 26.3	NG 47.4	GC 31.6	SI 47.4
S 47.4	W 42.1	C 47.4	LC 38.9
LH 47.4	KC 42.1	CC 47.4	SB 44.4

The market does not beat them. They beat themselves, because though they have brains they cannot sit tight. — Jesse Livermore

FRIDAY **15**

CL 57.9	NG 63.2	GC 57.9	SI 57.9
S 42.1	W 27.8	C 52.6	LC 27.8
LH 38.9	KC 31.6	CC 47.4	SB 47.4

Regret is an appalling waste of energy; you can't build on it; it is only good for wallowing in. — Katherine Mansfield

SATURDAY **16**

Father's Day

SUNDAY **17**

INSIDER INFORMATION FOR COMMODITIES: THE COMMITMENT OF TRADERS REPORT

In the stock market, all persons who work for a listed company and may have access to advance information regarding earnings or major company developments are labeled as "insiders." In the commodity markets, things are not as clear-cut, but the holdings — of major groups — must be reported to the Commodity Futures Trading Commission (CFTC). Futures positions are classified into three main categories: Large Commercials, Large Speculators, and non-reportable. All positions are classified as number of futures contracts outstanding, or open interest.

Commercials (or Hedgers) are those who are involved in the business of either producing or consuming the underlying. Commercials use futures contracts to offset price volatility in the underlying commodity. Though only those commercials who meet reportable contract holdings are labeled large, viewing this category of the *Commitment of Traders* report allows everyone to see the holdings — and by extension the view — of this group. Non-Commercials (Funds, or Large Speculators) are speculative traders with no interest in the underlying physical commodity who meet or exceed reportable position levels. Generally, this group are hedge funds and Commodity Pool Operators (CPO's). The last group, known as "Non-Reportable" is comprised of both small commercials — or those with a physical interest in the commodity that do not exceed reporting levels — and small speculators — or those with speculative positions less than reportable levels. This is generally the "public" on the speculative side and small producers/consumers on the commercial side.

Reportable Position Levels

Commodity	# of Contracts
Wheat	150
Corn	250
Soybeans	150
Live Cattle	100
Lean Hogs	100
Sugar No. 11	500
Cocoa	100
Coffee	50
Gold	200
Silver	150
Crude Oil	350
Natural Gas	200

Each Friday — or the following Monday if the regular reporting day is a holiday — the CFTC releases the positions of the 3 main classifications of futures holdings as of the previous Tuesday: Non-Commercials (Funds), Commercials (Hedgers), and Non-Reportable (small traders).

SAMPLE COMMITMENT OF TRADERS REPORT

SOYBEANS – CHICAGO BOARD OF TRADE — **CODE – 005602**
FUTURES ONLY POSITION AS OF 4/18/06

Non-Commercial			Commercial		Total		Non-Reportable	
Long	Short	Spreads	Long	Short	Long	Short	Long	Short
Contracts of 5,000 Bushels								
53.521	95,543	64.978	199,015	120,940	317,514	279,461	58.297	96.350
Changes from Previous Week / Change in Open Interest: -9,603								
-2.617	-9,665	4,164	-8,135	2,082	-6,588	-3,419	-3,015	-6,184
Percent of Open Interest for Each Category of Traders								
14.2	24.9	17.3	53.0	32.2	84.5	74.4	15.5	25.6
Number of Traders in Each Category (Total Traders: 411)								
118	127	140	95	104	305	322		

Viewing the *Commitment of Traders* can give the trader an idea of which side his position falls within the spectrum of other groups within the market. Normally, reportable positions (the Commercials/Hedgers and the Non-Commercials/Funds) are known as the smart money. But because these two groups typically make up the bulk of open interest, traders should view these groups separately.

The *Commitment of Traders Report* provides market participants with insight into the psychology of the market pricing but traders should remember the old adage that "bulls are slaughtered, bears are skinned, and pigs never make money." For more information on the *Commitments of Traders Report*, as well as current information, visit www.CFTC.gov or www.COMMODITYALMANAC.com.

JUNE

MONDAY **18**

CL 47.4	NG 57.9	GC 57.9	SI 57.9
S 42.1	W 21.1	C 31.6	LC 33.3
LH 63.2	KC 61.1	CC 73.7	SB 52.6

A statistician is someone who can draw a straight line from an unwarranted assumption to a foregone conclusion. — Anonymous

TUESDAY **19**

CL 33.3	NG 42.1	GC 61.1	SI 47.4
S 52.6	W 61.1	C 61.1	LC 42.1
LH 68.4	KC 36.8	CC 42.1	SB 77.8

Science is organized knowledge. Wisdom is organized life. — Immanuel Kant (German philosopher, 1724–1804)

WEDNESDAY **20**

CL 33.3	NG 44.4	GC 55.6	SI 27.8
S 47.4	W 68.4	C 55.6	LC 38.9
LH 57.9	KC 27.8	CC 61.1	SB 57.9

Profits can be made safely only when the opportunity is available and not just because they happen to be desired or needed. . . . Willingness and ability to hold funds uninvested while awaiting real opportunities is a key to success in the battle for investment survival. — Gerald M. Loeb

THURSDAY **21**

CL 63.2	NG 63.2	GC 27.8	SI 47.4
S 10.5	W 26.3	C 31.6	LC 42.1
LH 38.9	KC 47.4	CC 52.6	SB 38.9

You make money on Wall Street by being very selective and being patient, waiting for those opportunities that are irresistible, where the percentages are very heavily in your favor. — Seth Glickenhaus

FRIDAY **22**

CL 68.4	NG 38.9	GC 61.1	SI 47.4
S 47.4	W 47.4	C 44.4	LC 52.6
LH 42.1	KC 31.6	CC 47.4	SB 36.8

Reality is the name we give to our disappointments. — Mason Cooley

SATURDAY **23**

SUNDAY **24**

JULY ALMANAC

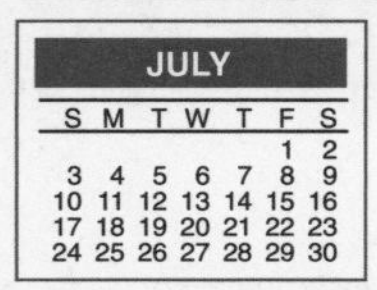

S	M	T	W	T	F	S
					1	2
3	4	5	6	7	8	9
10	11	12	13	14	15	16
17	18	19	20	21	22	23
24	25	26	27	28	29	30

AUGUST

S	M	T	W	T	F	S
1	2	3	4	5	6	7
8	9	10	11	12	13	14
15	16	17	18	19	20	21
22	23	24	25	26	27	28
29	30	31				

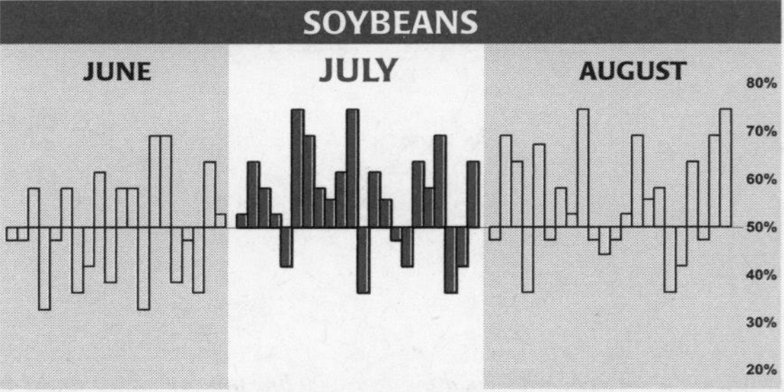

Market Probability Chart above is a graphic representation of Soybean futures taken from the Market Probability Calendar on page 144

PETROLEUM FUTURES: September Crude Oil up 15 / down 4 ◆ 8 of 10 June breaks reversed higher in July ◆ July/August period strong for Crude Oil ◆ October Natural Gas down 8 / up 7 ◆ Worst Julys follow June strength.

METALS FUTURES: October Gold up 6 / down 13 in July ◆ 6 of last 7 June rallies reversed to weakness in July ◆ July mixed for September Silver (up 9 / down 10) ◆ 7 of 9 July rallies reversed to weakness in August, while 7 of 10 July breaks continued through August.

GRAIN FUTURES: Worst month on record for Soybeans ◆ November Soybeans down an average of -24 1/2 cents/bu ◆ 9 of 12 July breaks continue in August ◆ December CBOT Wheat rallies in July continue through August (8 of 10) ◆ Worst month on record for Corn ◆ 8 of 12 July breaks basis December Corn reversed in August.

LIVESTOCK FUTURES: October Live Cattle up 15 / down 4 ◆ 9 of 9 last June rallies continued in July ◆ October Lean Hogs up 11 / down 8 ◆ July strength reversed in August (7 of 11).

SOFTS FUTURES: September Coffee up 7 / down 12 ◆ 11 of 16 last June breaks continued to downside in July ◆ 6 of 8 July breaks continued through August ◆ September Cocoa mixed (up 9 / down 10) ◆ October Sugar up 10 / down 8.

COMMODITY SPOTLIGHT SOYBEANS

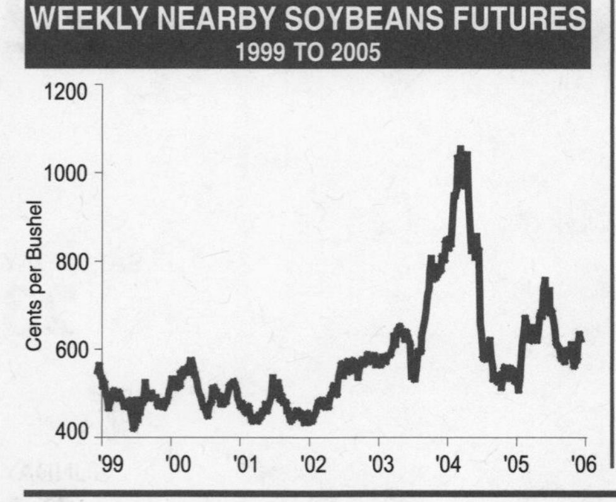

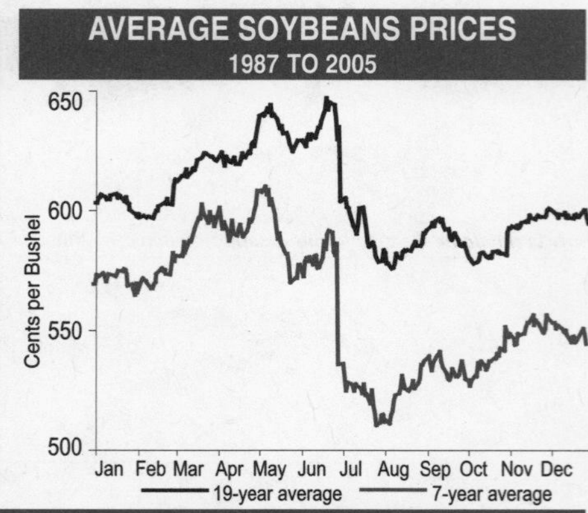

The Soybean crop is destroyed three times — at Planting, Pollination, and Harvest. The marketplace anticipates this destruction by building risk premium in anticipation of risk and removing the premiums as crop progress is made.

JUNE/JULY

MONDAY
25

CL	31.6	**NG**	57.9	**GC**	47.4	**SI**	47.4
S	47.4	**W**	61.1	**C**	47.4	**LC**	47.4
LH	52.6	**KC**	47.4	**CC**	42.1	**SB**	57.9

The dictionary is the only place that success comes before work. Hard work is the price we must pay for success. I think you can accomplish anything if you're willing to pay the price. — Vince Lombardi

TUESDAY
26

CL	47.4	**NG**	52.6	**GC**	47.4	**SI**	52.6
S	47.4	**W**	57.9	**C**	47.4	**LC**	66.7
LH	47.4	**KC**	42.1	**CC**	47.4	**SB**	63.2

A fool's brain digests philosophy into folly, science into superstition, and art into pedantry. Hence University education.
— George Bernard Shaw (Irish dramatist, 1856–1950)

WEDNESDAY
27

CL	31.6	**NG**	44.4	**GC**	42.1	**SI**	26.3
S	47.4	**W**	42.1	**C**	42.1	**LC**	47.4
LH	27.8	**KC**	52.6	**CC**	68.4	**SB**	68.4

The possession of gold has ruined fewer men than the lack of it. — Thomas Bailey Aldridge (1903)

THURSDAY
28

CL	63.2	**NG**	38.9	**GC**	33.3	**SI**	52.6
S	38.9	**W**	31.6	**C**	44.4	**LC**	63.2
LH	52.6	**KC**	36.8	**CC**	52.6	**SB**	52.6

Patience and perseverance have a magical effect before which difficulties disappear and obstacles vanish.
— John Quincy Adams (6th U.S. President, 1767–1848)

FRIDAY
29

CL	47.4	**NG**	73.7	**GC**	63.2	**SI**	63.2
S	52.6	**W**	42.1	**C**	61.1	**LC**	47.4
LH	47.4	**KC**	52.6	**CC**	57.9	**SB**	57.9

The years teach much which the days never know.
— Ralph Waldo Emerson (American author, poet, and philosopher, *Self-Reliance*, 1803–1882)

SATURDAY
30

SUNDAY
1

BEWARE OF POST POLLINATION HIGHS IN SOYBEANS

The U.S. Soybean crop is planted in April/May and pollinates (blooms) during July. After July, given the deep root system of the Soybean plant, the crop is almost impervious to weather with a few exceptions. Many Chicago traders consider the crop "made" after the second week of July.

With future supply more known after blooming, it is no wonder that July is the worst-month record for Soybean prices during the 1987 to 2005 period, for the market must grapple not only with U.S. supply but that of South America as well.

Given the increasing likelihood of future supply, rallies above the previous January-through-May price ranges create an attractive selling (short) opportunity as Soybean futures do not typically hold these lofty levels. November Soybeans have exceeded their earlier season highs in June or July 11 times (57.9%). However, 8 of these 11 rallies (72.7%) have failed to finish the month of July above those previous highs. By the end of July, November Soybeans have finished an average of -35 cents/bu below their January-through-May highs, with an average break of -71 cents/bu below the earlier seasonal highs.

Based on the above and a belief in the fact that the American farmer is an excellent producer, traders should be extremely wary of rallies in June or July that exceed the January-to-May highs of November Soybeans. Remember, supply tends to happen and supply weighs on prices.

NOVEMBER SOYBEANS CENTS PER BUSHEL CHANGES

Date	Jan/May High	Jan/May Low	Jun/Jul High	Jun/Jul Low	Jun Close	Break Jan/May High to Jun/Jul Low	Jan/May High to Jul Close	
1987	612	460 1/4	624 1/2	507 1/2	525 3/4	-104 1/2	-86 1/4	Late Season New Highs
1988	816	608 1/2	1046	754	787 1/2	-62	-28 1/2	Late Season New Highs
1989	760 1/2	628	712	577	578 3/4	-183 1/2	-181 3/4	
1990	682	588 1/2	680 1/2	591	610	-91	-72	
1991	638 1/2	579	618	517	600 1/2	-121 1/2	-38	
1992	641	571 1/2	651	551	552	-90	-89	Late Season New Highs
1993	613 3/4	579 1/4	757 1/2	576	688	-37 3/4	74 1/4	Late Season New Highs
1994	693 1/4	607	699	554	565 3/4	-139 1/4	-127 1/2	Late Season New Highs
1995	634	573 1/4	661	590	614	-44	-20	Late Season New Highs
1996	810	692	825	720 1/2	733	-89 1/2	-77	Late Season New Highs
1997	750	657	696 3/4	577	658	-173	-92	
1998	684 1/2	585 1/2	657	560	560 3/4	-124 1/2	-123 3/4	
1999	575	464 3/4	487 1/4	405 1/4	433 1/4	-169 3/4	-141 3/4	
2000	594 1/2	485 1/2	544	445 1/2	454	-149	-140 1/2	
2001	516 1/2	417 1/2	538	429	512 1/2	-87 1/2	-4	Late Season New Highs
2002	488	428 1/2	560	467	536 1/2	-21	48 1/2	Late Season New Highs
2003	585	502 1/2	588	507 1/2	509	-77 1/2	-76	Late Season New Highs
2004	799	633	734 1/2	568	569	-231	-230	
2005	686	519 1/2	770	660 1/2	686 3/4	-25 1/2	0 3/4	Late Season New Highs
	Averages					**-106 1/2**	**-74**	
	# Up					**0**	**3**	
	Jun/Jul High Greater than Jan/May High					**-70 3/4**	**-35**	

RESERVE YOUR *2008 ALMANAC* TODAY!

Special Pre-pub Offer! Save 20%

Take advantage of the opportunity to purchase the *2008 Almanac* at 20% off the regular list price! To order, just call us toll free at 800-356-5016 (in Canada call 800-567-4797) or fax us at 800-597-3299 or order online at www.stocktradersalmanac.com. Be sure to use **promo code ALMA8** when you are placing your order to receive your special discount.

RESERVE YOUR *2008 STOCK TRADER'S ALMANAC* NOW!

☐ **Please reserve _____ copies of the *2008 Stock Trader's Almanac.***

☐ **Please reserve _____ copies of the *2008 Commodity Trader's Almanac.***

Just $27.96 each (regularly $34.95) plus shipping & handling!

Deeper discounts are available for orders of 5 copies or more—call us at 800-356-5016 for details.

Shipping: US: first item $5.00, each additional $3.00; International: first item $10.50, each additional $7.00. Bulk discounts for 5 or more copies available. Call 800-356-5016.

$_______________ payment enclosed

☐ Check made payable to **John Wiley & Sons, Inc.** *(US Funds only, drawn on a US bank)*

☐ Charge Credit Card (check one): ☐ Visa ☐ Mastercard ☐ AmEx

Name ____________________ E-mail address ____________________

Address ____________________ Account # ____________________

City ____________________ Expiration Date ____________________

State __________ Zip __________ Signature ____________________

☐ **BECOME A SUBSCRIBER! I want to stay up-to-date! Please send me future editions of the (circle one): *Stock Trader's Almanac* or the *Commodity Trader's Almanac.*** You will automatically be shipped (along with the bill) future editions of the *Almanac* at the yearly pre-publication discount. It's so easy and convenient!

PROMO CODE: ALMA8

ISBN 0-470-10985-8 STA, 0-470-10986-6 CTA

SEND ME MORE OF THE *2007 STOCK TRADER'S ALMANAC* !

☐ Please send me _______ copies of the *2007 Stock Trader's Almanac* (ISBN 0471783773)

☐ Please send me _______ copies of the *2007 Commodity Trader's Almanac* (ISBN 0471792195)

$34.95 for single copies plus shipping

Shipping: US: first item $5.00, each additional $3.00; International: first item $10.50, each additional $7.00. Bulk discounts for 5 or more copies available. Call 800-356-5016.

$_______________ payment enclosed

☐ Check made payable to **John Wiley & Sons, Inc.**

☐ Charge Credit Card (check one): ☐ Visa ☐ Mastercard ☐ AmEx

Name ____________________ E-mail address ____________________

Address ____________________ Account # ____________________

City ____________________ Expiration Date ____________________

State __________ Zip __________ Signature ____________________

RESERVE YOUR *2008 STOCK TRADER'S ALMANAC* NOW AND SAVE 20%.

Mail the postage paid card below to reserve your copy.

NO POSTAGE NECESSARY IF MAILED IN THE UNITED STATES

BUSINESS REPLY MAIL
FIRST-CLASS MAIL PERMIT NO. 2277 HOBOKEN NJ

POSTAGE WILL BE PAID BY ADDRESSEE

F REID
JOHN WILEY & SONS INC
111 RIVER ST MS 5-01
HOBOKEN NJ 07030-9442

JULY

MONDAY
2

CL	47.4	**NG**	73.7	**GC**	63.2	**SI**	63.2
S	52.6	**W**	42.1	**C**	61.1	**LC**	47.4
LH	47.4	**KC**	52.6	**CC**	57.9	**SB**	57.9

Believe those who are seeking the truth; doubt those who find it. — Andre Gide

(Shortened Trading Day)

TUESDAY
3

CL	55.6	**NG**	31.6	**GC**	57.9	**SI**	77.8
S	52.6	**W**	42.1	**C**	63.2	**LC**	57.9
LH	57.9	**KC**	63.2	**CC**	66.7	**SB**	57.9

Make it idiot-proof and someone will make a better idiot. — Bumper sticker

Independence Day (Market Closed)

WEDNESDAY
4

Now there is one outstandingly important fact regarding Spaceship Earth (or "the markets"), and that is that no instruction book came with it. — Buckminster Fuller (American architect, author, 1895–1983)

THURSDAY
5

CL	47.4	**NG**	36.8	**GC**	38.9	**SI**	52.6
S	42.1	**W**	44.4	**C**	52.6	**LC**	55.6
LH	26.3	**KC**	42.1	**CC**	47.4	**SB**	47.4

Setting a goal is not the main thing. It is deciding how you will go about achieving it and staying with that plan. — Tom Landry (Head Coach Dallas Cowboys 1960–1988)

FRIDAY
6

CL	57.9	**NG**	57.9	**GC**	38.9	**SI**	47.4
S	55.6	**W**	52.6	**C**	26.3	**LC**	47.4
LH	73.7	**KC**	31.6	**CC**	55.6	**SB**	55.6

The difference between fiction (or "markets") and reality? Fiction has to make sense. — Tom Clancy

SATURDAY
7

SUNDAY
8

SUMMERS HEAT UP HEATING OIL ABSOLUTELY AND RELATIVELY

They say the best time to buy an umbrella from a street vendor is on a sunny day when demand is low. The same may be true for Heating Oil futures.

From the end of July through September, January Heating Oil futures have gained ground 13 times during the 19-year period from 1987 through 2005. On average, Heating Oil futures have gained 7.46 cents/gallon. The rationale for this rally in Heating Oil prices may be the building of inventories on the wholesale level ahead of expected increased residential usage when the weather turns cold.

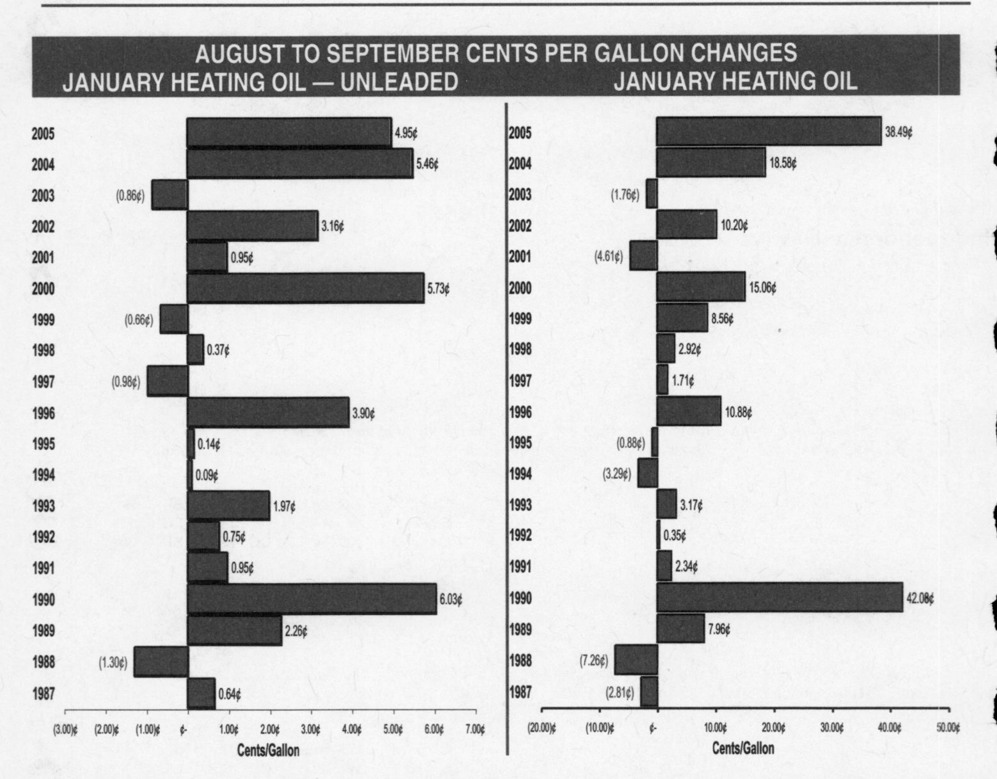

The Heating Oil — Unleaded chart shows the change between the two contracts on a relative basis while the Heating Oil Chart simply shows the absolute change of the January futures from August through September.

Unleaded Gasoline futures have gained during the aforementioned period, but not as strongly nor as consistently. January Heating Oil futures have gained relative to January Unleaded Gasoline futures in 15 of the 19 years studied.

On average, January Heating Oil futures have gained +1.77 cents/gallon by either increasing more than or decreasing less than January Unleaded Gasoline futures during August and September.

Traders wishing to take advantage of Heating Oil's gain during the end of summer may opt for establishing a long Heating Oil / Short Unleaded spread using the January contracts. The normal margin requirement is 75% less than the combined positions, making this a more affordable position to establish, with a better batting average historically, and possibly less volatility.

JULY

MONDAY
9

CL 42.1	NG 47.4	GC 61.1	SI 52.6
S 47.4	W 42.1	C 31.6	LC 61.1
LH 55.6	KC 55.6	CC 42.1	SB 36.8

Creativity requires the courage to let go of certainties. — Erich Fromm

TUESDAY
10

CL 68.4	NG 52.6	GC 52.6	SI 63.2
S 36.8	W 42.1	C 31.6	LC 36.8
LH 22.2	KC 57.9	CC 42.1	SB 47.4

Fortune favors the brave. — Virgil (Roman poet, *Aeneid*, 70–19 B.C.)

WEDNESDAY
11

CL 63.2	NG 42.1	GC 27.8	SI 55.6
S 47.4	W 47.4	C 42.1	LC 55.6
LH 26.3	KC 68.4	CC 38.9	SB 47.4

Everything is vague to a degree you do not realize till you have tried to make it precise.
"The Philosophy of Logical Atomism" — Bertrand Russell (British mathematician and philosopher, 1872–1970)

THURSDAY
12

CL 55.6	NG 36.8	GC 42.1	SI 42.1
S 42.1	W 47.4	C 52.6	LC 52.6
LH 47.4	KC 42.1	CC 57.9	SB 57.9

There have been three great inventions since the beginning of time: The fire, the wheel, and central banking. — Will Rogers

FRIDAY
13

CL 55.6	NG 47.4	GC 57.9	SI 47.4
S 47.4	W 57.9	C 42.1	LC 42.1
LH 52.6	KC 57.9	CC 57.9	SB 66.7

It is on our failures that we base a new and different and better success. — Havelock Ellis

SATURDAY
14

SUNDAY
15

PRICE PATTERNS MADE SIMPLE AND LOGICAL

For generations, traders have relied on price patterns in the commodities markets to predict the future. Their logic for this is that price represents the net sum buying and selling of all market participants, and price is a useful indicator by itself.

The following sample price charts show the three common technical price patterns. Each pattern shows the expected move — or target — that theory holds should follow these particular market cycles.

COMMON PRICE PATTERNS

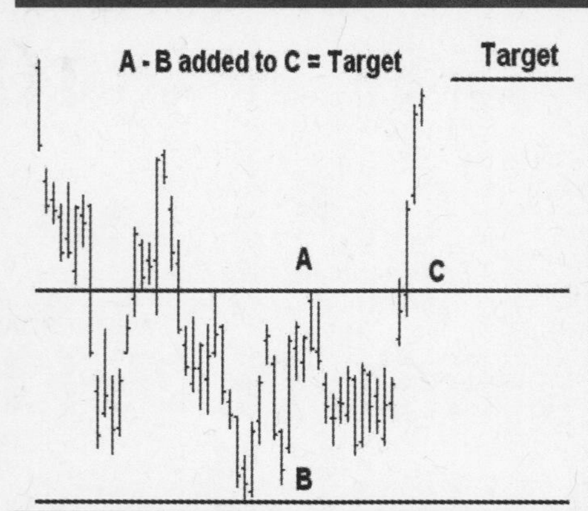

Trading Range: A period of characteristically low volatility, surrounded on either side by a high (A) and a low (B) in prices — also known as resistance and support.

When prices break out of the range, prices should continue in the direction of the breakout by a distance equal to the width (A-B) of the range.

Ranges usually occur after prolonged trends — or movement — in a given direction. Often the breakout of the range will continue in the same direction as the previously prevailing trend.

Triangles: A period classified by decreasing volatility in the form of lower highs (A) and higher lows (B).

Like a spring pushed together, the potential energy of the market is stored, and eventually set free, by a breakout above or below the midpoint of the highs (A) or lows (B) of the pattern.

Following a breakout, prices should move an equal distance of the width of the pattern (A-B) in short order.

Small triangles which appear within trends are usually referred to as "Flags."

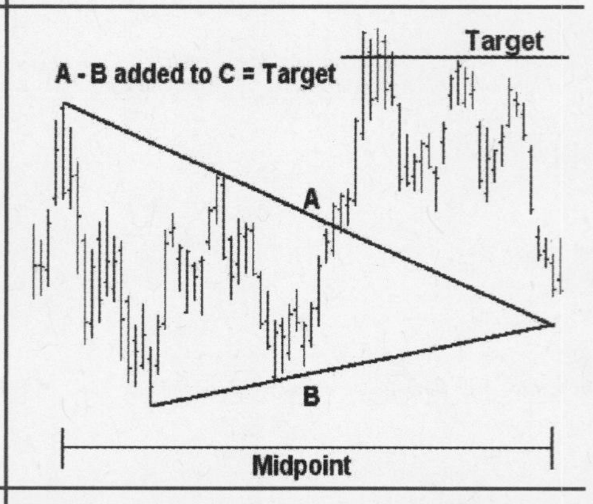

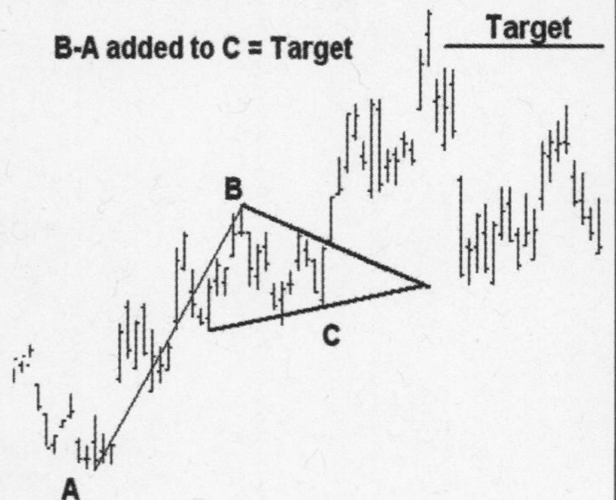

Flags: Flags are small triangles which appear within a strong trend (A to B). Following a strong movement (A to B), prices consolidate in a pattern of lower highs (B) and higher lows (C).

Traders identifying a potential flag should wait for a breakout above the high point (B) in a bull flag, or the low point (B) in a bear flag, as flags tend to be most reliable when the breakout occurs in the direction of the previously prevailing trend.

Following a flag, the market should move an equidistance between the start of the trend and the start of the flag (A-B) above the opposite extreme of the pattern (C) — i.e., "the target price equals C+(A-B)."

JULY

MONDAY 16

CL	57.9	**NG**	33.3	**GC**	73.7	**SI**	63.2
S	73.7	**W**	57.9	**C**	57.9	**LC**	63.2
LH	73.7	**KC**	47.4	**CC**	63.2	**SB**	68.4

Investors operate with limited funds and limited intelligence, they don't need to know everything. As long as they understand something better than others, they have an edge.
— George Soros (Financier, philanthropist, political activist, author, and philosopher, b. 1930)

TUESDAY 17

CL	63.2	**NG**	47.4	**GC**	36.8	**SI**	63.2
S	47.4	**W**	52.6	**C**	36.8	**LC**	47.4
LH	55.6	**KC**	38.9	**CC**	57.9	**SB**	47.4

Without speculation there can be no economic activity reaching beyond the immediate present. — Ludwig von Mises

WEDNESDAY 18

CL	38.9	**NG**	42.1	**GC**	36.8	**SI**	36.8
S	36.8	**W**	42.1	**C**	36.8	**LC**	47.4
LH	57.9	**KC**	63.2	**CC**	27.8	**SB**	63.2

A good trader has to have three things: a chronic inability to accept things at face value, to feel continuously unsettled, and to have humility. — Michael Steinhardt

THURSDAY 19

CL	57.9	**NG**	33.3	**GC**	73.7	**SI**	63.2
S	73.7	**W**	57.9	**C**	57.9	**LC**	63.2
LH	73.7	**KC**	47.4	**CC**	63.2	**SB**	68.4

Little minds are tamed and subdued by misfortune; but great minds rise above them. — Washington Irving (American essayist, historian, novelist, *The Legend of Sleepy Hollow*, U.S. ambassador to Spain 1842–46, 1783–1859)

FRIDAY 20

CL	47.4	**NG**	47.4	**GC**	57.9	**SI**	61.1
S	36.8	**W**	68.4	**C**	33.3	**LC**	47.4
LH	44.4	**KC**	52.6	**CC**	66.7	**SB**	63.2

Those who contemplate the beauty of the earth find reserves of strength that will endure as long as life lasts. — Rachel Carson

SATURDAY 21

SUNDAY 22

THE JULY REVERSE BAROMETER IN SOYBEANS

The U.S. Soybean crop is "made" by the 2nd week of July in most cases, meaning the crop has bloomed (pollinated) and has established a strong enough root system to withstand most of what nature can throw at it. Future supply is fairly secure.

The likelihood of future supply is readily apparent by the fact that July is the worst month on record for Soybean futures — during the 1987 to 2005 period. However, traders should always remember that the market discounts the obvious. The plethora of supply coming at harvest is far from a sure deal, and as such, Soybean prices often rebound or correct after their violent July moves.

November Soybean futures' price direction in August has been the opposite of July's 14 of the last 19 years (73.7%). Because July is historically the weakest month on record for Soybean futures, the strong reversal tendency of August favors strength. On average, November Soybeans have rallied +36 1/2 cents/bushel in August, with the strongest rallies occurring when August is moving in the opposite direction of July — which is usually down. August breaks are even more powerful, averaging -63 cents/bu.

Given the tendency for November Soybeans to reverse their July trends in August, market participants should look at July breaks as buying opportunities, and July rallies as a chance to sell crop-year highs. Hence, establishing positions in the opposite direction of July's movement or re-examining positions in July may well be warranted, though not without great risk. But, beware, August moves in the grains are usually quickly reversed as well.

JULY SOYBEANS CENTS PER BUSHEL CHANGES

Date	Jun Close	Jul Change	August Change	Comment	Aug Rally Jul Close to Aug High	Aug Break Jul Close to Aug Low	Aug Change
1987	550 1/2	- 24 3/4	- 21 1/2	Continuation	4 1/4	- 38 1/4	- 21 1/2
1988	971 1/2	- 184	80	Reversal	115 1/2	- 91	80
1989	653 1/2	- 74 3/4	8 3/4	Reversal	23 1/4	- 40	8 3/4
1990	650 1/2	- 40 1/2	3 3/4	Reversal	35 3/4	- 57 1/4	3 3/4
1991	536 3/4	63 3/4	- 10	Reversal	49 1/2	- 121	- 10
1992	618 3/4	- 66 3/4	- 11	Continuation	5 1/4	- 29 3/4	- 11
1993	658 1/2	29 1/2	- 24 1/2	Reversal	21	- 61	- 24 1/2
1994	628 3/4	- 63	8	Reversal	12 1/2	- 27 1/4	8
1995	595	19	9	Continuation	10 1/2	- 39 1/2	9
1996	746 1/4	- 13 1/4	61 1/2	Reversal	69	- 81 1/2	61 1/2
1997	617 1/2	40 1/2	- 32 1/2	Reversal	9	- 63	- 32 1/2
1998	616 3/4	- 56	- 49 1/4	Continuation	- 5 1/4	- 45	- 49 1/4
1999	460 3/4	- 27 1/2	49 3/4	Reversal	69 3/4	- 58	49 3/4
2000	476 3/4	- 22 3/4	51	Reversal	51 1/2	- 59 1/2	51
2001	464	48 1/2	- 26 1/2	Reversal	7 1/2	- 46 1/2	- 26 1/2
2002	506 3/4	29 3/4	8 1/4	Continuation	43	- 59	8 1/4
2003	552 1/2	- 43 1/2	80	Reversal	88	- 87 1/4	80
2004	669	- 100	58 1/4	Reversal	60	- 77	58 1/4
2005	666 1/4	20 1/2	- 88	Reversal	22 1/4	- 113 1/2	- 88
	Average	**- 24 1/2**	**8 1/4**		**36 1/2**	**- 63**	**8 1/4**
	# Up	**7**	**11**		**18**	**0**	**11**
	# Reversals			**14**			
Average Continuation		**- 20**	**- 13**		**11 1/2**	**- 42 1/4**	**- 13**
Average Reversal		**- 24 3/4**	**10 3/4**		**42**	**- 69**	**10 3/4**

JULY

MONDAY

23

CL 42.1	NG 31.6	GC 63.2	SI 57.9
S 36.8	W 47.4	C 27.8	LC 47.4
LH 44.4	KC 42.1	CC 52.6	SB 57.9

I'm a great believer in luck, and I find the harder I work the more I have of it. — Thomas Jefferson

TUESDAY

24

CL 63.2	NG 55.6	GC 33.3	SI 52.6
S 42.1	W 57.9	C 36.8	LC 47.4
LH 47.4	KC 33.3	CC 44.4	SB 44.4

Great ideas often receive violent opposition from mediocre minds.
— Albert Einstein (German/American physicist, 1921 Nobel Prize, 1879–1955)

WEDNESDAY

25

CL 57.9	NG 42.1	GC 47.4	SI 52.6
S 47.4	W 47.4	C 63.2	LC 61.1
LH 31.6	KC 57.9	CC 42.1	SB 36.8

If a man can see both sides of a problem, you know that none of his money is tied up in it. — Verda Ross

THURSDAY

26

CL 72.2	NG 36.8	GC 47.4	SI 44.4
S 31.6	W 38.9	C 31.6	LC 36.8
LH 78.9	KC 27.8	CC 47.4	SB 52.6

All you need to succeed is a yellow pad and a pencil. — Andre Meyer (Top deal-maker at Lazard Freres)

FRIDAY

27

CL 42.1	NG 42.1	GC 36.8	SI 38.9
S 47.4	W 42.1	C 42.1	LC 68.4
LH 68.4	KC 42.1	CC 36.8	SB 77.8

More people and increased income cause resources to become scarcer in the short run. Heightened scarcity causes prices to rise. The higher prices present opportunity and prompt investors to search for solutions. These solutions eventually lead to prices dropping lower than before the scarcity occurred.
— Julian Simon (Businessman, Professor of Business Administration, *The Ultimate Resource*, 1996, 1932–1998)

SATURDAY

28

SUNDAY

29

AUGUST ALMANAC

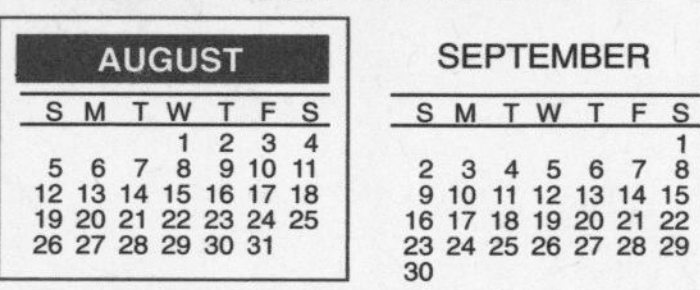

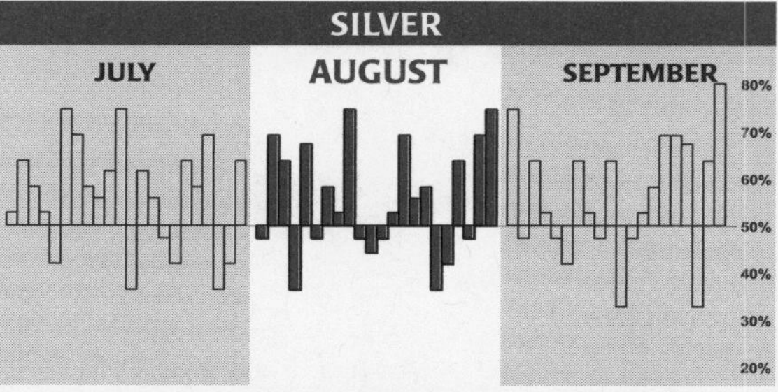

Market Probability Chart above is a graphic representation of Silver futures taken from the Market Probability Calendar on page 139

PETROLEUM FUTURES: December Crude Oil up 12 / down 7 ◆ 6 of last 7 August breaks have reversed in September ◆ January Natural Gas up 10 / down 6 ◆ Best Augusts have followed strong Julys ◆ 7 of 10 August rallies continued in September.

METALS FUTURES: October Gold up 7 / down 12 in August ◆ August rallies have continued through September (7 of 7) ◆ September Silver down 14 / up 5 ◆ 7 of 9 July rallies have been reversed in August ◆ 7 of 10 July breaks have continued through August.

GRAIN FUTURES: November Soybeans up 11 / down 8 ◆ 9 of last 12 July breaks have reversed in August ◆ 6 of 8 August breaks have continued through September basis November Soybeans ◆ December CBOT Wheat up 13 / down 6 ◆ 8 of 10 last July rallies continued in August basis September Wheat ◆ December Corn up 12 / down 7 in August ◆ 8 of 12 July breaks reversed in August.

LIVESTOCK FUTURES: October Live Cattle up 6 / down 13 ◆ Worst August breaks have followed rare July breaks (4 of 4) ◆ 7 of 9 August rallies have continued in September basis December Cattle ◆ 10 of 12 August breaks in October Hogs have reversed in September.

SOFTS FUTURES: 8 of 10 August rallies basis December Coffee have reversed in September ◆ October Sugar up 7 / down 12 ◆ 5 of 8 July breaks have continued through August basis October Sugar ◆ 7 of last 10 September rallies have reversed in October basis December Cocoa.

COMMODITY SPOTLIGHT SILVER

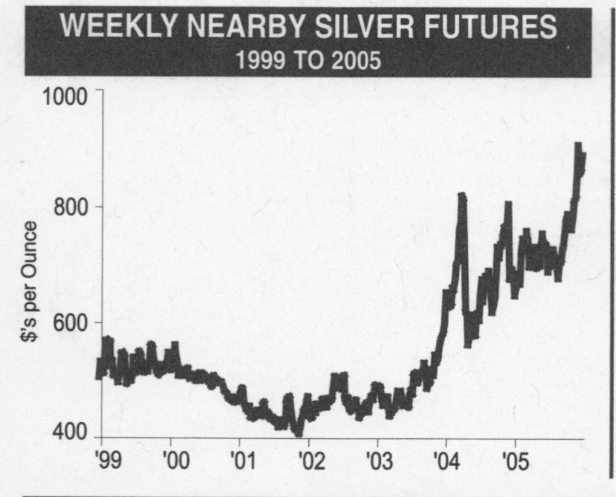

Though Silver has a long history as a precious metal, today demand comes from industry. Silver prices tend to reflect the state of the general economy as they are demand-driven.

JULY/AUGUST

MONDAY
30

CL 44.4	NG 47.4	GC 66.7	SI 73.7
S 61.1	W 47.4	C 47.4	LC 57.9
LH 55.6	KC 68.4	CC 36.8	SB 57.9

A bull market tends to bail you out of all your mistakes. Conversely, bear markets make you PAY for your mistakes.
— Richard Russell (*Dow Theory Letters*)

TUESDAY
31

CL 66.7	NG 47.4	GC 36.8	SI 36.8
S 47.4	W 47.4	C 33.3	LC 47.4
LH 55.6	KC 47.4	CC 57.9	SB 47.4

Speculation anticipates future price changes; its economic function consists in evening out price differences between different places and different points in time and, through the pressure which prices exert on production and consumption, in adapting stocks and demands to each other. — Ludwig von Mises

WEDNESDAY
1

CL 47.4	NG 52.6	GC 57.9	SI 68.4
S 42.1	W 52.6	C 47.4	LC 68.4
LH 38.9	KC 42.1	CC 31.6	SB 44.4

In this game, the market has to keep pitching, but you don't have to swing.
You can stand there with the bat on your shoulder for six months until you get a fat pitch. — Warren Buffett

THURSDAY
2

CL 68.4	NG 44.4	GC 47.4	SI 42.1
S 44.4	W 63.2	C 66.7	LC 42.1
LH 47.4	KC 61.1	CC 33.3	SB 63.2

Our ideals resemble the stars, which illuminate the night. No one will ever be able to touch them.
But the men who, like the sailors on the ocean, take them for guides, will undoubtedly reach their goal. — Carl Schurz

FRIDAY
3

CL 63.2	NG 68.4	GC 47.4	SI 42.1
S 26.3	W 52.6	C 47.4	LC 47.4
LH 47.4	KC 52.6	CC 57.9	SB 42.1

You don't learn to hold your own in the world by standing on guard, but by attacking and getting well-hammered yourself.
— George Bernard Shaw (Irish dramatist, 1856–1950)

SATURDAY
4

SUNDAY
5

WATCH FOR AUGUST WEAKNESS IN SILVER ESPECIALLY DURING BEARISH TRENDS

The severity, and even likelihood, of an August drop in September Silver prices can be foretold quite accurately by looking at the April-through-July trend. Since 1987, September Silver futures have increased in value 9 times (47.4%) and decreased 10 times (52.6%) from April through July.

Following the last 9 April to July rallies, September Silver futures have declined in August 8 times (88.9%) by an average of -31.8 cents/ounce.

Four out of 5 of the August rallies in September Silver have been preceded by weakness during the April-to-July period. The average change in August is a paltry -9.6 cents/bu.

April-through-July price trends offer an excellent reverse clue towards August prices, especially when prices are strong.

SEPTEMBER SILVER FUTURES CENTS PER OUNCE CHANGES

Chronological Data						Ranked by April-to-July Change				
Date	Apr Close	Jul Close	Apr-Jul Change	Aug Close	Aug Change	Rank	Year	Apr-Jul Change	Aug Change	Averages
1987	817.8	835.0	17.2	738.3	-96.7	1	1993	96.3	-57.0	
1988	666.9	685.5	18.6	655.6	-29.9	2	2004	45.7	21.1	
1989	580.7	531.3	-49.4	504.5	-26.8	3	2003	45.4	-1.1	
1990	510.2	482.2	-28.0	475.9	-6.3	4	2005	27.7	-48.1	
1991	406.4	407.8	1.4	380.7	-27.1	5	1988	18.6	-29.9	
1992	404.7	393.7	-11.0	373.0	-20.7	6	1987	17.2	-96.7	-31.8
1993	444.5	540.8	96.3	483.8	-57.0	7	2002	2.4	-16.1	
1994	542.8	533.2	-9.6	544.3	11.1	8	1999	1.8	-31.3	
1995	584.2	505.2	-79.0	531.1	25.9	9	1991	1.4	-27.1	
1996	539.0	514.8	-24.2	517.4	2.6	10	2000	-2.0	-3.5	
1997	474.1	449.0	-25.1	461.6	12.6	11	1994	-9.6	11.1	
1998	624.0	545.8	-78.2	461.8	-84.0	12	1992	-11.0	-20.7	
1999	544.7	546.5	1.8	515.2	-31.3	13	2001	-16.4	-6.6	
2000	505.8	503.8	-2.0	500.3	-3.5	14	1996	-24.2	2.6	
2001	439.2	422.8	-16.4	416.2	-6.6	15	1997	-25.1	12.6	-9.6
2002	457.4	459.8	2.4	443.7	-16.1	16	1990	-28.0	-6.3	
2003	466.6	512.0	45.4	510.9	-1.1	17	1989	-49.4	-26.8	
2004	610.3	656.0	45.7	677.1	21.1	18	1998	-78.2	-84.0	
2005	698.5	726.2	27.7	678.1	-48.1	19	1995	-79.0	25.9	
Average			-3.5		-20.1					
# Up			9		5					
# Down			10		14					
Following Apr-to-Jul strength										
# Up					1					
# Down					8					
Averages					-31.8					

AUGUST

MONDAY 6

CL	36.8	NG	44.4	GC	52.6	SI	57.9
S	26.3	W	27.8	C	26.3	LC	47.4
LH	26.3	KC	42.1	CC	38.9	SB	63.2

The secret to business is to know something that nobody else knows. — Aristotle Onassis (Greek shipping billionaire)

TUESDAY 7

CL	66.7	NG	73.7	GC	33.3	SI	42.1
S	47.4	W	63.2	C	47.4	LC	57.9
LH	61.1	KC	47.4	CC	47.4	SB	47.4

If you bet on a horse, that's gambling. If you bet you can make three spades, that's entertainment. If you bet cotton will go up three points, that's business. See the difference? — Blackie Sherrod

WEDNESDAY 8

CL	47.4	NG	47.4	GC	47.4	SI	52.6
S	52.6	W	57.9	C	55.6	LC	68.4
LH	52.6	KC	47.4	CC	47.4	SB	47.4

It is unwise to be too sure of one's own wisdom. It is healthy to be reminded that the strongest might weaken and the wisest might err. — Mohandas K. Gandhi

THURSDAY 9

CL	57.9	NG	57.9	GC	73.7	SI	42.1
S	66.7	W	57.9	C	73.7	LC	42.1
LH	36.8	KC	52.6	CC	47.4	SB	31.6

The strongest arguments prove nothing so long as the conclusions are not verified by experience. Experimental science is the queen of sciences and the goal of all speculation. — Roger Bacon

FRIDAY 10

CL	52.6	NG	72.2	GC	57.9	SI	63.2
S	78.9	W	57.9	C	57.9	LC	47.4
LH	15.8	KC	31.6	CC	47.4	SB	63.2

Self-respect is the fruit of discipline; the sense of dignity grows with the ability to say no to oneself.
— Abraham Lincoln (16th U.S. President, 1809–1865)

SATURDAY 11

SUNDAY 12

AUGUST RALLIES IN CORN SHOULD BE SOLD

The U.S. Corn crop — which accounts for almost 42% of world production — pollinates in late June and early July. After silking (pollination) the crop doughs and dents during the rest of July and August. By late August/early September, the crop is mature, awaiting some field drying time and eventual harvest. The crop is usually impervious at this point to most threats, and therefore future supply is very secure come harvest.

However, August heat is a worrisome event. With average corn-belt temperatures in excess 80° F, the Corn crop — especially a vulnerable crop — could suffer damage and a loss of yield. But, such events are extremely rare.

During the 19-year period ending in 2005, December Corn futures have rallied in August — primarily on fear of crop loss — a total of 12 times (63.2%). But following these 12 August rallies, December Corn futures have reversed and broken in September 10 times (83.3%), dropping by an average of -13 1/4 cents/bu.

September rallies tend to be smaller than normal following an August rally, while breaks tend to be more severe. Following the last 12 August increases, December Corn futures have had an average rally of 8 cents/bu, versus an average September rally in all years of +18 cent/bu. December Corn futures breaks in September following a strong August have averaged -18 cents/bu., an increase of almost 30% in magnitude compared to the norm.

Traders should view August rallies with great trepidation. With harvest fast approaching, price pressures may be around the corner.

DECEMBER CORN CENTS PER BUSHEL CHANGES

Date	Jul Close	Aug Change	Aug Rally Jul Close to Aug High	Aug Break Jul Close to Aug Low	Sep Close	Sep Change	Sep Rally Aug Close to Sep High	Sep Break Aug Close to Sep Low
1987	173 1/2	-7	1/2	-11 3/4	179 3/4	13 1/4	15 3/4	-2 1/4
1988	283 3/4	12 3/4	32 1/4	-4	285 3/4	-10 3/4	9 1/2	-16 1/2
1989	220 1/2	16 1/4	20 3/4	-2	233	-3 3/4	3 1/4	-10 1/4
1990	255 1/2	-22 1/4	- 1/4	-23	228	-5 1/4	4 1/2	-11 3/4
1991	263 1/4	-8 1/2	8 3/4	-28	249 1/4	-5 1/2	3 1/4	-10
1992	222 3/4	-5 1/2	4 1/4	-9	215 1/4	-2	9 1/2	-4 1/2
1993	241 3/4	-4 1/4	8 1/4	-5 3/4	244 3/4	7 1/4	13	-5
1994	222	3/4	4 3/4	-4 1/4	215 3/4	-7	5 1/4	-8 3/4
1995	281 1/4	12 1/2	12 3/4	-11 1/4	311 3/4	18	21	-4
1996	319 3/4	24	35 1/4	-5 1/4	296 3/4	-47	2 1/4	-49 3/4
1997	267 3/4	1 1/2	10 1/4	-19 1/4	257 3/4	-11 1/2	4 3/4	-13 3/4
1998	223 3/4	-24 1/4	1/4	-24 1/2	209	9 1/2	15 1/2	-2 1/2
1999	214 1/2	4 3/4	29	1/4	208 1/4	-11	7 1/4	-11 1/2
2000	192 1/4	4 1/4	5 1/4	-6 3/4	197 3/4	1 1/4	3 1/4	-9 3/4
2001	230 1/4	2	7 1/2	-10	214 1/2	-17 3/4	- 1/4	-18 1/2
2002	256 1/2	11 1/2	32	-2 1/2	251 1/2	-16 1/2	28	-18 1/2
2003	212	29 3/4	31	1	220 1/4	-21 1/2	5 1/2	-21 3/4
2004	225 1/2	12 1/4	19 3/4	- 1/2	205 1/2	-32 1/4	7 1/4	-33 3/4
2005	248 1/4	-31 3/4	2 3/4	-33 1/4	205 1/2	-11	6	-14
Average		**1 2/4**	**14**	**-10 1/2**		**-8**	**8 3/4**	**-14**
# Up		**12**	**18**	**2**		**5**	**18**	**0**
Following an Up August								
# Up						**2**	**11**	**0**
Average						**-13 1/4**	**8**	**-18**

AUGUST

MONDAY 13

CL 73.7	NG 52.6	GC 36.8	SI 47.4
S 63.2	W 57.9	C 52.6	LC 47.4
LH 63.2	KC 42.1	CC 55.6	SB 31.6

Two things are infinite: the universe and human stupidity; and I'm not sure about the universe.
— Albert Einstein (German/American physicist, 1921 Nobel Prize, 1879–1955)

TUESDAY 14

CL 47.4	NG 44.4	GC 42.1	SI 57.9
S 47.4	W 52.6	C 47.4	LC 66.7
LH 72.2	KC 42.1	CC 31.6	SB 47.4

I know the price of success: dedication, hard work, and an unremitting devotion to the things you want to see happen.
— Frank Lloyd Wright (American architect)

WEDNESDAY 15

CL 44.4	NG 47.4	GC 57.9	SI 52.6
S 47.4	W 52.6	C 52.6	LC 38.9
LH 33.3	KC 36.8	CC 63.2	SB 52.6

There are two ways to slide easily through life: to believe everything or to doubt everything; both ways save us from thinking.
— Alfred Korzybski

THURSDAY 16

CL 47.4	NG 47.4	GC 68.4	SI 52.6
S 63.2	W 68.4	C 52.6	LC 63.2
LH 33.3	KC 52.6	CC 36.8	SB 42.1

The trouble with gardening (trading) is that it does not remain an avocation. It becomes an obsession. — Phyllis McGinley

FRIDAY 17

CL 47.4	NG 57.9	GC 36.8	SI 44.4
S 44.4	W 47.4	C 57.9	LC 47.4
LH 47.4	KC 52.6	CC 52.6	SB 47.4

I prefer to be true to myself, even at the hazard of incurring the ridicule of others, rather than to be false, and to incur my own abhorrence. — Frederick Douglass

SATURDAY 18

SUNDAY 19

IF GOLD GLITTERS IN AUGUST, IT MAY WELL BECOME MORE PRECIOUS

December Gold futures have continued their August rally in each of the last 5 years since 2000. During the 19-year period from 1987 to 2005, December Gold futures have continued their August rally into September following each of the last 7 rallies in August: 2005, 2004, 2003, 2002, 2001, 1994, and 1990.

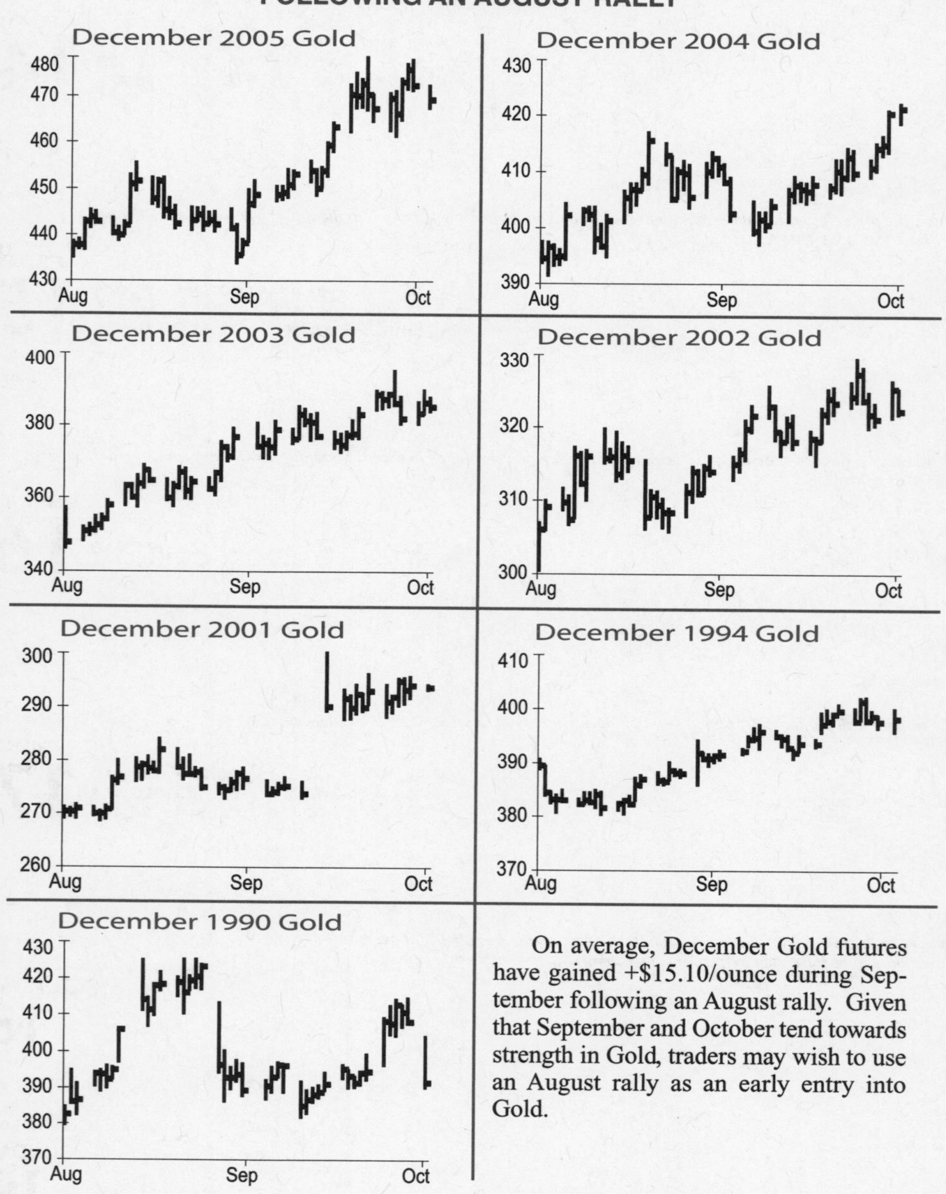

On average, December Gold futures have gained +$15.10/ounce during September following an August rally. Given that September and October tend towards strength in Gold, traders may wish to use an August rally as an early entry into Gold.

AUGUST

MONDAY 20

CL 52.6	NG 66.7	GC 57.9	SI 77.8
S 52.6	W 38.9	C 27.8	LC 47.4
LH 72.2	KC 52.6	CC 26.3	SB 42.1

The secret of success is constancy to purpose. — Benjamin Disraeli (British prime minister, 1804–1881)

TUESDAY 21

CL 68.4	NG 47.4	GC 47.4	SI 38.9
S 57.9	W 52.6	C 38.9	LC 27.8
LH 31.6	KC 47.4	CC 57.9	SB 68.4

Experience is simply the name we give our mistakes. — Oscar Wilde (Irish-born writer and wit)

WEDNESDAY 22

CL 55.6	NG 47.4	GC 44.4	SI 47.4
S 42.1	W 42.1	C 47.4	LC 31.6
LH 57.9	KC 57.9	CC 63.2	SB 36.8

Every time everyone's talking about something, that's the time to sell. — George Lindemann (Billionaire, *Forbes*)

THURSDAY 23

CL 57.9	NG 38.9	GC 36.8	SI 42.1
S 63.2	W 72.2	C 52.6	LC 42.1
LH 42.1	KC 78.9	CC 68.4	SB 57.9

Look for an impending crash in the economy when the best-seller lists are filled with books on business strategies and quick-fix management ideas. — Peter Drucker (Management consultant, "The man who invented the corporate society," born in Austria 1909)

FRIDAY 24

CL 36.8	NG 47.4	GC 47.4	SI 47.4
S 42.1	W 52.6	C 47.4	LC 36.8
LH 52.6	KC 52.6	CC 55.6	SB 44.4

Science cannot resolve moral conflicts, but it can help to more accurately frame the debates about those conflicts. — Heinz Pagels

SATURDAY 25

SUNDAY 26

SEPTEMBER ALMANAC

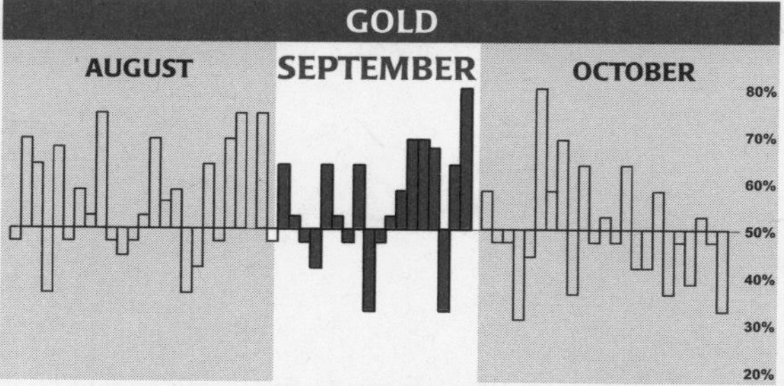

Market Probability Chart above is a graphic representation of Gold futures taken from the Market Probability Calendar on page 134

PETROLEUM FUTURES: Crude Oil up 13 / down 6 ◆ Best Septembers follow August weakness basis December Crude Oil ◆ September rallies are fleeting as 9 of 13 have been reversed in October ◆ January Natural Gas up 10 / down 5 ◆ 7 of 10 August rallies have continued through September ◆ 7 of last 10 September rallies have been reversed in October.

METALS FUTURES: Strongest month on record for Gold — gained a total of $117.30/ounce from 1987 – 2005 ◆ Strong demand from jewelry trade bolsters prices, especially following last 7 August rallies — all of which have seen September gains ◆ 2nd-strongest month on record for Silver ◆ Up 13 / down 6 ◆ September Silver rallies usually reversed in October (11 of 13) basis December Silver.

GRAIN FUTURES: November Soybean futures down an average -10 3/4 cents/bu on harvest pressure ◆ September's monthly trend sets the tone for October (14 of 19) ◆ December Corn up 5 / down 14 ◆ 10 of 12 August rallies reversed in September basis December Corn ◆ Rare September rallies tend to continue through October (4 of 5).

LIVESTOCK FUTURES: Best Septembers follow August strength in Live Cattle ◆ December Live Cattle up 13 / down 6 ◆ September strength continued through October (10 of 13) ◆ December Hogs up 15 / down 4 ◆ Strongest month on record for Hogs (average change of +1.77 cents/lb) ◆ Best Septembers follow August weakness (10 of 12) ◆ However, September strength often reversed in October (12 of 15).

SOFTS FUTURES: December Coffee up 5 / down 14 ◆ Worst September follows August strength ◆ September begins main crop harvest on Ivory Coast (world's largest Cocoa producer) ◆ Rare September rallies reversed in October (8 of 8).

COMMODITY SPOTLIGHT GOLD

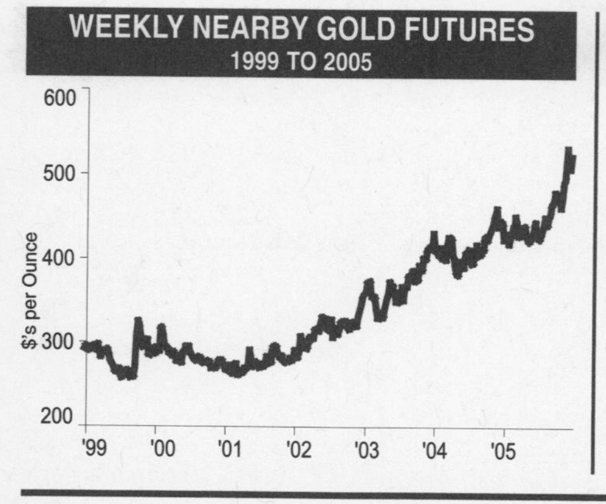

At its core, Gold is a commodity used and consumed. However, Gold also has an intrinsic, emotional value as well which can drive prices much further than would be rationally expected.

AUGUST/SEPTEMBER

MONDAY **27**

CL 42.1	NG 44.4	GC 38.9	SI 36.8
S 61.1	W 52.6	C 52.6	LC 33.3
LH 36.8	KC 73.7	CC 42.1	SB 38.9

...the most successful positions I've taken have been those about which I've been most nervous (and ignored that emotion anyway). Courage is not about being fearless; courage is about acting appropriately even when you are fearful.
— Daniel Turov (*Turov on Timing*)

TUESDAY **28**

CL 63.2	NG 31.6	GC 26.3	SI 42.1
S 36.8	W 26.3	C 26.3	LC 63.2
LH 52.6	KC 47.4	CC 68.4	SB 47.4

Whenever you see a successful business, someone once made a courageous decision.
— Peter Drucker (Management consultant, "The man who invented the corporate society," born in Austria 1909)

WEDNESDAY **29**

CL 47.4	NG 36.8	GC 42.1	SI 44.4
S 47.4	W 44.4	C 42.1	LC 52.6
LH 42.1	KC 57.9	CC 52.6	SB 47.4

Cheapening the cost of necessities and conveniences of life is the most powerful agent of civilization and progress.
— Thomas Elliott Perkins (1888)

THURSDAY **30**

CL 68.4	NG 63.2	GC 47.4	SI 31.6
S 36.8	W 47.4	C 38.9	LC 47.4
LH 36.8	KC 52.6	CC 52.6	SB 47.4

If I had my life to live over again, I would elect to be a trader of goods rather than a student of science. I think barter is a noble thing. — Albert Einstein (German/American physicist, 1921 Nobel Prize, 1934, 1879–1955)

FRIDAY **31**

CL 73.7	NG 31.6	GC 61.1	SI 57.9
S 68.4	W 77.8	C 68.4	LC 66.7
LH 68.4	KC 68.4	CC 57.9	SB 57.9

Make money and the whole nation will conspire to call you a gentleman. — George Bernard Shaw (Irish dramatist, 1856–1950)

SATURDAY **1**

SUNDAY **2**

SEPTEMBER THROUGH HOLIDAY SEASON BULLISH FOR GOLD

Over half the consumption of Gold in a given year can be accounted for by the jewelry industry. The busiest time of the year for the jewelry industry is the holiday shopping season — which accounts for roughly 40% of the yearly sales according to *Professional Jeweler* magazine.

Preparation for the shopping season usually begins in September, as European manufacturers/fabricators come back from vacations, and retail outlets begin ordering inventory to meet holiday demand. This increase in demand makes the September-through-December period the strongest on record for Gold futures.

The average September / December rally in the last 19 years has been +$29.50/ounce, while in the last 5 years, rallies have averaged a whopping +$50.00/ounce. The average September / December break is -$15.00/ounce since 1987, but in the last 5 years, it has been only -$6.70/ounce, despite increased volatility.

On a closing basis, February Gold futures have settled December higher than August by an average of +$8.50/ounce since 1987. However, in the last 5 years, December's close has averaged +$35.20/ounce gain over the August settlement.

Given the strong demand pull for Gold in the 4th quarter, traders should be looking for above-average rallies and smaller-than-normal breaks in the coming months.

FEBRUARY GOLD DOLLARS PER OUNCE CHANGES

Date	Aug Close	Sep/Dec High	Sep/Dec Low	Sep/Dec Rally Aug Close to Sep/Dec High	Sep/Dec Break Aug Close to Sep/Dec Low	Dec Close	Sep/Dec Change
1987	464.6	507.4	461.0	42.8	-3.6	488.9	24.3
1988	446.1	445.0	401.0	-1.1	-45.1	412.3	-33.8
1989	369.2	425.6	364.7	56.4	-4.5	405.2	36.0
1990	393.4	418.5	365.5	25.1	-27.9	396.2	2.8
1991	356.0	374.9	349.8	18.9	-6.2	355.2	-0.8
1992	347.0	356.0	330.5	9.0	-16.5	333.3	-13.7
1993	377.4	393.9	344.5	16.5	-32.9	391.9	14.5
1994	394.0	405.0	377.7	11.0	-16.3	384.4	-9.6
1995	389.5	393.4	382.5	3.9	-7.0	388.1	-1.4
1996	393.9	394.0	367.6	0.1	-26.3	371.2	-22.7
1997	329.1	348.8	283.3	19.7	-45.8	289.9	-39.2
1998	280.6	307.7	282.9	27.1	2.3	289.2	8.6
1999	258.1	338.0	255.5	79.9	-2.6	289.6	31.5
2000	284.7	285.1	266.2	0.4	-18.5	273.6	-11.1
2001	277.4	297.5	271.7	20.1	-5.7	279.0	1.6
2002	314.6	355.7	310.0	41.1	-4.6	348.2	33.6
2003	377.5	418.4	368.0	40.9	-9.5	416.1	38.6
2004	414.0	458.7	398.7	44.7	-15.3	438.4	24.4
2005	441.2	544.5	442.7	103.3	1.5	518.9	77.7
	Since 1987						
	Averages			**29.5**	**-15.0**		**8.5**
	# Up			**18**	**2**		**11**
	Since 2005						
	Averages			**50.0**	**-6.7**		**35.2**
	# Up			**5**	**1**		**5**

Rally defined as high price between September through December – August close. Break defined as low price between September and December – August close.

SEPTEMBER

Labor Day (Market Closed)

MONDAY
3

[Be]come more humble as the market goes your way. — Bernard Baruch

TUESDAY
4

CL 73.7	NG 31.6	GC 61.1	SI 57.9
S 68.4	W 77.8	C 68.4	LC 66.7
LH 68.4	KC 68.4	CC 57.9	SB 57.9

The only real mistake is the one from which we learn nothing. — John Powell

WEDNESDAY
5

CL 47.4	NG 38.9	GC 38.9	SI 42.1
S 61.1	W 47.4	C 52.6	LC 42.1
LH 84.2	KC 63.2	CC 42.1	SB 52.6

[If] all the economists in the world were laid end to end, they still wouldn't reach a conclusion.
— George Bernard Shaw (Irish dramatist, 1856–1950)

THURSDAY
6

CL 63.2	NG 47.4	GC 47.4	SI 47.4
S 73.7	W 68.4	C 57.9	LC 72.2
LH 78.9	KC 42.1	CC 42.1	SB 47.4

Beware of inside information…all inside information. — Jesse Livermore (*How to Trade in Stocks*)

FRIDAY
7

CL 52.6	NG 68.4	GC 52.6	SI 47.4
S 73.7	W 42.1	C 52.6	LC 42.1
LH 57.9	KC 47.4	CC 52.6	SB 33.3

A man will fight harder for his interests than his rights. — Napoleon Bonaparte (Emperor of France 1804–1815, 1769–1821)

SATURDAY
8

SUNDAY
9

THE SEPTEMBER SLAMMER AND COCOA HARVEST PRESSURES

The Cocoa tree typically produces two crops each year. On the Ivory Coast — the largest Cocoa-producing nation in the world — the main Cocoa harvest runs from October to March which is roughly five to six months after the wet season. The main crop accounts for roughly 75% to 80% of the total Cocoa produced in Africa, while the May-through-August mid-crop harvest accounts for the remainder.

Some market behaviors are so well-ingrained in the psyche of the marketplace that traders give them nicknames. One such market bias is the tendency for Cocoa futures to break in September and October. As such, traders on the New York Coffee, Sugar, and Cocoa Exchange (CSCE) call this one the "September Slammer" for good reason.

During the 19-year period beginning in 1987, December Cocoa futures have broken during September/October period 14 times (73.6%), falling an average of -$77/ton.

The average September/October break has averaged -$134/ton using the December futures. The average rally during this period has been a relatively weak $82/ton in comparison.

Given the large amount of supply hitting the market, traders should beware of an impending break during the September/October period in Cocoa prices.

DECEMBER COCOA DOLLARS PER TON CHANGES

Date	Aug Close	Sep/Oct High	Sep/Oct Low	Oct Close	Sep/Oct Rally Aug Close to Sep/Oct High	Sep/Oct Break Aug Close to Sep/Oct Low	Sep/Oct Change
1987	1988	1978	1785	1807	-10	-203	-181
1988	1256	1384	1103	1309	128	-153	53
1989	1149	1157	956	977	8	-193	-172
1990	1319	1353	1125	1153	34	-194	-166
1991	1091	1305	1115	1208	214	24	117
1992	1092	1109	918	932	17	-174	-160
1993	1079	1221	1053	1120	142	-26	41
1994	1357	1388	1240	1327	31	-117	-30
1995	1336	1344	1245	1311	8	-91	-25
1996	1352	1418	1329	1353	66	-23	1
1997	1717	1739	1574	1603	22	-143	-114
1998	1614	1634	1485	1506	20	-129	-108
1999	951	1093	858	874	142	-93	-77
2000	795	846	752	755	51	-43	-40
2001	949	1130	885	1017	181	-64	68
2002	2002	2405	1842	1927	403	-160	-75
2003	1761	1740	1360	1440	-21	-401	-321
2004	1686	1639	1390	1469	-47	-296	-217
2005	1404	1575	1328	1351	171	-76	-53
	Average				**82**	**-134**	**-77**
	# Up				**16**	**1**	**5**

Rally defined as high price between September/October – August close. Break defined as low price between September/October – August close.

SEPTEMBER

MONDAY
10

CL	47.4	**NG**	57.9	**GC**	63.2	**SI**	57.9
S	42.1	**W**	42.1	**C**	47.4	**LC**	77.8
LH	57.9	**KC**	57.9	**CC**	47.4	**SB**	55.6

The beginning of wisdom is found in doubting; by doubting we come to the question, and by seeking we may come upon the truth. — Pierre Abelard

TUESDAY
11

CL	42.1	**NG**	52.6	**GC**	42.1	**SI**	33.3
S	72.2	**W**	57.9	**C**	63.2	**LC**	68.4
LH	52.6	**KC**	42.1	**CC**	42.1	**SB**	44.4

"In Memory"

If you don't know who you are, the stock market is an expensive place to find out. — George Goodman (1959)

WEDNESDAY
12

CL	63.2	**NG**	61.1	**GC**	38.9	**SI**	63.2
S	42.1	**W**	44.4	**C**	36.8	**LC**	44.4
LH	47.4	**KC**	47.4	**CC**	42.1	**SB**	38.9

In order to be a great writer (or "trader") a person must have a built-in, shockproof crap detector. — Ernest Hemingway

Rosh Hashanah

THURSDAY
13

CL	52.6	**NG**	47.4	**GC**	42.1	**SI**	38.9
S	36.8	**W**	44.4	**C**	47.4	**LC**	47.4
LH	68.4	**KC**	31.6	**CC**	52.6	**SB**	55.6

Your emotions are often a reverse indicator of what you ought to be doing. — John F. Hindelong (Dillon, Reed)

FRIDAY
14

CL	47.4	**NG**	47.4	**GC**	42.1	**SI**	42.1
S	52.6	**W**	31.6	**C**	27.8	**LC**	66.7
LH	52.6	**KC**	42.1	**CC**	57.9	**SB**	55.6

The average man desires to be told specifically which particular stock to buy or sell. He wants to get something for nothing. He does not wish to work. — William Lefevre (*Reminiscences of a Stock Operator*)

SATURDAY
15

SUNDAY
16

SEPTEMBER BULLS ARE SLAUGHTERED DURING OCTOBER IN THE HOG MARKET

Hog slaughter rates tend to reach their peak in September, and stay relatively steady near their peaks through the end of the year. Spring pigs usually approach slaughter weight by the end of the year and thus the market is flush with supply.

However, demand for Pork is high and the below-average slaughter of summer often creates limited supplies. This is readily apparent by the fact that September is the strongest month on record for Hog futures — gaining an average of +1.77 cents/lb in 15 of the 19 years between 1987 and 2005.

However, September rallies tend to be fleeting despite their frequency and strength. December Hog futures have declined during October in 16 of the last 19 years (84.2%) by an average of -1.44 cents/lb. The average October break is -3.44 cents/lb. On average, December Hogs break by -5.62 cents/lb from their September rally peak to their October break trough, showing traders that bullish traders in September may well have a tough row to hoe in October.

DECEMBER LEAN HOG CENTS PER POUND CHANGES

Date	Aug Close	Sep Close	Sep Change	Sep Rally Aug Close to Sep High	Sep Break Aug Close to Sep Low	Oct Change	Oct Rally Sep Close to Oct High	Oct Break Sep Close to Oct Low
1987	65.80	61.18	-4.63	1.55	-5.65	-3.13	3.65	-3.20
1988	55.68	58.13	2.45	3.45	-2.78	-2.53	1.08	-3.00
1989	57.40	59.95	2.55	2.80	-2.60	2.97	4.77	-0.48
1990	66.93	71.20	4.28	5.78	0.03	-1.25	4.60	-2.23
1991	59.15	60.43	1.28	3.68	-0.77	-4.05	0.65	-4.35
1992	54.85	57.93	3.08	3.20	-0.25	-0.60	2.83	-0.90
1993	62.70	64.05	1.35	4.05	-0.40	2.23	5.53	0.58
1994	53.30	49.20	-4.10	0.98	-4.45	-1.55	0.52	-4.88
1995	59.93	62.98	3.05	4.20	-0.32	-3.93	0.42	-4.03
1996	72.35	77.43	5.08	6.08	-0.60	-3.93	2.03	-7.85
1997	67.38	63.43	-3.95	1.47	-3.95	-1.20	0.58	-3.40
1998	36.95	40.40	3.45	4.85	-1.43	-3.00	4.20	-3.18
1999	43.43	46.63	3.20	4.43	-3.85	-0.10	3.08	-2.33
2000	50.30	54.20	3.90	4.03	-0.15	-3.03	0.97	-3.70
2001	54.33	54.83	0.50	2.88	-1.03	-3.18	2.33	-8.13
2002	35.30	40.55	5.25	5.58	-1.70	2.58	3.00	-2.22
2003	53.93	53.60	-0.32	5.58	-1.03	-0.27	7.43	-2.45
2004	63.73	69.13	5.40	8.08	-1.83	-1.68	0.13	-5.63
2005	61.55	63.35	1.80	2.33	-1.55	-1.68	2.30	-4.08
	Average		**1.77**	**3.94**	**-1.81**	**-1.44**	**2.64**	**-3.44**
	# Up		**15**	**19**	**1**	**3**	**19**	**1**

SEPTEMBER

MONDAY
17

CL	63.2	**NG**	57.9	**GC**	47.4	**SI**	52.6
S	47.4	**W**	33.3	**C**	31.6	**LC**	52.6
LH	73.7	**KC**	42.1	**CC**	52.6	**SB**	42.1

When I have to depend upon hope in a trade, I get out of it. — Jesse Livermore

TUESDAY
18

CL	33.3	**NG**	57.9	**GC**	42.1	**SI**	42.1
S	47.4	**W**	47.4	**C**	42.1	**LC**	38.9
LH	47.4	**KC**	42.1	**CC**	38.9	**SB**	47.4

Victory goes to the player who makes the next-to-last mistake. — Savielly Grigorievitch Tartakower (Chess master, 1887–1956)

WEDNESDAY
19

CL	47.4	**NG**	42.1	**GC**	36.8	**SI**	63.2
S	57.9	**W**	73.7	**C**	44.4	**LC**	36.8
LH	44.4	**KC**	52.6	**CC**	47.4	**SB**	38.9

Gardening (and "trading") requires lots of water — most of it in the form of perspiration. — Lou Erickson

THURSDAY
20

CL	57.9	**NG**	44.4	**GC**	63.2	**SI**	57.9
S	63.2	**W**	61.1	**C**	57.9	**LC**	57.9
LH	44.4	**KC**	63.2	**CC**	57.9	**SB**	33.3

Self-trust is the first secret of success. — Ralph Waldo Emerson (American author, poet, and philosopher, 1803–1882)

FRIDAY
21

CL	68.4	**NG**	66.7	**GC**	63.2	**SI**	57.9
S	61.1	**W**	42.1	**C**	63.2	**LC**	33.3
LH	47.4	**KC**	44.4	**CC**	47.4	**SB**	55.6

Unless you've interpreted changes before they've occurred, you'll be decimated trying to follow them. — Robert J. Nurock

Yom Kippur

SATURDAY
22

SUNDAY
23

WALKING THE WALK AND TALKING THE TALK UNDERSTANDING LIVESTOCK VERNACULAR

All professions use terms and jargon which at first seem impenetrable. The Livestock futures are no different.

The first thing a participant in the Livestock futures market should understand is the terminology regarding markets. There are four different Livestock futures markets, all traded on the Chicago Mercantile Exchange (CME): Live Cattle (LC), Feeder Cattle (FC), Lean Hogs (LH), and Pork Bellies (PB).

Live Cattle refers to cattle of slaughter weight — between 900 and 1,400 pounds (lbs). Feeder Cattle (FC) are cattle weighing between 600 and 800 lbs that are put into feedlots to be fattened up to slaughter (or "Live") weight through a three–six month regimen of intensive feeding. Though Live Cattle are sold for slaughter, they are sold (or "marketed") on the basis of their weight pre-slaughter. As such, Live Cattle are often referred to as "Fats," while Feeder Cattle are referred to as "Thins."

Unlike the Cattle market, pork products are marketed on a post-slaughter, or "hanging weight" basis. Lean Hogs are not slimmed down versions of Hogs. "Lean" refers to post-slaughter hanging-carcass weight. Prior to February 1997, the Chicago Mercantile Exchange (CME) traded Hog futures on a Live weight basis, but now they trade on a Lean basis. Typically, a "Lean" Hog weighs about 74% of a "Live" Hog. The other pork futures contract is Pork Bellies — used to make bacon.

Sales of livestock from breeders/feeders to slaughter houses are referred to as "Marketings," while the sale from a breeder to a feeder is referred to as a placement — especially in the cattle industry. Disappearance is the death toll of cattle placed on feed. Farrowings are births of pigs following a gestation period of approximately 114 days.

Information about the population of Cattle on Feed — or Cattle placed on feedlots in any given month — is readily available from the United States Agricultural Department (USDA) at www.USDA.gov. Each month the USDA releases the Cattle on Feed report which highlights the numbers of Cattle entering (Placements) as well as exiting (Marketings and Disappearance) feedlots. Twice a year, the USDA releases a Cattle census in the form of the Cattle Inventory Report near the end of January and July. This report gives traders the government estimate of the Cattle population by class of cattle.

The USDA also releases a quarterly report on the population of Hogs, as well as information regarding breeding (farrowing) intentions. The quarterly Hogs and Pigs report by the USDA is issued near the end of March, June, September, and December, covering the prior months' issues.

The USDA also releases a daily slaughter estimate report which gives the number of Cattle and Hogs slaughtered the previous week. In combination, all of these reports help the astute Livestock trader keep up to date with current supply trends in the Livestock futures markets. But traders should be warned that even though these reports contain valuable information, the marketplace anticipates the release so accurately that traders on the Chicago Mercantile Exchange have nicknamed the monthly Cattle on Feed report, "Cattle on Fade," as often prices will move in the opposite direction of what logic would dictate after reading the report. "Fade" is a floor-trading term meaning to do the opposite.

SEPTEMBER

MONDAY
24

CL 68.4	NG 47.4	GC 68.4	SI 63.2
S 31.6	W 61.1	C 27.8	LC 44.4
LH 47.4	KC 57.9	CC 42.1	SB 61.1

f a battered stock refuses to sink any lower no matter how many negative articles appear in the papers, hat stock is worth a close look. — James L. Fraser (*Contrary Investor*)

TUESDAY
25

CL 66.7	NG 47.4	GC 73.7	SI 52.6
S 44.4	W 63.2	C 44.4	LC 52.6
LH 47.4	KC 57.9	CC 57.9	SB 38.9

Only those who dare to fail greatly can ever achieve greatly. — Robert F. Kennedy

WEDNESDAY
26

CL 33.3	NG 47.4	GC 47.4	SI 42.1
S 47.4	W 47.4	C 47.4	LC 52.6
LH 27.8	KC 63.2	CC 57.9	SB 38.9

Restlessness and discontent are the first necessities of progress. — Thomas Alva Edison (American inventor, 1093 patents, 1847–1931)

THURSDAY
27

CL 63.2	NG 47.4	GC 42.1	SI 44.4
S 52.6	W 57.9	C 55.6	LC 44.4
LH 36.8	KC 26.3	CC 31.6	SB 52.6

t is a funny thing about life; if you refuse to accept anything but the best, you very often get it. — W. Somerset Maugham

FRIDAY
28

CL 78.9	NG 52.6	GC 31.6	SI 47.4
S 52.6	W 72.2	C 47.4	LC 44.4
LH 63.2	KC 61.1	CC 66.7	SB 47.4

es, we have to divide up our time like that, between our politics and our equations. But to me our equations are far more important, for politics are only a matter of present concern. A mathematical equation stands forever.
— Albert Einstein (German/American physicist, 1921 Nobel Prize, 1879–1955)

SATURDAY
29

SUNDAY
30

OCTOBER ALMANAC

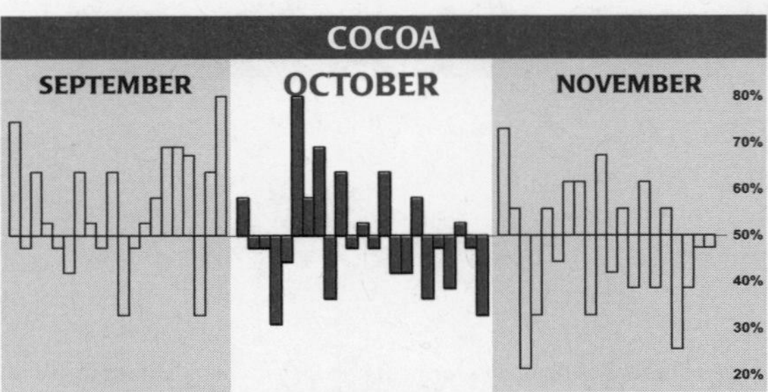

Market Probability Chart above is a graphic representation of Cocoa futures taken from the Market Probability Calendar on page 179

PETROLEUM FUTURES: 9 of 13 September rallies in December Crude have been reversed in October ◆ December Crude up 8 / down 11 in October ◆ January Natural Gas up 6 / down 9 in October ◆ 7 of last 10 September rallies have resulted in October losses ◆ 9 of 12 October breaks have continued through November basis March Natural Gas.

METALS FUTURES: December Gold up 7 / down 12 ◆ 6 of 7 October rallies continue through November ◆ December Silver up 4 / down 14 ◆ 11 of 13 September rallies saw breaks in October.

GRAIN FUTURES: Worst Octobers' basis January Soybeans followed September weakness ◆ October strength in Soybeans continues through November (7 of 8) ◆ December CBOT Wheat up 12 / down 7 ◆ Rare September Corn rallies tend to continue through October (4 of 5) ◆ October breaks tend to continue in December Corn (6 of 9).

LIVESTOCK FUTURES: December Live Cattle up 13 / down 6 ◆ September strength continues through October in Cattle (10 of 13) ◆ October Cattle weakness tends to be reversed in November (7 of 8) basis February Cattle ◆ December Lean Hogs down 16 / up 3 ◆ September strength typically reversed in October (12 of 15) basis December Hogs ◆ October weakness creates bargains through year-end.

SOFTS FUTURES: December Cocoa down 15 / up 4 in October ◆ Worst month on record for Cocoa, down -$984/ton from 1987 – 2005 ◆ Weak Septembers create buying opportunities in March Sugar during October ◆ October rallies in March Sugar tend to continue through November (8 of 12).

COMMODITY SPOTLIGHT COCOA

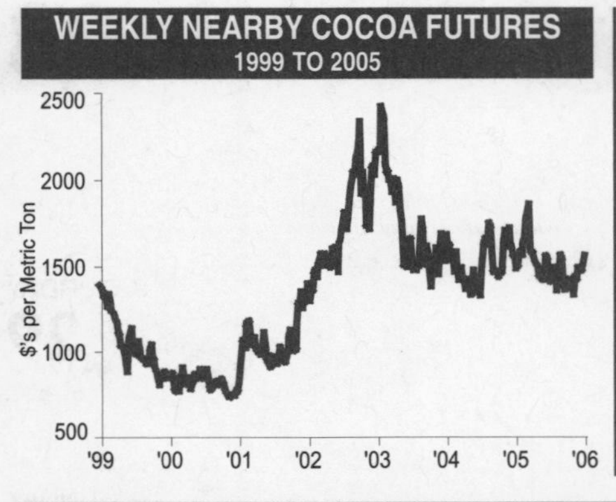

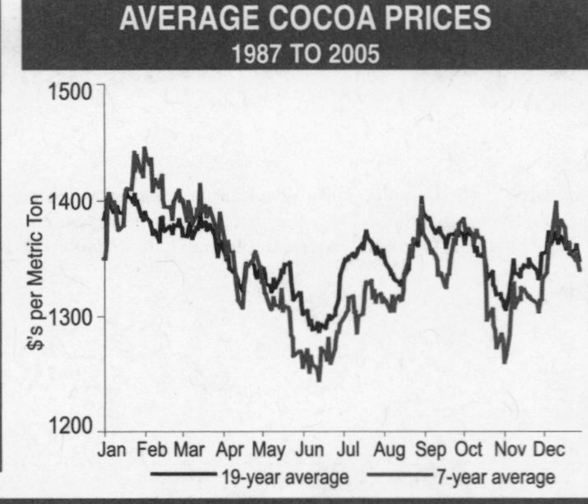

Cocoa prices tend towards weakness during the beginning of the main and mid-crop harvests. Only in years of plight or political uncertainty do prices hold up to the onslaught of supply.

OCTOBER

MONDAY **1**

CL 57.9	NG 61.1	GC 52.6	SI 55.6
S 26.3	W 57.9	C 31.6	LC 52.6
LH 63.2	KC 26.3	CC 44.4	SB 47.4

When one door closes, another door opens; but we so often look so long and so regretfully upon the closed door, that we do not see the ones which open for us. — Alexander Graham Bell

TUESDAY **2**

CL 47.4	NG 44.4	GC 44.4	SI 42.1
S 47.4	W 42.1	C 55.6	LC 63.2
LH 52.6	KC 36.8	CC 38.9	SB 36.8

The most important single factor in shaping security markets is public psychology. — Gerald M. Loeb

WEDNESDAY **3**

CL 47.4	NG 52.6	GC 57.9	SI 44.4
S 36.8	W 57.9	C 42.1	LC 55.6
LH 52.6	KC 55.6	CC 57.9	SB 52.6

Change does not necessarily assure progress, but progress implacably requires change. Education is essential to change, for education creates both new wants and the ability to satisfy them. — Henry Steele Commager

THURSDAY **4**

CL 31.6	NG 52.6	GC 63.2	SI 61.1
S 47.4	W 36.8	C 44.4	LC 31.6
LH 44.4	KC 57.9	CC 61.1	SB 72.2

Wall Street never changes. The pockets change, the suckers change, the stocks change, but Wall Street never changes because human nature never changes. — Jesse Livermore

FRIDAY **5**

CL 44.4	NG 57.9	GC 47.4	SI 47.4
S 47.4	W 47.4	C 68.4	LC 73.7
LH 57.9	KC 52.6	CC 52.6	SB 38.9

When you get into a tight place and everything goes against you, till it seems as though you could not hang on a minute longer, never give up then, for that is just the place and time that the tide will turn.
— Harriet Beecher Stowe (American writer and abolitionist)

SATURDAY **6**

SUNDAY **7**

SEPTEMBER COCOA RALLIES SLAMMED IN OCTOBER

December Cocoa futures have posted gains in September only 8 times during the 19-year period from 1987 through 2005. Following these 8 rallies, prices reversed and settled the month of October lower.

The average gain in September during the aforementioned 8 years was +$79/ton. Following these 8 September rallies, December Cocoa futures proceeded to break by an average of -$81/ton. Four of the 8 years saw breaks in October of a higher magnitude than the September rallies: 1999, 2000, 2002, and 2005.

September Cocoa rallies can be powerful, as 6 of the last 8 rallies have continued higher at the beginning of October, exceeding the September monthly high.

The average decline from the September close to the October low has been -$113/ton. In 2002, December Cocoa futures broke from a September settlement of $2191/ton to an October low of $1842/ton, or -$349/ton.

Given that December Cocoa futures have posted losses in the September-through-October period 15 of the 19 years studied (78.9%) (see page 84), traders should view September rallies as an opportunity to either establish short (sell) positions, or to liquidate long (buy) positions — or at least manage position stop losses more aggressively.

DECEMBER COCOA FUTURES IN SEPTEMBER AND OCTOBER DURING YEARS OF SEPTEMBER STRENGTH

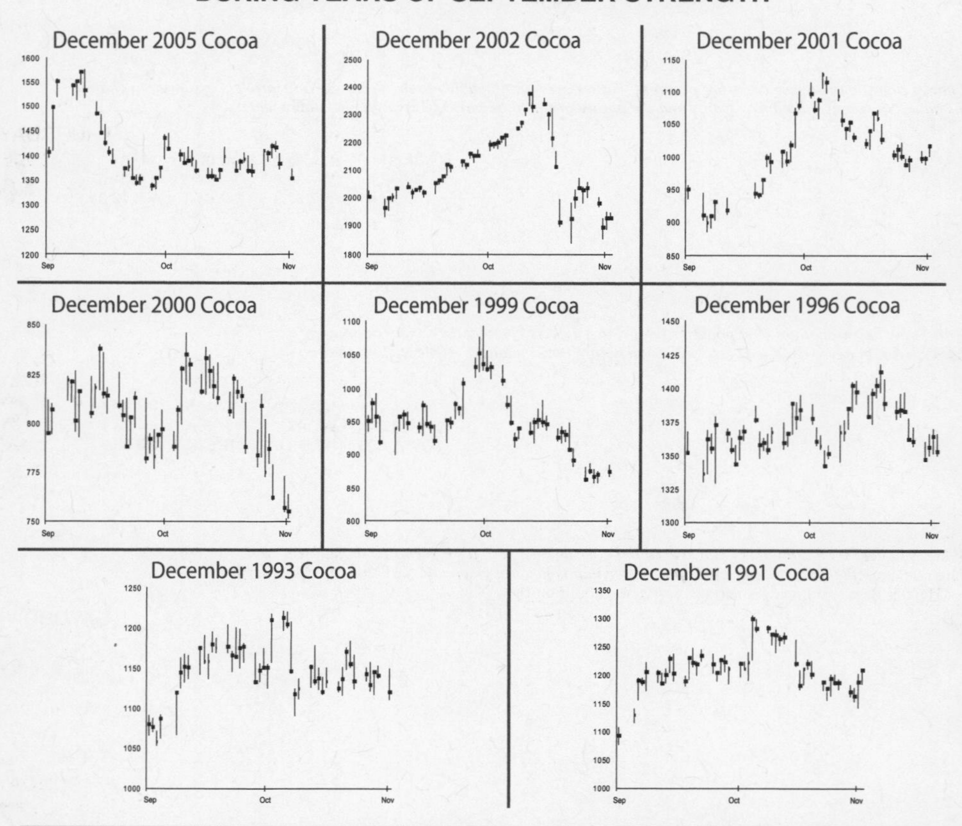

OCTOBER

Columbus Day (Bond Market Closed)

MONDAY

8

CL 78.9	**NG** 57.9	**GC** 61.1	**SI** 47.4
S 55.6	**W** 73.7	**C** 52.6	**LC** 52.6
LH 42.1	**KC** 61.1	**CC** 42.1	**SB** 52.6

o me, the "tape" is the final arbiter of any investment decision. I have a cardinal rule: Never fight the tape! — Martin Zweig

TUESDAY

9

CL 57.9	**NG** 63.2	**GC** 52.6	**SI** 47.4
S 63.2	**W** 44.4	**C** 44.4	**LC** 47.4
LH 42.1	**KC** 47.4	**CC** 55.6	**SB** 52.6

You can't say civilization don't advance — for in every war, they kill you in a new way. — Will Rogers

WEDNESDAY

10

CL 68.4	**NG** 55.6	**GC** 36.8	**SI** 21.1
S 68.4	**W** 47.4	**C** 61.1	**LC** 63.2
LH 47.4	**KC** 57.9	**CC** 31.6	**SB** 42.1

he heights by great men reached and kept were not attained by sudden flight,
but they, while their companions slept, were toiling upward in the night. — Henry Wadsworth Longfellow

THURSDAY

11

CL 36.8	**NG** 36.8	**GC** 42.1	**SI** 44.4
S 52.6	**W** 42.1	**C** 63.2	**LC** 78.9
LH 52.6	**KC** 44.4	**CC** 42.1	**SB** 84.2

Analysts are supposed to be critics of corporations. They often end up being public relations spokesmen for them.
— Ralph Wanger (Chief Investment Officer, Acorn Fund)

FRIDAY

12

CL 63.2	**NG** 52.6	**GC** 42.1	**SI** 42.1
S 47.4	**W** 63.2	**C** 57.9	**LC** 47.4
LH 61.1	**KC** 68.4	**CC** 42.1	**SB** 31.6

He who knows nothing is confident of everything. — Anonymous

SATURDAY

13

SUNDAY

14

OCTOBER PERFORMANCE SETS THE TREND IN GOLD

The major demand period for the largest consumer of Gold — the jewelry industry — is the end-of-year holiday shopping season. Jewelry sales in the final quarter of the year usually make up 40% of yearly sales.

Jewelers buying in October is a critical benchmark for future performance, with December Gold following October's trend through November in 13 of the last 19 years (68.4%).

Following October strength, December Gold has continued higher through November on 6 of 7 occasions (85.7%). After October weakness, December Gold has continued lower in November on 7 of 12 occasions (58.3%).

Goldbugs and traders alike should take note that 5 of the 6 errors in October's predictive ability have occurred following October weakness, and thus should remember that the holiday shopping season is typically a strong period for Gold futures — see page 82.

DECEMBER GOLD DOLLARS PER OUNCE CHANGES

Date	Oct Close	Oct Change	Oct Close to Nov High	Oct Close to Nov Low	Nov Change	Trend
1987	471.2	12.4	25.8	-15.2	19.8	Continuation
1988	415.1	15.9	13.8	-2.5	9.7	Continuation
1989	377.6	5.6	42.1	-1.9	34.0	Continuation
1990	381.3	-26.8	10.2	-5.3	2.0	Reversal
1991	359.5	2.2	11.2	-5.9	8.4	Continuation
1992	340.1	-9.3	0.7	-11.2	-5.8	Continuation
1993	369.6	12.5	11.6	-8.9	0.2	Continuation
1994	384.9	-12.7	3.0	-5.2	-4.2	Continuation
1995	384.3	-2.2	7.2	-2.8	2.9	Reversal
1996	379.1	-1.4	6.7	-6.8	-6.1	Continuation
1997	312.1	-24.8	4.8	-16.1	-15.2	Continuation
1998	293.7	-5.3	5.4	-5.0	-1.2	Continuation
1999	300.3	0.8	0.1	-12.3	-10.2	Reversal
2000	266.4	-10.5	4.8	-1.9	3.7	Reversal
2001	280.5	-13.5	2.0	-8.6	-6.6	Continuation
2002	318.4	-6.8	7.0	-1.9	-1.6	Continuation
2003	384.6	-1.5	17.4	-8.1	12.2	Reversal
2004	429.4	9.0	25.4	-11.4	21.9	Continuation
2005	466.9	-5.4	35.4	-10.8	27.7	Reversal
	Averages	**-3.3**	**12.3**	**-7.5**	**4.8**	
	# Up	**7**	**19**	**0**	**11**	
	Following Up Oct					
	Averages	**8.3**	**18.6**	**-8.3**	**12.0**	
	# Up	**7**	**19**	**0**	**6**	
	Following Down Oct					
	Averages	**-10.0**	**8.7**	**-7.0**	**0.7**	
	# Down	**12**	**0**	**19**	**7**	

OCTOBER

MONDAY 15

CL 47.4	NG 33.3	GC 42.1	SI 36.8
S 55.6	W 42.1	C 42.1	LC 31.6
LH 36.8	KC 47.4	CC 47.4	SB 55.6

here is science, logic, reason; there is thought verified by experience. And then there is California (or trading). — Edward Abbey

TUESDAY 16

CL 52.6	NG 52.6	GC 36.8	SI 47.4
S 33.3	W 57.9	C 38.9	LC 57.9
LH 42.1	KC 63.2	CC 52.6	SB 47.4

The weakest link in any system is the loose nut behind the wheel. — J. Mark Kinoff

WEDNESDAY 17

CL 47.4	NG 33.3	GC 42.1	SI 36.8
S 55.6	W 42.1	C 42.1	LC 31.6
LH 36.8	KC 47.4	CC 47.4	SB 55.6

n an uptrend, if a higher high is made but fails to carry through, and prices dip below the previous high, the trend is apt to reverse. The converse is true for downtrends. — Victor Sperandeo (*Trader Vic — Methods of a Wall Street Master*)

THURSDAY 18

CL 63.2	NG 52.6	GC 42.1	SI 42.1
S 47.4	W 63.2	C 57.9	LC 47.4
LH 61.1	KC 68.4	CC 42.1	SB 31.6

The trend is your friend...until it ends or ends! — Anonymous

FRIDAY 19

CL 42.1	NG 52.6	GC 44.4	SI 36.8
S 63.2	W 36.8	C 27.8	LC 47.4
LH 57.9	KC 31.6	CC 47.4	SB 44.4

To fly, we have to have resistance. — Maya Lin

SATURDAY 20

SUNDAY 21

OCTOBER SUGAR TRENDS SET TONE FOR REST OF YEAR

Sweet candy treats are strongly associated with the approaching holiday season. Be it dancing sugar plums, sweet rice cakes, or other tasty morsels, most end-of-year holiday celebrations incorporate sugar-laden treats. In preparation for the onslaught of holiday demand, distributors buy March Sugar in October to meet consumer demand.

Since 1987, March Sugar futures have rallied in October 12 times (63.2%), gaining an average of +0.13 cents/lb. Following these 12 strong Octobers, March Sugar futures have continued to gain through November and December 10 times.

On average March Sugar futures have had a year-end rally of +1.01 cents/lb. However, following only strong Octobers, the year-end rally increases in magnitude, while year-end breaks decrease in magnitude. On a monthly settlement basis, March Sugar futures have gained +0.85 cents/lb on average during the October-through-December period following strong Octobers, a substantially larger gain than is achieved in all years.

Traders should look upon October strength as a precursor year-end strength in March Sugar futures.

MARCH SUGAR FUTURES CENTS PER POUND CHANGES

Date	Oct Close	Oct Change	Nov/Dec High	Nov/Dec Low	Dec Close	Oct Close to Dec Close	Dec Rally Oct Close to Nov/Dec High	Dec Break Oct Close to Nov/Dec High
1987	7.59	0.63	9.55	7.31	9.49	1.90	1.96	-0.28
1988	10.59	0.95	12.00	9.91	11.15	0.56	1.41	-0.68
1989	13.97	-0.19	15.38	12.78	13.16	-0.81	1.41	-1.19
1990	9.42	-0.69	10.33	9.33	9.37	-0.05	0.91	-0.09
1991	8.98	-0.03	9.27	8.12	9.00	0.02	0.29	-0.86
1992	8.77	0.06	9.00	8.12	8.39	-0.38	0.23	-0.65
1993	10.62	0.17	11.03	9.88	10.77	0.15	0.41	-0.74
1994	12.80	0.40	15.38	12.73	15.17	2.37	2.58	-0.07
1995	10.56	0.38	11.65	10.52	11.60	1.04	1.09	-0.04
1996	10.30	-0.59	11.00	10.21	10.99	0.69	0.70	-0.09
1997	12.39	0.83	12.55	11.86	12.22	-0.17	0.16	-0.53
1998	7.71	0.06	8.50	7.42	7.86	0.15	0.79	-0.29
1999	6.88	-0.05	7.10	5.62	6.12	-0.76	0.22	-1.26
2000	9.90	0.45	10.33	8.67	10.20	0.30	0.43	-1.23
2001	6.74	0.11	7.85	6.61	7.39	0.65	1.11	-0.13
2002	7.36	0.92	7.89	6.58	7.61	0.25	0.53	-0.78
2003	5.93	-0.51	6.79	5.66	5.67	-0.26	0.86	-0.27
2004	8.60	-0.46	9.08	8.35	9.04	0.44	0.48	-0.25
2005	11.33	0.10	14.89	11.13	14.68	3.35	3.56	-0.20
	Averages	**0.13**				**0.50**	**1.01**	**-0.51**
	# Up	**12**				**13**	**19**	**0**
	Following Up Oct							
	Averages					**0.85**	**1.19**	**-0.47**
	# Up					**10**	**12**	**0**

DO YOU HAVE THE ALMANAC ADVANTAGE?

CUSTOMIZE AND UPDATE YOUR ALMANAC!

You can find out what seasonal trends are on schedule and which are not....how to take advantage of them...what market-moving events are coming up...and what the indicators say about the next move.

Subscribe to the **Almanac Investor Platform** and receive full access to our online interactive research tools and reports, plus receive our monthly Almanac Investor Newsletter and our Almanac Investor E-Alerts!

IT'S EASY TO SUBSCRIBE...

- **Online at stocktradersalmanac.com using promo code STA7**
- **Call us toll-free at 800-356-5016**
- **Fax us at 800-597-3299**
- **Mail the self-addressed card on the reverse side to our attention**

NO POSTAGE NECESSARY IF MAILED IN THE UNITED STATES

BUSINESS REPLY MAIL
FIRST-CLASS MAIL PERMIT NO. 2277 HOBOKEN NJ

POSTAGE WILL BE PAID BY ADDRESSEE

F REID
JOHN WILEY & SONS INC
111 RIVER ST MS 5-01
HOBOKEN NJ 07030-9442

OCTOBER

MONDAY **22**

CL 42.1	NG 55.6	GC 47.4	SI 68.4
S 47.4	W 57.9	C 47.4	LC 66.7
LH 55.6	KC 47.4	CC 57.9	SB 52.6

If the models are telling you to sell, sell, sell, but only buyers are out there, don't be a jerk. Buy!
— William Silber, Ph.D. (N.Y.U., *Newsweek*, 1986)

TUESDAY **23**

CL 57.9	NG 42.1	GC 63.2	SI 66.7
S 63.2	W 47.4	C 47.4	LC 36.8
LH 21.1	KC 47.4	CC 47.4	SB 36.8

Many of life's failures are people who did not realize how close they were to success when they gave up.
— Thomas Alva Edison (American inventor, 1093 patents, 1847–1931)

WEDNESDAY **24**

CL 36.8	NG 57.9	GC 31.6	SI 26.3
S 44.4	W 42.1	C 33.3	LC 66.7
LH 47.4	KC 68.4	CC 63.2	SB 72.2

Most people would die sooner than think; in fact, they do. — Bertrand Russell (British mathematician and philosopher, 1872–1970)

THURSDAY **25**

CL 47.4	NG 42.1	GC 42.1	SI 47.4
S 47.4	W 42.1	C 42.1	LC 63.2
LH 57.9	KC 57.9	CC 42.1	SB 47.4

Opportunity is missed by most because it is dressed in overalls and looks like work.
— Thomas Alva Edison (American inventor, 1093 patents, 1847–1931)

FRIDAY **26**

CL 38.9	NG 36.8	GC 47.4	SI 57.9
S 42.1	W 42.1	C 42.1	LC 47.4
LH 27.8	KC 52.6	CC 22.2	SB 38.9

To know values is to know the meaning of the market. — Charles Dow

SATURDAY **27**

SUNDAY **28**

NOVEMBER ALMANAC

NOVEMBER						
S	M	T	W	T	F	S
				1	2	3
4	5	6	7	8	9	10
11	12	13	14	15	16	17
18	19	20	21	22	23	24
25	26	27	28	29	30	

DECEMBER						
S	M	T	W	T	F	S
						1
2	3	4	5	6	7	8
9	10	11	12	13	14	15
16	17	18	19	20	21	22
23	24	25	26	27	28	29
30	31					

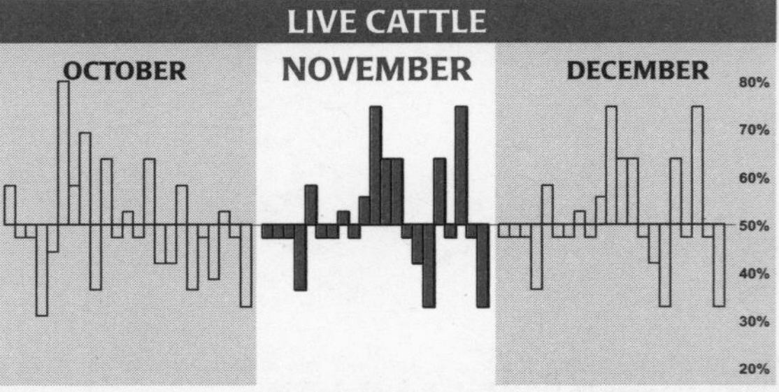

Market Probability Chart above is a graphic representation of Live Cattle futures taken from the Market Probability Calendar on page 159

PETROLEUM FUTURES: January Crude up 9 / down 10 ◆ November's trend sets the tone for December pricing in January Crude Oil (14 of 19) ◆ 7 of 9 November rallies continued in December ◆ 7 of 10 November breaks continued through December ◆ March Natural Gas down 12 / up 4 ◆ Worst Novembers follow October weakness ◆ November weakness continued through December (7 of 11).

METALS FUTURES: February Gold up 11 / down 8 ◆ November strength usually follows rare October rallies (6 of 7) ◆ November weakness in Gold continues through December (6 of 8) ◆ Silver and other Industrial metals begin to gain on Gold as jewelry demand diminishes.

GRAIN FUTURES: January Soybeans up 13 / down 6 ◆ Best Novembers follow October strength in Soybeans ◆ November rallies reversed in December 8 of 12 ◆ Mixed month for March Corn and Wheat (up 7 / down 12) and March CBOT wheat (up 9 / down 10).

LIVESTOCK FUTURES: Best Novembers have followed October weakness in February Live Cattle (up 7 of 8) ◆ November breaks reversed in December (5 of 7) basis February Live Cattle ◆ Cattle tends towards strength through January.

SOFTS FUTURES: October breaks in March Coffee continue through November (7 of 10) ◆ March Sugar up 13 / down 6 ◆ Best Novembers in Sugar follow October strength ◆ Mixed month for Cocoa (up 10 / down 9) ◆ 7 of 10 November rallies reversed in December basis March Cocoa due to main crop harvest pressures on Ivory Coast.

COMMODITY SPOTLIGHT LIVE CATTLE

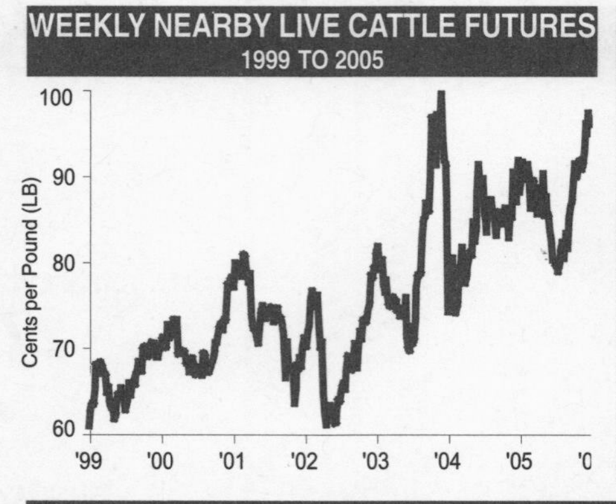

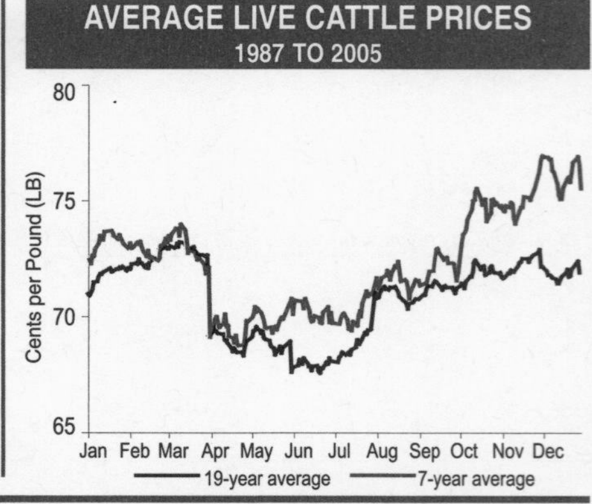

Slaughter peaks typically in August and registers its lows in February. In anticipation of this cycle Cattle tends towards strength in winter and weakness in spring.

MONDAY **29**

CL 52.6	NG 72.2	GC 38.9	SI 33.3
S 31.6	W 42.1	C 44.4	LC 33.3
LH 42.1	KC 38.9	CC 52.6	SB 66.7

[The Fed] is very smart, but [it] doesn't run the markets. In the end, the markets will run [the Fed]. The markets are bigger than any man or any group of men. The markets can even break a president. — Richard Russell (*Dow Theory Letters*, August 4, 2004)

TUESDAY **30**

CL 47.4	NG 52.6	GC 52.6	SI 57.9
S 38.9	W 36.8	C 27.8	LC 44.4
LH 42.1	KC 57.9	CC 52.6	SB 33.3

The average man doesn't wish to be told that it is a bull or a bear market. What he desires is to be told specifically which particular stock to buy or sell. He wants to get something for nothing. He does not wish to work. He doesn't even wish to have to think. — Jesse Livermore

Halloween 

WEDNESDAY **31**

CL 33.3	NG 52.6	GC 47.4	SI 47.4
S 31.6	W 42.1	C 38.9	LC 57.9
LH 38.9	KC 52.6	CC 42.1	SB 36.8

Strong people make as many mistakes as weak people. Difference is that strong people (and succesful traders) admit their mistakes, laugh at them, learn from them. That is how they become strong (and succesful). — Richard Needham

THURSDAY **1**

CL 52.6	NG 44.4	GC 36.8	SI 31.6
S 63.2	W 47.4	C 42.1	LC 68.4
LH 57.9	KC 57.9	CC 38.9	SB 44.4

There are two ways to slide easily through life: to believe everything or to doubt everything; both ways save us from thinking. — Theodore Rubin

FRIDAY **2**

CL 42.1	NG 47.4	GC 47.4	SI 42.1
S 63.2	W 61.1	C 52.6	LC 36.8
LH 52.6	KC 44.4	CC 47.4	SB 47.4

Liberty without learning is always in peril and learning without liberty is always in vain. — John F. Kennedy (35th U.S. President, 1917–1963)

SATURDAY **3**

Daylight Saving Time Ends

SUNDAY **4**

PLACEMENTS AND TRANSPORTATION MAKE BEEF BULLISH INTO FEBRUARY

Commodities — such as Wheat and Beef — are primarily transported by barge. The U.S. river system is an excellent way to transport large amounts of product, with commodities making up the bulk of barge traffic.

During the winter months, river routes — such as the Mississippi and Snake — often become difficult to navigate. Barge rates often rise during the winter, and commodity supplies build up in the interior. This can be readily seen in the Cattle market.

Live Cattle — or steers weighing in excess of 900 lbs — often cannot be moved to slaughter plants during the winter months, or the slaughter plants have difficulty moving supplies to consumers on the coast. This can create a "hole" in supply, which may be exaggerated by the fact that fewer than average cattle are at slaughter weight during the winter, given the natural breeding/slaughter cycle in the cattle market.

This dynamic is readily apparent by the magnitude of the winter rally in February Live Cattle futures. On average, in the November-through-February period, February Live Cattle futures have had an average winter rally of +4.35 cents/bu, finishing February above its end-of-October level 15 times since 1987 (78.9%).

However, riding a winter rally is not without risk. Winter breaks are a reality as well, averaging a break of -3.40 cents/pound in February Live Cattle. Given the tendency for Live Cattle (both February and April contracts) to rally at the tail end of winter in the new year, weakness in November or December may represent an excellent opportunity to establish a bullish (long) position in the Cattle market.

APRIL LIVE CATTLE CENTS PER POUND CHANGES

Date	Oct Close	Nov/Feb High	Nov/Feb Low	Feb Close	Oct Close to Feb Close	Winter Rally Oct Close to Nov/Dec High	Winter Break Oct Close to Nov/Dec Low
1987	62.53	73.55	60.75	71.50	8.98	11.03	-1.78
1988	75.38	78.45	72.65	78.05	2.68	3.08	-2.72
1989	74.20	77.88	73.43	75.45	1.25	3.68	-0.78
1990	75.23	80.35	74.20	80.23	5.00	5.13	-1.02
1991	74.25	79.18	70.45	77.40	3.15	4.93	-3.80
1992	71.78	80.50	71.58	80.23	8.45	8.72	-0.20
1993	76.33	77.15	74.03	77.10	0.77	0.83	-2.30
1994	69.90	75.25	68.20	74.28	4.38	5.35	-1.70
1995	67.55	68.45	62.73	63.93	-3.63	0.90	-4.83
1996	65.25	70.40	64.00	69.63	4.38	5.15	-1.25
1997	72.35	73.05	62.98	64.38	-7.97	0.70	-9.37
1998	66.43	68.75	59.90	68.03	1.60	2.33	-6.53
1999	70.43	73.50	69.75	71.18	0.75	3.08	-0.67
2000	74.93	81.58	74.25	81.38	6.45	6.65	-0.67
2001	73.35	76.53	67.25	74.20	0.85	3.18	-6.10
2002	74.85	80.15	74.30	75.83	0.98	5.30	-0.55
2003	81.48	84.60	68.60	76.85	-4.63	3.13	-12.88
2004	85.13	90.30	82.00	86.05	0.92	5.18	-3.13
2005	91.08	95.55	86.75	87.23	-3.85	4.47	-4.33
	Average				**1.61**	**4.36**	**-3.40**
	# Up				**15**	**19**	**0**

NOVEMBER

MONDAY 5

CL 21.1	NG 36.8	GC 63.2	SI 52.6
S 52.6	W 52.6	C 44.4	LC 47.4
LH 68.4	KC 66.7	CC 38.9	SB 33.3

When I'm bearish and I sell a stock, each sale must be at a lower level than the previous sale. When I am buying, the reverse is true. I must buy on a rising scale. I don't buy long stocks on a scale down, I buy on a scale up. — Jesse Livermore

TUESDAY 6

Election Day

CL 38.9	NG 55.6	GC 38.9	SI 47.4
S 61.1	W 36.8	C 31.6	LC 47.4
LH 52.6	KC 47.4	CC 42.1	SB 52.6

There are no creeds in mathematics. — Peter Drucker (Management consultant, "The man who invented the corporate society," born in Austria 1909)

WEDNESDAY 7

CL 42.1	NG 31.6	GC 55.6	SI 63.2
S 52.6	W 61.1	C 52.6	LC 73.7
LH 68.4	KC 57.9	CC 47.4	SB 47.4

If you think you can do a thing or think you can't do a thing, you're right. — Henry Ford

THURSDAY 8

CL 47.4	NG 47.4	GC 52.6	SI 63.2
S 57.9	W 72.2	C 57.9	LC 52.6
LH 52.6	KC 61.1	CC 63.2	SB 66.7

I was in search of a one-armed economist so that the guy could never make a statement and then say: "on the other hand." — Harry S. Truman

FRIDAY 9

CL 52.6	NG 47.4	GC 52.6	SI 44.4
S 42.1	W 57.9	C 44.4	LC 61.1
LH 44.4	KC 57.9	CC 52.6	SB 57.9

Never adopt permanently any type of asset or any selection method. Try to stay flexible, open-minded, and skeptical. — Sir John Templeton (Founder Templeton Funds, philanthropist, 1994)

SATURDAY 10

SUNDAY 11

Veterans' Day

NOVEMBER TRENDS CONTINUE IN DECEMBER IN CRUDE OIL

Refineries pay taxes on inventories at the end of the year. Couple taxes with the fact that refineries tend to slow production during the Christmas holiday season — as workers take time off — and you can see the quandary refineries are in during December.

However, they tend to tell their positions by their November action, as can be seen in the performance of March Crude Oil futures during December. During the 1987-to-2005 period, March Crude Oil futures have posted gains in November 9 times (47.4%) and losses 10 times (52.6%).

Despite November's mixed performance, November Crude Oil performance offers great insight into December's performance. Following the 9 November rallies in March, Crude prices have continued higher in December in 7 years (77.7%). After the 10 November breaks, Crude Oil prices have continued lower in 7 years (70.0%). In other words, November's trend has correctly predicted December's performance in 14 of the last 19 years (73.7%).

November's trend is predictive of December's magnitude of change. Following strong Novembers, March Crude Oil has experienced an average December rally of $2.29/barrel, and December break of -$1.16/barrel. Comparatively, following November weakness, March Crude Oil's December rally has only averaged +$0.78/barrel, while the December break has averaged a solid -$2.73/barrel.

Traders should watch November's trend for a strong indication of what to expect both in terms of direction and magnitude for March Crude Oil in December.

MARCH CRUDE OIL FUTURES DOLLARS PER BARREL CHANGES

Date	Nov Close	Nov Change	Oct/Nov Trend	Dec Rally Nov Close to Dec High	Dec Break Nov Close to Dec Low	Dec Change	Nov Trend
1987	18.30	-1.31	Down	0.25	-3.60	-1.71	Continued
1988	15.07	1.41	Up	1.68	-0.24	1.62	Continued
1989	19.47	0.19	Up	2.18	-0.09	2.02	Continued
1990	29.22	-1.94	Down	-0.12	-5.22	-1.42	Continued
1991	21.10	-1.51	Down	-0.03	-2.70	-1.98	Continued
1992	19.90	-0.69	Down	0.25	-1.04	-0.19	Continued
1993	15.91	-1.55	Down	0.07	-1.59	-1.41	Continued
1994	17.98	0.14	Up	0.07	-1.41	-0.27	Reversed
1995	17.73	0.55	Up	1.35	0.06	1.33	Continued
1996	22.93	0.57	Up	2.19	-0.73	1.74	Continued
1997	19.47	-1.56	Down	-0.13	-1.77	-1.64	Continued
1998	12.14	-2.82	Down	1.01	-1.04	0.05	Reversed
1999	23.17	1.75	Up	2.82	-0.37	1.62	Continued
2000	31.90	1.63	Up	0.40	-6.76	-5.92	Reversed
2001	19.84	-1.69	Down	1.76	-1.39	0.27	Reversed
2002	26.44	0.23	Up	6.36	-0.24	4.15	Continued
2003	29.84	1.55	Up	3.56	-0.64	2.44	Continued
2004	49.18	-1.68	Down	0.00	-8.18	-5.55	Continued
2005	58.68	-2.32	Down	4.77	-0.73	3.22	Reversed
	Average	-0.48		**1.50**	-1.98	-0.09	
	# Up	**9**		**15**	**1**	**10**	
	Following Up Nov Trends						
	Average	**0.89**		**2.29**	-1.16	**0.97**	
	# Up	**9**		**9**	**1**	**7**	
	Following Down Nov Trends						
	Average	-1.71		**0.78**	-2.73	-1.04	
	# Down	**10**		**4**	**10**	**7**	

NOVEMBER

MONDAY **12**

CL 63.2	**NG** 52.6	**GC** 63.2	**SI** 68.4
S 52.6	**W** 38.9	**C** 47.4	**LC** 47.4
LH 47.4	**KC** 31.6	**CC** 68.4	**SB** 47.4

To change one's life: Start immediately. Do it flamboyantly. No exceptions.
— William James (Philosopher, psychologist, 1842–1910)

TUESDAY **13**

CL 38.9	**NG** 42.1	**GC** 63.2	**SI** 63.2
S 57.9	**W** 42.1	**C** 66.7	**LC** 61.1
LH 57.9	**KC** 47.4	**CC** 36.8	**SB** 44.4

If you don't profit from your investment mistakes, someone else will. — Yale Hirsch

WEDNESDAY **14**

CL 52.6	**NG** 44.4	**GC** 57.9	**SI** 57.9
S 63.2	**W** 36.8	**C** 38.9	**LC** 72.2
LH 57.9	**KC** 68.4	**CC** 42.1	**SB** 52.6

Knowledge born from actual experience is the answer to why one profits; lack of it is the reason one loses. — Gerald M. Loeb

THURSDAY **15**

CL 57.9	**NG** 47.4	**GC** 38.9	**SI** 52.6
S 55.6	**W** 38.9	**C** 38.9	**LC** 66.7
LH 68.4	**KC** 42.1	**CC** 52.6	**SB** 36.8

There are times in politics (or "trading") when you must be on the right side and lose. — John Kenneth Galbraith

FRIDAY **16**

CL 47.4	**NG** 52.6	**GC** 47.4	**SI** 52.6
S 47.4	**W** 47.4	**C** 26.3	**LC** 44.4
LH 47.4	**KC** 47.4	**CC** 44.4	**SB** 42.1

Those who cannot remember the past are condemned to repeat it.
— George Santayana (American philosopher, poet, 1863–1952)

SATURDAY **17**

SUNDAY **18**

SPRING HOGS RULE SUPREME: APRIL HOGS GAIN ABSOLUTELY AND RELATIVELY

A spring pig is one which is born in the spring. Spring is a time of heavy breeding in the Hog market. Usually spring pigs become Christmas hams, a fact that is evident by the high slaughter rates in November and December.

The excess supply of Pork at the end of the year tends to pressure the last of the winter contracts — February. During the last 19 years, February Hog futures have declined during the December/January period slightly more than half the time (10 of 19). However, as the supply is worked off and slaughter rates drop in the New Year, the 1st of the spring contracts (April Hogs) tends towards strength, gaining in 15 of the last 19 years (78.9%).

Traders can take advantage of relative strength of April Hogs versus February Hogs through a trading strategy known as an intra-market spread — see page 26. Since 1987, April Hogs have gained relative to February Hogs 15 times (78.9%) from the beginning of December through the end of January. On average, April Hog futures have gained +1.50 cents/lb relative to February Hogs during this period.

The normal production cycle of pork puts downward pressure on February Hogs, while at the same time supporting April Hog futures in December and January. Armed with this knowledge, traders can choose the appropriate futures contract to suit their market opinion, or establish spread positions between them to take advantage of this phenomenon.

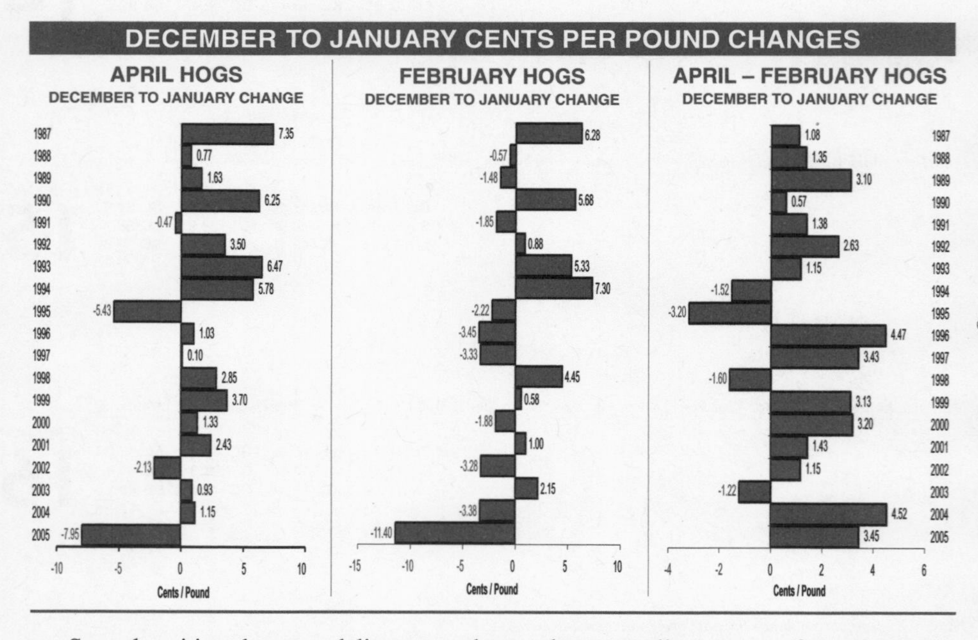

Spread positions between delivery months may be an excellent strategy for traders. The long April/short February Hog spread has historically been much less volatile than an outright long April Hog position during December and January. However, the returns from the strategy have historically been extremely similar within average gain of +1.50 cents/lb versus a +1.52 cent/lb gain from simply buying April Hogs.

NOVEMBER

MONDAY 19

CL 38.9	NG 42.1	GC 63.2	SI 63.2
S 57.9	W 42.1	C 66.7	LC 61.1
LH 57.9	KC 47.4	CC 36.8	SB 44.4

Major bottoms are usually made when analysts cut their earnings estimates and companies report earnings which are below expectations. — Edward Babbitt, Jr. (Avatar Associates)

TUESDAY 20

CL 36.8	NG 44.4	GC 55.6	SI 57.9
S 47.4	W 66.7	C 52.6	LC 52.6
LH 52.6	KC 31.6	CC 47.4	SB 47.4

When a falling stock becomes a screaming buy because it cannot conceivably drop further, try to buy it 30 percent lower. — Al Rizzo (1986)

WEDNESDAY 21

CL 63.2	NG 47.4	GC 47.4	SI 52.6
S 42.1	W 55.6	C 26.3	LC 57.9
LH 42.1	KC 44.4	CC 63.2	SB 55.6

Pliability: Consider and reconsider the facts, and your opinions. Stubbornness as to opinions — "cockiness" — must be entirely eliminated. — Bernard Baruch

Thanksgiving (Market Closed)

THURSDAY 22

Buy when you are scared to death; sell when tickled to death. — Market maxim (*The Cabot Market Letter*, April 12, 2001)

(Shortened Trading Day)

FRIDAY 23

CL 55.6	NG 61.1	GC 52.6	SI 38.9
S 63.2	W 36.8	C 44.4	LC 47.4
LH 55.6	KC 47.4	CC 38.9	SB 52.6

Thomas Alva Edison said, "Genius is 5% inspiration and 95% perspiration!" Unfortunately, many startup "genius" entrepreneurs mistakenly switch the two percentages around, and then wonder why they can't get their projects off the ground. — Yale Hirsch

SATURDAY 24

SUNDAY 25

DECEMBER ALMANAC

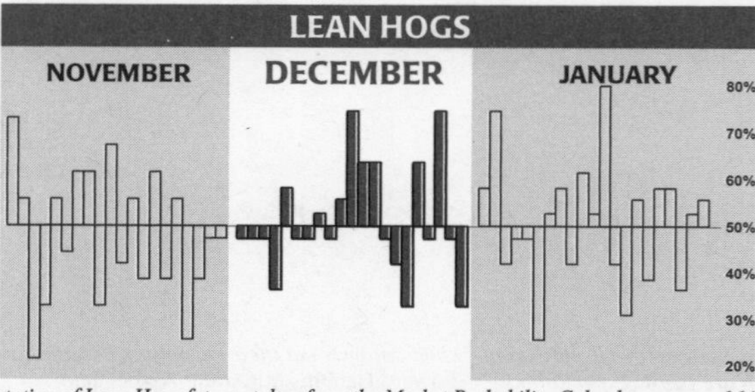

Market Probability Chart above is a graphic representation of Lean Hogs futures taken from the Market Probability Calendar on page 164

PETROLEUM FUTURES: November's trend in Crude Oil tends to be continued in December ◆ December strength continues in January ◆ March Natural Gas up 5 / down 11 ◆ Worst Decembers tend to follow strong Novembers.

METALS FUTURES: November weakness in February Gold carries through to December (6 of 8) ◆ December weakness continues through January (8 of 12) ◆ 13 of 19 December trends have continued through January basis March Silver ◆ 7 of 10 up Decembers have continued through January ◆ 6 of 9 down Decembers have continued through January.

GRAIN FUTURES: 12 of 19 December trends have been reversed in March CBOT Wheat ◆ Expect December weakness in January Soybeans following November rallies (8 of 12) ◆ 7 of 8 December rallies have reversed in January basis March Soybeans.

LIVESTOCK FUTURES: February Live Cattle tends towards strength at year-end ◆ 11 of 13 December rallies have continued through January ◆ December weakness in February Hogs tends to be reversed in January (7 of 10).

SOFTS FUTURES: March Sugar up 12 / down 7 ◆ December's highs and lows violated in January (15 of 19) in the direction of the December closing trend basis March Sugar ◆ November rallies in March Cocoa reversed in December (7 of 10) ◆ 9 of 11 December breaks basis March Cocoa continued through January.

COMMODITY SPOTLIGHT LEAN HOGS

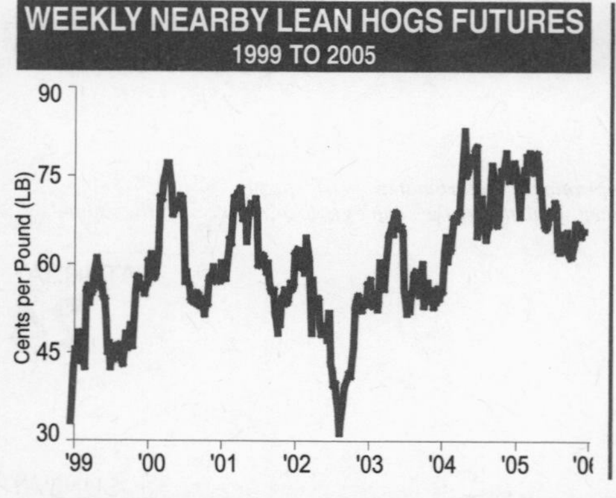

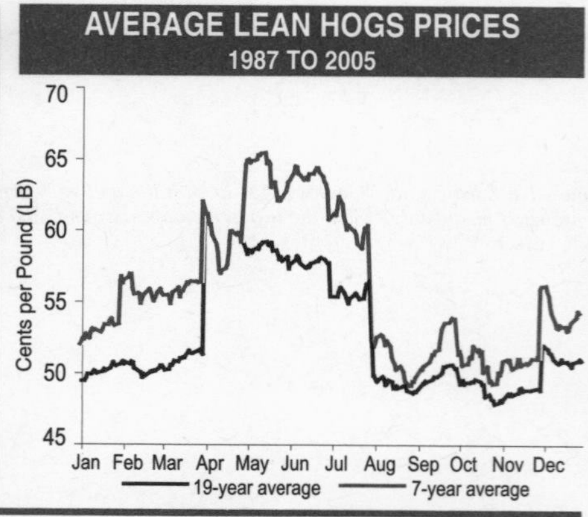

The lack of slaughter-ready Hogs during summer coupled with high demand tends to cause high prices. However, abundant supplies in the fall after spring farrowings tends to depress prices.

NOVEMBER/DECEMBER

MONDAY
26

CL 47.4	NG 38.9	GC 47.4	SI 42.1
S 57.9	W 36.8	C 47.4	LC 61.1
LH 38.9	KC 47.4	CC 57.9	SB 36.8

Do not let what you cannot do interfere with what you can do. — John Wooden (Coach UCLA basketball, born 1910)

TUESDAY
27

CL 63.2	NG 52.6	GC 55.6	SI 36.8
S 47.4	W 47.4	C 52.6	LC 57.9
LH 52.6	KC 26.3	CC 36.8	SB 57.9

Securities pricing is in every sense a psychological phenomenon that arises from the interaction of human beings with fear. Why not greed and fear as the equation is usually stated? Because greed is simply fear of not having enough. — John Bollinger (Bollinger Capital Management, created Bollinger Bands, *Capital Growth Letter, Bollinger on Bollinger Bands*)

WEDNESDAY
28

CL 57.9	NG 47.4	GC 57.9	SI 61.1
S 55.6	W 52.6	C 27.8	LC 36.8
LH 61.1	KC 26.3	CC 42.1	SB 63.2

When it comes to getting things done, we need fewer architects (or "analysts") and more bricklayers (or "traders"). — Colleen C. Barrett

THURSDAY
29

CL 27.8	NG 42.1	GC 36.8	SI 44.4
S 72.2	W 38.9	C 33.3	LC 47.4
LH 52.6	KC 33.3	CC 36.8	SB 47.4

The influence of speculation cannot alter the average level of prices over a given period; what it can do is to diminish the gap between the highest and the lowest prices. Price fluctuations are reduced by speculation, not aggravated, as the popular legend has it. — Ludwig von Mises

FRIDAY
30

CL 42.1	NG 52.6	GC 36.8	SI 21.1
S 63.2	W 36.8	C 47.4	LC 47.4
LH 36.8	KC 68.4	CC 47.4	SB 73.7

There is only one side of the market and it is not the bull side or the bear side, but the right side. — Jesse Livermore

SATURDAY
1

SUNDAY
2

YEAR-END TREND IN HOGS REVERSED IN JANUARY

Year-end trends in the Hog market set the tone for January. In the final months of the year Hog slaughter rates tend to peak at their highest levels. Consumption also tends to be high. But transportation is difficult; hence supplies often build in the interior of the nation near production facilities, causing tight supplies elsewhere during many winters. This dynamic sets the tone for prices at the start of the New Year.

Since 1987, April Hog futures have rallied from the end of October through December 12 times (63.2%) and broken 7 times (36.8%). During this time frame, April Hog futures have moved in the opposite direction of this trend during January 78.9% of the time (15 of 19 years).

Following the last 12 occurrences of October-through-December strength, April Hog futures have declined in January 8 times (66.7%), with an average January break -2.54 cents/pound. Following the last 7 October through December breaks, April Hogs have reversed in January 4 times (57.1%) with an average January rally of +6.30 cents/pound.

Traders should look at end-of-year movements as a guide to what can happen in the New Year. Remember, the trend of the market is not always your "friend" for it can bend or end.

APRIL LEAN HOG CENTS PER POUND CHANGES

Date	Oct Close	Oct to Dec Change	Jan Change	Jan Rally Dec Close to Jan High	Jan Break Dec Close to Jan Low	Year-End Trend Comment
1987	52.43	-0.47	7.70	10.60	-0.45	Reversed
1988	59.00	2.83	-3.08	0.88	-5.28	Reversed
1989	58.65	1.98	2.70	5.93	-0.42	Continued
1990	63.60	-0.27	4.90	6.68	-1.30	Reversed
1991	54.70	-4.10	3.48	4.45	-0.27	Reversed
1992	54.33	2.97	1.90	2.83	-1.15	Continued
1993	65.13	-1.68	6.40	6.70	-0.40	Reversed
1994	51.30	2.63	-0.35	1.75	-1.70	Reversed
1995	63.05	1.73	-4.85	-2.00	-5.58	Reversed
1996	69.95	6.27	-1.47	1.18	-1.97	Reversed
1997	59.00	-2.75	1.38	3.15	-1.20	Reversed
1998	46.10	-8.90	5.83	8.05	-1.65	Reversed
1999	51.45	4.15	4.65	4.80	0.52	Continued
2000	52.23	5.18	-0.25	2.80	-0.75	Reversed
2001	55.25	4.80	0.85	2.15	-0.95	Continued
2002	53.45	4.28	-0.88	2.43	-3.28	Reversed
2003	59.83	-4.93	4.30	4.50	0.25	Reversed
2004	64.75	12.05	-1.25	1.80	-2.50	Reversed
2005	65.68	2.80	-6.65	0.43	-7.47	Reversed
	Average	**1.50**	**1.33**	**3.64**	**-1.87**	
	# Up	**12**	**11**	**18**	**2**	
	# Reversed					**15**
	Following Up Oct to Dec Change					
	Average	**4.30**	-0.72	**2.08**	-2.54	
	# Up	**12**	**4**	**11**	**1**	
	Following Down Oct to Dec Change					
	Average	-3.30	**4.85**	**6.30**	**-0.72**	
	# Up	**7**	**7**	**7**	**1**	

DECEMBER

MONDAY **3**

CL 47.4	NG 36.8	GC 47.4	SI 57.9
S 52.6	W 61.1	C 47.4	LC 47.4
LH 63.2	KC 47.4	CC 61.1	SB 47.4

It is not how right or how wrong you are that matters, but how much money you make when right and how much you do not lose when wrong. — George Soros (Financier, philanthropist, political activist, author, and philosopher, b. 1930)

TUESDAY **4**

CL 47.4	NG 47.4	GC 47.4	SI 52.6
S 52.6	W 61.1	C 52.6	LC 52.6
LH 68.4	KC 57.9	CC 36.8	SB 73.7

Change is the law of life. And those who look only to the past or present are certain to miss the future.
— John F. Kennedy (35th U.S. President, 1917–1963)

Chanukah

WEDNESDAY **5**

CL 47.4	NG 44.4	GC 36.8	SI 47.4
S 38.9	W 31.6	C 27.8	LC 26.3
LH 31.6	KC 36.8	CC 52.6	SB 47.4

The worse a situation becomes, the less it takes to turn it around, the bigger the upside.
— George Soros (Financier, philanthropist, political activist, author, and philosopher, b. 1930)

THURSDAY **6**

CL 36.8	NG 52.6	GC 52.6	SI 57.9
S 42.1	W 57.9	C 61.1	LC 52.6
LH 36.8	KC 57.9	CC 72.2	SB 63.2

History is a collection of agreed-upon lies. — Voltaire (French philosopher)

FRIDAY **7**

CL 57.9	NG 57.9	GC 52.6	SI 55.6
S 52.6	W 57.9	C 42.1	LC 55.6
LH 57.9	KC 42.1	CC 47.4	SB 33.3

Creativity comes from trust. Trust your instincts. And never hope more than you work. — Rita Mae Brown

SATURDAY **8**

SUNDAY **9**

DECEMBER CATTLE RALLIES CONTINUE THEIR BULLISH TRENDS IN JANUARY

Unlike the pork market which tends to see increased supply during the winter, cattle slaughter rates tend to decline in the 4th quarter. The supply of beef tends to be extremely tight during January, especially when slaughter rates are low in November/December.

There is a strong correlation between slaughter rates and Live Cattle futures prices. When slaughter rates are low, Live Cattle prices tend to be strong. High slaughter rates pressure Live Cattle prices. This relationship is especially strong in the period surrounding the New Year.

In the last 19 years, April Live Cattle futures have followed their December direction in January 13 times (68.4%). However, the relationship between December supplies and slaughter patterns and January performance is even stronger when supplies are tight.

Since 1987, April Live Cattle futures have posted gains in December 13 times. January strength has followed December strength 11 times (84.6%).

Traders should not be afraid of buying into higher prices in December in the April Live Cattle market, as price trends tend to continue. Supply problems tend to be exaggerated in the New Year, so often December rallies are continued through January.

APRIL LIVE CATTLE CENTS PER POUND CHANGES

Date	Nov Close	Dec Close	Dec Change	Jan Change	Trend Comment	Jan Rally Dec Close to Jan High	Jan Break Dec Close to Jan Low
1987	63.68	65.43	1.75	2.38	Continuation	4.83	-0.33
1988	73.70	75.48	1.77	0.95	Continuation	1.18	-2.32
1989	73.83	75.68	1.85	0.35	Continuation	2.03	-0.58
1990	75.95	76.48	0.52	1.05	Continuation	1.20	-2.27
1991	74.53	73.03	-1.50	4.13	Reversal	4.27	-0.18
1992	74.43	76.68	2.25	0.17	Continuation	2.78	-0.13
1993	74.85	75.73	0.88	0.73	Continuation	1.43	-0.80
1994	68.63	72.90	4.28	1.25	Continuation	2.35	0.05
1995	67.60	66.38	-1.22	-2.53	Continuation	0.63	-3.65
1996	64.98	65.55	0.58	1.28	Continuation	1.65	-0.45
1997	72.35	68.78	-3.57	-1.30	Continuation	0.92	-2.83
1998	64.83	63.03	-1.80	2.05	Reversal	3.48	-0.57
1999	71.35	71.58	0.23	0.47	Continuation	1.93	-0.58
2000	75.40	79.13	3.72	-2.30	Reversal	1.88	-2.75
2001	72.30	73.68	1.38	1.85	Continuation	2.28	-0.77
2002	77.98	78.90	0.93	1.07	Continuation	1.25	-1.80
2003	83.93	71.50	-12.43	1.93	Reversal	6.20	-1.00
2004	85.73	85.63	-0.10	2.70	Reversal	4.68	0.03
2005	93.25	95.05	1.80	-3.47	Reversal	0.50	-4.22
# Continuations					**13**		
Average			**0.07**	**0.67**		**2.39**	**-1.32**
# Up			**13**	**15**		**19**	**2**
Following an Up December							
Average			**1.69**	**0.44**		**1.94**	**-1.30**
# Up			**13**	**11**		**13**	**1**
Following a Down December							
Average			**-3.77**	**1.16**		**3.36**	**-1.37**
# Up			**6**	**4**		**6**	**1**

DECEMBER

MONDAY **10**

CL 47.4	NG 44.4	GC 63.2	SI 52.6
S 42.1	W 47.4	C 38.9	LC 52.6
LH 47.4	KC 47.4	CC 38.9	SB 47.4

You win some, you lose some. And then there's that little-known third category.
— Albert Gore (U.S. Vice President 1993-2000, former 2000 presidential candidate, quoted at the 2004 DNC)

TUESDAY **11**

CL 47.4	NG 55.6	GC 42.1	SI 33.3
S 57.9	W 63.2	C 61.1	LC 52.6
LH 36.8	KC 52.6	CC 42.1	SB 27.8

Freedom is not something that anybody can be given. Freedom is something people take, and people are as free as they want to be. — James Baldwin

WEDNESDAY **12**

CL 52.6	NG 57.9	GC 44.4	SI 57.9
S 36.8	W 36.8	C 44.4	LC 66.7
LH 36.8	KC 52.6	CC 47.4	SB 55.6

A realist believes that what is done or left undone in the short run determines the long run.
— Sydney J. Harris (American journalist and author, 1917–1986)

THURSDAY **13**

CL 47.4	NG 52.6	GC 68.4	SI 52.6
S 68.4	W 52.6	C 61.1	LC 52.6
LH 52.6	KC 52.6	CC 36.8	SB 47.4

Nothing gives one person so much advantage over another as to remain always cool and unruffled under all circumstances.
— Thomas Jefferson

FRIDAY **14**

CL 55.6	NG 47.4	GC 57.9	SI 27.8
S 31.6	W 27.8	C 52.6	LC 57.9
LH 61.1	KC 47.4	CC 36.8	SB 42.1

All through time, people have basically acted the same way in the market as a result of greed, fear, ignorance and hope — that is why the numerical formations and patterns recur on a constant basis. — Jesse Livermore

SATURDAY **15**

SUNDAY **16**

NOVEMBER / DECEMBER RALLIES REVERSED IN JANUARY IN SOYBEANS

One of the best-known tendencies in the commodity markets is the February Break in the grain markets. Futures markets usually anticipate the known by playing off the unknown, often nullifying the patterns and causing them to be ever-changing or disappear. Case in point . . . Soybean futures and the February Break.

The changing nature of the February Break cycle is apparent in the performance of March Soybeans in February. March Soybean futures have rallied in 11 of the last 19 Februarys, posting an average gain of +12 cents/bu. Though no February Break looks to consistently happen, a January Break does, especially when prices rally in the last quarter (October through December).

In the last 19 years, March Soybean futures have gained from October through December 11 times (57.9%). Following these 4th-quarter rallies, March Soybeans have finished the month of January lower 9 times (81.8%), with an average January break of -29 1/2 cents/bushel.

Traders should look for well-known patterns to be anticipated and begin a little earlier as the years go by. Traders are also well-served to look for the underlying reasons behind these cycles, and then understand what environments the behaviors are most persistent in.

MARCH SOYBEANS CENTS PER BUSHEL CHANGES

Date	Prv Oct Close	Prv Dec Close	Prv Oct to Dec Change	Jan Rally Prv Dec Close to Jan High	Jan Break Prv Dec Close to Jan Low	Jan Change	Comment
1987	547	614 3/4	67 3/4	26 1/2	-13 3/4	-5 1/4	Reversal
1988	801 1/4	819 1/4	18	13 1/2	-78 3/4	-46 1/2	Reversal
1989	585 1/4	582 1/4	-3	4 1/4	-28 3/4	-21 1/4	Continuation
1990	624 1/2	574 3/4	-49 3/4	14 1/2	-25 1/4	-8	Continuation
1991	575	557	-18	28 3/4	-8 1/2	15	Reversal
1992	558 3/4	574 1/4	15 1/2	13 3/4	-7 1/4	-0 1/4	Reversal
1993	636 1/4	712 1/2	76 1/4	8 1/2	-31	-25 3/4	Reversal
1994	564	561 1/2	-2 1/2	1 1/2	-14 1/4	-14	Continuation
1995	692 3/4	744 3/4	52	25 1/4	-24 1/2	-6	Reversal
1996	673 1/2	687 3/4	14 1/4	66 1/4	0 1/4	50 1/2	Continuation
1997	701 3/4	676 1/4	-25 1/2	13 3/4	-18 1/4	-3 1/2	Continuation
1998	576 3/4	541 1/4	-35 1/2	16 1/2	-34 3/4	-34 1/2	Continuation
1999	490 3/4	469 3/4	-21	59 1/4	-6 1/2	38 1/4	Reversal
2000	478 3/4	509 3/4	31	0 1/4	-53 1/2	-50 1/4	Reversal
2001	441 3/4	422 1/4	-19 1/2	32 1/4	-6 1/2	8	Reversal
2002	562 1/4	565	2 3/4	20	-21	-1	Reversal
2003	784	794	10	61	-8 1/2	25 1/2	Continuation
2004	540 1/4	547 1/4	7	3 3/4	-37 1/4	-32 1/2	Reversal
2005	584 1/4	613 1/2	29 1/4	19 1/2	-50	-19 1/4	Reversal
Average			**7 3/4**	**22 1/2**	**-24 3/4**	**-7**	
# Up			**11**	**19**	**1**	**5**	
Following an Up October to December							
Average			**29 1/2**	**23 1/2**	**-29 1/2**	**-10**	
# Up			**11**	**11**	**1**	**2**	

DECEMBER

MONDAY **17**

CL 73.7	NG 66.7	GC 55.6	SI 63.2
S 57.9	W 63.2	C 63.2	LC 63.2
LH 63.2	KC 47.4	CC 73.7	SB 47.4

If you're going through hell, keep going. — Winston Churchill (British statesman, 1874–1965)

TUESDAY **18**

CL 63.2	NG 36.8	GC 63.2	SI 47.4
S 36.8	W 44.4	C 42.1	LC 55.6
LH 36.8	KC 63.2	CC 47.4	SB 36.8

With globalization, the big [countries] don't eat the small, the fast eat the slow.
— Thomas L. Friedman (Op-ed columnist, referring to the Arab nations, *New York Times*)

WEDNESDAY **19**

CL 47.4	NG 55.6	GC 68.4	SI 66.7
S 63.2	W 66.7	C 57.9	LC 52.6
LH 33.3	KC 52.6	CC 47.4	SB 42.1

Six essential qualities that are the key to success: Sincerity, personal integrity, humility, courtesy, wisdom, charity.
— William Menninger

THURSDAY **20**

CL 42.1	NG 47.4	GC 47.4	SI 47.4
S 61.1	W 61.1	C 38.9	LC 38.9
LH 38.9	KC 55.6	CC 47.4	SB 66.7

I keep hearing "Should I buy? Should I buy?" When I start hearing "Should I sell?" that's the bottom.
— Nick Moore (Portfolio manager, Jurika & Voyles, *TheStreet.com,* Mar. 12, 2001)

FRIDAY **21**

CL 33.3	NG 38.9	GC 52.6	SI 57.9
S 42.1	W 36.8	C 47.4	LC 84.2
LH 44.4	KC 55.6	CC 47.4	SB 26.3

Whenever a well-known bearish analyst is interviewed {Cover story} in the financial press, it usually coincides with an important near-term market bottom. — Clif Droke (Clifdroke.com, November 15, 2004)

SATURDAY **22**

SUNDAY **23**

DECEMBER STRENGTH IS TELLING FOR CRUDE OIL'S JANUARY DIRECTION

Refineries must pay taxes on year-end inventories of petroleum products (CL/HU/HO). Tax pressures on inventories coupled with poor supply/demand dynamics have caused March Crude Oil futures to decline in 9 of the 19 years studied between 1987 and 2005.

However, in the years when the supply/demand balance shifts in such a way as not to encourage refinery sales and March Crude Oil futures rally in December, January tends to see strength as well. Following the last 10 rallies during December, March Crude Oil has continued higher in January 7 times (70.0%), posting above-average strength in January.

On average during the last 19 years, March Crude Oil futures have rallied by an average of +$2.45/bbl; following December strength, January rallies have averaged $2.75/bbl, and January breaks have been smaller as well. As such, traders may be well served to look at end of year strength in Crude Oil as a sign of higher prices in the new year.

MARCH CRUDE OIL DOLLARS PER BARREL CHANGES

Date	Dec Close	Dec Change	Jan Rally Dec Close to Jan High	Jan Break Dec Close to Jan Low	Jan Change
1987	16.59	-1.71	1.16	-0.79	0.35
1988	16.69	1.62	2.16	-0.16	0.34
1989	21.49	2.02	1.69	-0.59	1.19
1990	27.80	-1.42	3.00	-9.20	-6.26
1991	19.12	-1.98	0.62	-1.37	-0.22
1992	19.71	-0.19	1.04	-1.36	0.55
1993	14.50	-1.41	1.32	-0.02	0.69
1994	17.71	-0.27	0.94	-0.46	0.68
1995	19.06	1.33	0.66	-1.98	-1.32
1996	24.67	1.74	1.38	-1.04	-0.52
1997	17.83	-1.64	0.23	-2.13	-0.62
1998	12.19	0.05	1.53	-0.35	0.56
1999	24.79	1.62	4.28	-1.22	2.85
2000	25.98	-5.92	4.59	0.09	2.68
2001	20.11	0.27	2.19	-1.61	-0.63
2002	30.59	4.15	3.36	-1.34	2.92
2003	32.28	2.44	2.97	0.07	0.77
2004	43.63	-5.55	6.12	-2.03	4.57
2005	61.90	3.22	7.30	-0.22	6.02
Averages		**-0.09**	**2.45**	**-1.35**	**0.77**
# Up		**10**	**19**	**2**	**13**
Following Up December					
# Up		**10**	**9**	**0**	**7**
Average		**1.85**	**2.75**	**-0.84**	**1.22**

(Shortened Trading Day)

MONDAY 24

CL 63.2	NG 55.6	GC 42.1	SI 38.9
S 42.1	W 47.4	C 47.4	LC 66.7
LH 66.7	KC 31.6	CC 31.6	SB 26.3

I have but one lamp by which my feet are guided, and that is the lamp of experience. I know no way of judging the future but by the past. — Edward Gibbon

Christmas Day (Market Closed)

TUESDAY 25

It isn't as important to buy as cheap as possible as it is to buy at the right time. — Jesse Livermore

WEDNESDAY 26

CL 47.4	NG 42.1	GC 47.4	SI 73.7
S 72.2	W 73.7	C 66.7	LC 73.7
LH 47.4	KC 47.4	CC 55.6	SB 66.7

Institutions tend to dump stock in a single transaction and buy, if possible, in smaller lots, gradually accumulating a position. Therefore, many more big blocks are traded on downticks than on upticks. — Justin Mamis

THURSDAY 27

CL 73.7	NG 63.2	GC 73.7	SI 68.4
S 44.4	W 38.9	C 61.1	LC 36.8
LH 57.9	KC 47.4	CC 77.8	SB 73.7

News on stocks is not important. How the stock reacts to it is important. — Michael L. Burke (*Investors Intelligence*)

FRIDAY 28

CL 47.4	NG 47.4	GC 38.9	SI 31.6
S 15.8	W 26.3	C 38.9	LC 47.4
LH 42.1	KC 52.6	CC 22.2	SB 47.4

To repeat what others have said requires education, to challenge it requires brains. — Mary Pettibone Poole

SATURDAY 29

SUNDAY 30

CONTRACT EXPIRATIONS BY COMMODITY

Contract Month	CRUDE OIL 1ST Notice Futures	CRUDE OIL Options Expiry	NATURAL GAS 1ST Notice Futures	NATURAL GAS Options Expiry	GOLD 1ST Notice Futures	GOLD Options Expiry	SILVER 1ST Notice Futures	SILVER Options Expiry	SOYBEANS 1ST Notice Futures	SOYBEANS Options Expiry	CBOT WHEAT 1ST Notice Futures	CBOT WHEAT Options Expiry
Jan(F)	12/19/06	12/14/06	12/27/06	12/26/06			12/29/06	12/26/06	12/28/06	12/21/06		
Feb(G)	01/22/07	01/17/07	01/29/07	01/26/07	01/31/07	01/25/07						
Mar(H)	02/20/07	02/14/07	02/26/07	02/23/07			02/28/07	02/22/06	02/27/07	02/23/07	02/27/07	02/23/07
Apr(J)	03/20/07	03/15/07	03/28/07	03/27/07	04/30/07	03/27/07						
May(K)	04/20/07	04/17/07	04/26/07	04/25/07			04/30/07	04/25/06	04/27/07	04/20/07	04/27/07	04/20/07
Jun(M)	05/22/07	05/17/07	05/29/07	05/25/07	06/29/07	05/24/07						
Jul(N)	06/20/07	06/15/07	06/27/07	06/26/07			06/29/07	06/26/06	06/28/07	06/22/07	06/28/07	06/22/07
Aug(Q)	07/20/07	07/17/07	07/27/07	07/26/07	07/31/07	07/26/07			07/30/07	07/24/07		
Sep(U)	08/21/07	08/16/07	08/29/07	08/28/07			08/31/07	08/28/06	08/30/07	08/24/07	08/30/07	08/24/07
Oct(V)	09/20/07	09/17/07	09/26/07	09/25/07	09/28/07	09/25/07						
Nov(X)	10/22/07	10/17/07	10/29/07	10/26/07					10/30/07	10/26/07		
Dec(Z)	11/16/07	11/13/07	11/28/07	11/27/07	11/30/07	11/27/07	11/30/07	11/27/06			11/29/07	11/23/07

Contract Month	CORN 1ST Notice Futures	CORN Options Expiry	LIVE CATTLE 1ST Notice Futures	LIVE CATTLE Options Expiry	LEAN HOGS 1ST Notice Futures	LEAN HOGS Options Expiry	COFFEE 1ST Notice Futures	COFFEE Options Expiry	SUGAR #11 1ST Notice Futures	SUGAR #11 Options Expiry	COCOA 1ST Notice Futures	COCOA Options Expiry
Feb(G)			02/05/07	02/02/07	02/14/07	02/14/07						
Mar(H)	02/27/07	02/23/07					02/20/07	02/09/07	02/28/07	02/09/07	02/14/07	02/02/07
Apr(J)			04/16/07	04/16/07	04/16/07	04/16/07						
May(K)	04/27/07	04/20/07					04/20/07	03/09/07	04/30/07	04/13/07	04/17/07	04/05/07
Jun(M)			06/04/07	06/01/07	05/14/07	05/14/07						
Jul(N)	06/28/07	06/22/07			07/16/07	07/16/07	06/21/07	06/08/07	06/29/07	06/08/07	06/18/07	06/01/07
Aug(Q)			08/06/07	08/03/07	08/14/07	08/14/07						
Sep(U)	08/30/07	08/24/07	09/10/07	09/07/07			08/23/07	08/10/07			08/20/07	08/03/07
Oct(V)			10/08/07	10/05/07	10/12/07	10/12/07			09/28/07	09/14/07		
Dec(Z)	11/29/07	11/20/07	12/10/07	12/07/07	12/14/07	12/14/07	11/20/07	11/09/07			11/15/07	11/02/07

DECEMBER/JANUARY 2008

MONDAY 31

CL 33.3	NG 57.9	GC 38.9	SI 27.8
S 26.3	W 42.1	C 26.3	LC 61.1
LH 63.2	KC 44.4	CC 31.6	SB 47.4

The winds and waves are always on the side of the ablest navigators. — Edward Gibbon

New Year's Day (Market Closed)

TUESDAY 1

Inflation is the one form of taxation that can be imposed without legislation.
— Milton Friedman (American economist, 1976 Nobel Prize, b. 1912)

WEDNESDAY 2

CL 57.9	NG 47.4	GC 78.9	SI 63.2
S 73.7	W 52.6	C 55.6	LC 52.6
LH 47.4	KC 42.1	CC 44.4	SB 73.7

No profession requires more hard work, intelligence, patience, and mental discipline than successful speculation. — Robert Rhea

THURSDAY 3

CL 72.2	NG 42.1	GC 26.3	SI 36.8
S 42.1	W 63.2	C 38.9	LC 38.9
LH 66.7	KC 66.7	CC 52.6	SB 47.4

If you are not willing to study, if you are not sufficiently interested to investigate and analyze the stock market yourself, then I beg of you to become an outright long-pull investor, to buy good stocks, and hold on to them; for otherwise your chances of success as a trader will be nil. — Humphrey B. Neill (*Tape Reading and Market Tactics*, 1931)

FRIDAY 4

CL 47.4	NG 52.6	GC 31.6	SI 42.1
S 68.4	W 63.2	C 57.9	LC 38.9
LH 63.2	KC 61.1	CC 42.1	SB 31.6

The dumbest people I know are those who know it all. — Malcolm Forbes

SATURDAY 5

SUNDAY 6

2008 STRATEGY CALENDAR

	MONDAY	TUESDAY	WEDNESDAY	THURSDAY	FRIDAY	SATURDAY	SUNDAY
	31	1 JANUARY	2	3	4	5	6
	7	8	9	10	11	12	13
JANUARY	14	15	16	17	18	19	20
	21 Martin Luther King Day	22	23	24	25	26	27
	28	29	30	31	1 FEBRUARY	2	3
	4	5	6 Ash Wednesday	7	8	9	10
FEBRUARY	11	12	13	14 ♥	15	16	17
	18 Presidents' Day	19	20	21	22	23	24
	25	26	27	28	29	1 MARCH	2
	3	4	5	6	7	8	9 Daylight Saving Time Begins
	10	11	12	13	14	15	16
MARCH	17 ♣ St. Patrick's Day	18	19	20	21 Good Friday	22	23 Easter
	24	25	26	27	28	29	30
	31	1 APRIL	2	3	4	5	6
	7	8	9	10	11	12	13
APRIL	14	15	16	17	18	19	20 Passover
	21	22	23	24	25	26	27
	28	29	30	1 MAY	2	3	4
	5	6	7	8	9	10	11 Mother's Day
MAY	12	13	14	15	16	17	18
	19	20	21	22	23	24	25
	26 Memorial Day	27	28	29	30	31	1 JUNE
	2	3	4	5	6	7	8
JUNE	9	10	11	12	13	14	15 Father's Day
	16	17	18	19	20	21	22
	23	24	25	26	27	28	29

Market closed on shaded weekdays; closes early when half-shaded.

2008 STRATEGY CALENDAR

MONDAY	TUESDAY	WEDNESDAY	THURSDAY	FRIDAY	SATURDAY	SUNDAY	
30	1 JULY	2	3	4 Independence Day	5	6	JULY
7	8	9	10	11	12	13	
14	15	16	17	18	19	20	
21	22	23	24	25	26	27	
28	29	30	31	1 AUGUST	2	3	AUGUST
4	5	6	7	8	9	10	
11	12	13	14	15	16	17	
18	19	20	21	22	23	24	
25	26	27	28	29	30	31	
1 SEPTEMBER Labor Day	2	3	4	5	6	7	SEPTEMBER
8	9	10	11	12	13	14	
15	16	17	18	19	20	21	
22	23	24	25	26	27	28	
29	30 Rosh Hashanah	1 OCTOBER	2	3	4	5	OCTOBER
6	7	8	9 Yom Kippur	10	11	12	
13 Columbus Day	14	15	16	17	18	19	
20	21	22	23	24	25	26	
27	28	29	30	31	1 NOVEMBER	2 Daylight Saving Time Ends	NOVEMBER
3	4 Election Day	5	6	7	8	9	
10	11 Veterans' Day	12	13	14	15	16	
17	18	19	20	21	22	23	
24	25	26	27 Thanksgiving	28	29	30	
1 DECEMBER	2	3	4	5	6	7	DECEMBER
8	9	10	11	12	13	14	
15	16	17	18	19	20	21	
22 Chanukah	23	24	25 Christmas	26	27	28	
29	30	31	1 JANUARY New Year's Day	2	3	4	

STANDARDS OF WEIGHT AND MEASURE

MEASURES OF WEIGHT	EQUIVALENT
1 Kilogram	32.15075 Troy Oz.
1 Kilogram	2.20462 Lbs.
1 Metric Quintal	220.462 Lbs.
1 Metric Ton	2204.62 Lbs.
1 Short Ton	2000 Lbs.
1 Long Ton	2240 Lbs.
1 Metric Ton	1000 Kilograms
1 Metric Ton	1.10231 Short Tons
1 Metric Ton	0.98421 Long Tons

MEASURES OF LENGTH AND AREA	
1 Centimeter	0.39370 Inches
1 Meter	39.370 Inches
1 Meter	3.2808 Feet
1 Kilometer	0.6214 Miles
1 Square Meter	1550.003 Square Inches
1 Square Meter	10.7639 Square Feet
1 Hectare	2.47105 Acres
1 Hectare	10.000 Square Meters

MEASURES OF TEMPERATURE	
Celsius Degrees	.556 x (fahrenheit degrees) -32
Fahrenheit Degrees	1.8 x (celsius degrees) +32

DOMESTIC AND METRIC CONVERSION FACTORS FOR BUSHELS AND YIELDS	
WEIGHT	**BUSHELS**
60 Lb. Bushel: Wheat, White Potatoes, Soybeans	
1 Metric Ton	36.74 Bushels
1 Metric Ton/Hectare	14.869 Bushels/Ac.
1 Quinta/Hectare	1.4869 Bushels/Ac.
1 Short Ton	33.33 Bushels
1 Long Ton	37.33 Bushels
56 Lb. Bushel: Corn, Rye, Sorghum Grain, Flaxseed	
1 Metric Ton	39.37 Bushels
1 Metric Ton/Hectare	15.932 Bushels/Ac.
1 Quinta/Hectare	1.5932 Bushels/Ac.
1 Short Ton	35.71 Bushels
1 Long Ton	40.00 Bushels

Source: National Bureau of Standards

UNDERSTANDING COMMODITY QUOTES

A futures contract is a legally binding agreement, made on the trading floor of a futures exchange, to buy or sell a commodity or financial instrument at some time in the future. Futures contracts are standardized according to quality, quantity, delivery time, and location for each commodity. The only variable is price, which is discovered on an exchange trading floor.

July 2007 Corn Futures
symbol — CN7 — year
month code

Futures quotes entail not only a standard Symbol designating the commodity, but also the contract month and year. The majority of quote providers on the internet put out futures quotes in a symbol, month, year format. For example, the commodity symbol for Corn — traded on the Chicago Board of Trade — is "C". Symbols are restricted to one or two characters generally, like "C" for Corn and "CL" for Crude Oil.

December 2007 Crude Oil Futures
symbol — CLZ7 — year
month code

The symbol is directly followed by a Month code. Month codes are done with alphabetical representations of the months. The month codes start with "F" designating January, and progress forward. The table to the right lists month codes.

Futures Month Codes		
F = January	K = May	U = September
G= February	M = June	V = October
H = March	N = July	X = November
J = April	Q = August	Z = December

Lastly, the contract year is designated by the last digit of the year (7 for 2007, 8 for 2008). Because a futures contract represents the obligation to make or accept delivery of a particular commodity (the symbol), at a specific time (the contract month and year), futures quotes must contain all of this information. For example, CN7 represents Corn (C) for delivery in July (N) of 2007, while CLZ7 would represent Crude Oil (CL) for delivery in December (Z) of 2007. All futures quotes are between 4 and 5 characters long — sometimes 6, as a few quote companies will designate years with two numbers, like 07 for 2007, differentiating it from a 2017 contract.

Though all futures contracts are standardized to size — as represented by the contract size — the units of price are different. For example, Crude Oil is quoted in dollars per barrel ($/bbl) so a price of 65.54 would be "sixty-five dollars and fifty-four cents per barrel." Other commodities, like Corn, are quoted in cents (cents/bushel). As such a corn price of 235 1/2 would be "two hundred and thirty-five and half cents per bushel" or $2.35 1/2 /bushel.

COMMODITY SYMBOLS AND PRICE QUOTE GUIDE

Commodity Name	Commodity Symbol	Contract Months	Units Per Contract	Sample Price	Read As
Crude Oil	CL	F,G,H,J,K,M,N,Q,U,V,X,Z	$/Barrel	6554	$65.54/barrel
Natural Gas	NG	F,G,H,J,K,M,N,Q,U,V,X,Z	Cents / BTU	6920	$0.6920/BTU
Gold	GC	G,J,M,Q,V,Z	$/Ounce	63550	$635.50/ounce
Silver	SI	H,K,N,U,Z	Cents/Ounce	13802	$13.802/ounce
Soybeans	S	F,H,K,N,Q,U,Z	Cents/Bushel	536 3/4	$5.36 3/4 / bushel
CBOT Wheat	W	H,K,N,U,Z	Cents/Bushel	235 1/2	$2.35 1/2 / bushel
Corn	C	H,K,N,U,Z	Cents/Bushel	262 1/4	$2.62 1/4 / bushel
Live Cattle	LC	G,J,M,Q,U,V,Z	Cents/Pound	7595	$0.7595 / pound
Lean Hogs	LH	G,J,K,M,N,Q,U,V,X,Z	Cents/Pound	6542	$0.65425 / pound
Coffee	KC	H,K,N,U,Z	Cents/Pound	10955	$10.955 / pound
Sugar #11	SB	F,H,K,N,V	Cents/Pound	1705	$0.1705 / pound
Cocoa	CC	H,K,N,U,Z	$/Ton	1535	$1535 / ton
Heating Oil	HO	F,G,H,J,K,M,N,Q,U,V,X,Z	Cents / Gallon	19270	$1.9270 / gallon
Unleaded Gas	HU	F,G,H,J,K,M,N,Q,U,V,X,Z	Cents / Gallon	19970	$1.9970 / gallon
Platinum	PL	F,J,K,N,V	$/Ounce	11799	$1,179.90 / ounce
KCBT Wheat	KW	H,K,N,U,Z	Cents/Bushel	438 1/2	$4.38 1/2 / bushel

READING WIDELY TRADED CONTRACT TABLES

The Widely Traded Contract Tables by commodity contain not only basic information regarding monthly trends, but also a plethora of information regarding the likelihood of trends continuing and reversing during the period studied, on a contract-specific basis. Please refer to the numbers next to fields for a brief explanation of the table.

1 Contract: refers to the specific contract month being studied.

2 Month: refers to the specific month's performance being studied.

3 Yrs Tested: the # of years in the study.

4 # Up: The # of years the month in question has had a higher settlement than the previous calendar month (i.e., Jan > Feb).

5 # Down: The # of years the month in question settles lower than the previous month.

6 Total Gain (Loss): The sum of all monthly changes during the number of years tested.

7 Average Gain (Loss): The average of all monthly changes being studied (6/3).

8 Previous Month: Below these rows, figures are given on trend continuation and reversals basis the abovementioned month. For example, all data in the top set of rows shows the performance of the May (K) futures following an up January.

9 % Closing Higher: The percentage of time the month in question has had a positive settlement (4/3).

10 # Higher Highs: The # of times the month in question's highest intra-day price has exceeded the previous month's highest price.

11 # Lower Lows: The # of times the month in question's lowest intra-day prices was less than the previous month's low price.

Sample Table		
1	Contract	Mar (H)
2	Month	JAN
3	Yrs Tested	19
4	# Up	10
5	# Down	9
6	Total Gain (Loss)	1 3/4
7	Average Gain (Loss)	0
8	*If Previous Month is Up, then FOLLOWING Month had the following Characteristics*	
1	Contract	May (K)
2	Month	FEB
3	Yrs Tested	11
4	# Up	2
5	# Down	9
9	% Closing Higher	18.2%
6	Total Gain (Loss)	-57 3/4
7	Average Gain (Loss)	-5 1/4
10	# Higher Highs	6
11	# Lower Lows	4
8	*If Previous Month is Down, then FOLLOWING Month had the following Characteristics*	
1	Contract	May (K)
2	Month	FEB
3	Yrs Tested	8
4	# Up	2
5	# Down	6
9	% Closing Lower	75.0%
6	Total Gain (Loss)	4 3/4
7	Average Gain (Loss)	2/4
10	# Higher Highs	3
11	# Lower Lows	6

For example, in the table above we can see that March CBOT Wheat was up 10/down 9 in January. During January March Wheat gained +1 3/4 cents per bu. During this 19-year period, May Wheat rallied in January 11 times, and broke 8. Following the 11 January rallies, May Wheat broke in February 9 times and rallied 2 times. In total, following a January rally, Wheat prices declined by -57 3/4 cents/bu making a higher monthly high in February 6 times and a lower monthly low 4 times. Following the 8 January breaks, May Wheat continued its decline through February 6 times, but managed a gain of +4 3/4 cents/bu in total during these 8 years.

Of course, the figures presented in the following tables only represent the historical tendencies of the markets' studies. Given that market cycles are ever-changing and adapting, all of these figures should be taken with a grain of salt. They may offer us insight into opportunities but are not a trading plan.

Pages 124 – 183 presents tables for 12 different commodity markets which cover the entire year, matching calendar months to what we believe are typically the most actively traded contract months.

DUAL DEMAND STRUCTURE OF CRUDE OIL DRIVES PRICES

Each barrel of Crude Oil produces roughly on average 19 gallons of gasoline and 9 gallons of distillate fuels (Heating Oil). It is by understanding the nature of the demand for petroleum products that one can understand the normal price action in the petroleum market.

It takes several weeks to months to convert a barrel of Crude Oil to either Unleaded Gasoline (HU) or Heating Oil (HO) for consumer usage. Wholesalers — known as "jobbers" — tend to buy ahead of normal retail demand, thus driving prices up (and down) ahead of perceived retail usage or playing "catch up" once retail usage manifests itself.

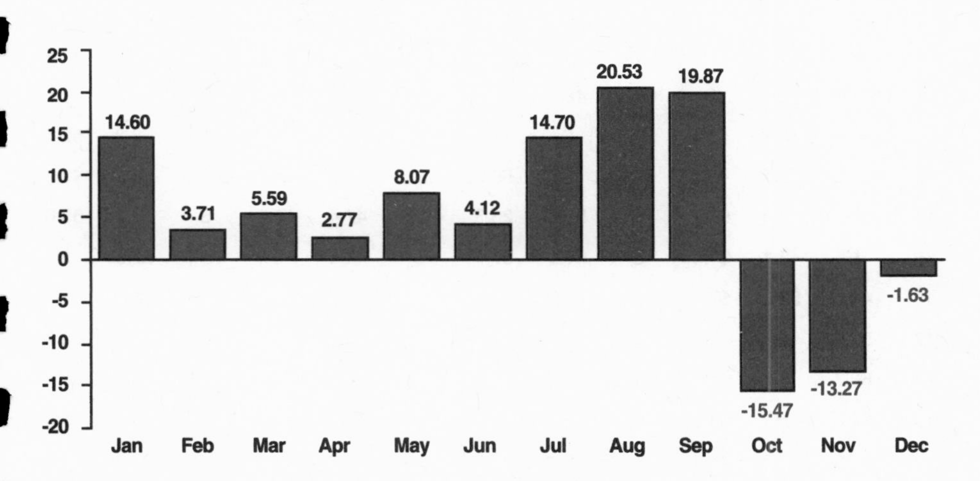

Traders should notice that the weakest period for Crude Oil prices is the October/November period, when gasoline demand is weak and much of the Heating Oil demand has been met — as most Heating Oil customers buy a season's worth of product at a time.

However, traders may wish to take to heart the fact that run-ups ahead of the quintessential "Summer Driving Season," which kicks off in March, and the "Winter Heating Season," which starts in October, have often seen the futures move to price in these events — offering a clue towards future direction.

No inventory system is as efficient as that of major refineries. They are very aware of usage trends and their own supply, and thus price their products to meet demand with great efficiency — for proof, simply look at Exxon/Mobile's earnings (XOM) which set a new record for the most cash a publicly traded company made in 2005.

CRUDE OIL FUTURES MARKET PROBABILITY CALENDAR FOR 2007

THE % CHANGE OF THE MARKET RISING ON ANY TRADING DAY OF THE YEAR

(Based on the number of times the widely traded contract rose on a particular trading day during January 1987-December 2005)

Contract	Mar (H)	Apr (J)	Jun (M)	Jun (M)	Sep (U)	Sep (U)	Sep (U)	Dec (Z)	Dec (Z)	Dec (Z)	Jan (F)	Mar (H)
Date	Jan	Feb	Mar	Apr	May	Jun	Jul	Aug	Sep	Oct	Nov	Dec
1	H	44.4	47.4	S	57.9	52.6	S	47.4	S	57.9	52.6	S
2	57.9	47.4	52.6	63.2	72.2	S	47.4	68.4	S	47.4	42.1	S
3	72.2	S	S	44.4	38.9	S	55.6	63.2	H	47.4	S	47.4
4	47.4	S	S	57.9	63.2	42.1	H	S	73.7	31.6	S	47.4
5	47.4	47.4	68.4	61.1	S	52.6	47.4	S	47.4	44.4	21.1	47.4
6	S	52.6	52.6	H	S	31.6	57.9	36.8	63.2	S	38.9	36.8
7	S	42.1	66.7	S	57.9	52.6	S	66.7	52.6	S	42.1	57.9
8	44.4	47.4	42.1	S	61.1	52.6	S	47.4	S	78.9	47.4	S
9	33.3	52.6	42.1	47.4	57.9	S	42.1	57.9	S	57.9	52.6	S
10	47.4	S	S	33.3	63.2	S	68.4	52.6	47.4	68.4	S	47.4
11	47.4	S	S	68.4	42.1	42.1	63.2	S	42.1	36.8	S	47.4
12	31.6	52.6	42.1	52.6	S	42.1	55.6	S	63.2	63.2	63.2	52.6
13	S	42.1	42.1	57.9	S	55.6	55.6	73.7	52.6	S	38.9	47.4
14	S	83.3	66.7	S	52.6	26.3	S	47.4	47.4	S	52.6	55.6
15	H	42.1	31.6	S	61.1	57.9	S	44.4	S	47.4	57.9	S
16	44.4	52.6	57.9	33.3	57.9	S	57.9	47.4	S	52.6	47.4	S
17	52.6	S	S	63.2	52.6	S	63.2	47.4	63.2	47.4	S	73.7
18	66.7	S	S	63.2	36.8	47.4	38.9	S	33.3	63.2	S	63.2
19	31.6	H	52.6	68.4	S	33.3	57.9	S	47.4	42.1	38.9	47.4
20	S	57.9	47.4	68.4	S	33.3	47.4	52.6	57.9	S	36.8	42.1
21	S	47.4	55.6	S	63.2	63.2	S	68.4	68.4	S	63.2	33.3
22	52.6	31.6	55.6	S	47.4	68.4	S	55.6	S	42.1	H	S
23	36.8	63.2	42.1	52.6	42.1	S	42.1	57.9	S	57.9	55.6	S
24	52.6	S	S	72.2	47.4	S	63.2	36.8	68.4	36.8	S	63.2
25	57.9	S	S	44.4	52.6	31.6	57.9	S	66.7	47.4	S	H
26	55.6	47.4	47.4	73.7	S	47.4	72.2	S	33.3	38.9	47.4	47.4
27	S	73.7	73.7	47.4	S	31.6	42.1	42.1	63.2	S	63.2	73.7
28	S	36.8	52.6	S	H	63.2	S	63.2	78.9	S	57.9	47.4
29	47.4		55.6	S	44.4	47.4	S	47.4	S	52.6	27.8	S
30	66.7		47.4	52.6	42.1	S	44.4	68.4	S	47.4	42.1	S
31	44.4		S		52.6		66.7	73.7		33.3		33.3

CRUDE OIL WIDELY TRADED CONTRACT MONTHLY SETTLEMENTS

Contract Month	Mar (H)	Apr (J)	Jun (M)	Jun (M)	Sep (U)	Sep (U)	Sep (U)	Dec (Z)	Dec (Z)	Dec (Z)	Jan (F)	Mar (H)
Date	JAN	FEB	MAR	APR	MAY	JUN	JUL	AUG	SEP	OCT	NOV	DEC
1987	18.75	16.60	18.53	18.73	19.00	20.09	21.37	19.43	19.48	19.96	18.51	16.59
1988	16.94	16.01	16.98	17.99	17.81	15.32	16.31	15.23	13.02	13.58	15.32	16.69
1989	17.03	18.15	19.50	20.42	18.39	19.50	18.31	18.62	19.87	19.94	19.89	21.49
1990	22.68	21.54	20.57	18.54	18.63	17.72	20.69	26.57	38.31	35.23	28.85	27.80
1991	21.54	19.16	19.48	20.96	21.31	20.54	21.68	22.00	22.13	23.37	21.48	19.12
1992	18.90	18.68	19.58	20.85	22.04	21.57	21.87	21.30	21.63	20.62	19.89	19.71
1993	20.26	20.60	20.64	20.53	20.31	19.11	17.88	18.74	18.93	16.92	15.43	14.50
1994	15.19	14.48	14.90	16.90	17.77	18.83	20.30	17.58	18.45	18.19	18.05	17.71
1995	18.39	18.49	18.95	20.38	18.70	17.25	17.56	17.40	17.28	17.64	18.18	19.06
1996	17.74	19.54	20.15	21.20	18.66	20.10	20.42	21.24	23.77	23.35	23.75	24.67
1997	24.15	20.30	20.42	20.21	21.01	19.84	20.14	19.83	21.12	21.08	19.15	17.83
1998	17.21	15.44	15.94	15.39	16.08	14.67	14.21	13.87	16.16	14.42	11.22	12.19
1999	12.75	12.27	16.73	18.66	16.76	19.30	20.53	21.91	24.14	21.75	24.59	24.79
2000	27.64	30.43	26.38	25.74	27.89	31.13	27.43	31.58	30.71	32.70	33.82	25.98
2001	28.66	27.39	26.57	28.46	28.43	26.09	26.35	27.34	23.68	21.18	19.44	20.11
2002	19.48	21.74	26.37	27.29	25.24	26.71	27.02	28.58	30.21	27.22	26.89	30.59
2003	33.51	36.75	29.19	25.80	27.75	29.73	30.54	30.83	28.92	29.11	30.41	32.28
2004	33.05	36.16	35.08	37.38	39.35	37.14	43.80	41.75	49.21	51.76	49.13	43.63
2005	48.20	51.75	56.42	49.72	53.03	57.64	60.57	69.58	66.23	59.76	57.32	61.90
2006	67.92	61.41	67.93									

CRUDE OIL WIDELY TRADED CONTRACT MONTHLY CHANGES

Contract Month	Mar (H)	Apr (J)	Jun (M)	Jun (M)	Sep (U)	Sep (U)	Sep (U)	Dec (Z)	Dec (Z)	Dec (Z)	Jan (F)	Mar (H)
Date	JAN	FEB	MAR	APR	MAY	JUN	JUL	AUG	SEP	OCT	NOV	DEC
1987	2.84	0.65	-1.78	2.12	-0.08	1.03	1.09	0.66	-1.28	0.05	0.46	-1.31
1988	-1.71	0.35	-0.77	1.11	1.06	-0.03	-2.49	0.96	-1.41	-2.21	0.60	1.41
1989	1.62	0.35	1.13	2.14	0.16	-0.01	1.11	-0.20	0.51	1.25	-0.03	0.19
1990	2.02	0.77	0.37	-0.96	-0.79	-1.34	-0.91	3.10	4.66	11.74	-2.78	-1.94
1991	-1.42	-6.06	-0.96	1.06	1.15	0.89	-0.77	0.94	0.57	0.13	1.17	-1.51
1992	-1.98	-0.13	-0.18	0.60	1.23	1.22	-0.47	0.19	-0.31	0.33	-0.92	-0.69
1993	-0.19	0.52	0.28	-0.03	0.10	-0.53	-1.20	-1.12	0.28	0.19	-1.87	-1.55
1994	-1.41	0.38	-0.55	0.06	1.33	1.15	1.06	1.02	-1.76	0.87	-0.44	0.14
1995	-0.27	0.51	0.15	0.73	1.03	-0.69	-1.45	0.13	0.21	-0.12	0.23	0.55
1996	1.33	-1.31	1.15	1.91	0.46	-0.35	1.44	0.47	2.02	2.53	-0.11	0.57
1997	1.74	-0.29	-2.88	0.56	-0.20	0.89	-1.17	0.19	-0.33	1.29	0.14	-1.56
1998	-1.64	-0.66	-1.56	-0.21	0.06	-0.64	-1.41	-0.68	-1.19	2.29	-1.64	-2.82
1999	0.05	0.39	-0.44	4.21	1.39	-1.01	2.54	1.30	1.69	2.23	-1.89	1.75
2000	1.62	2.73	2.36	-1.30	-0.62	3.03	3.24	-1.94	4.58	-0.87	1.01	1.63
2001	-5.92	2.37	0.37	-0.79	2.30	-0.22	-2.34	-0.47	1.75	-3.66	-2.44	-1.69
2002	0.27	-0.46	1.81	4.33	0.46	-1.14	1.47	0.00	2.55	1.63	-2.87	0.23
2003	4.15	3.28	2.42	-4.09	-2.10	2.61	1.98	0.91	1.51	-1.91	0.37	1.55
2004	2.44	0.27	3.44	0.66	2.59	3.11	-2.21	5.33	-0.24	7.46	3.02	-1.68
2005	-5.55	4.88	4.15	3.92	-4.17	0.10	4.61	3.74	6.72	-3.35	-6.14	-2.32
2006	3.22	6.39	3.87									
# Up	13	9	13	12	9	9	15	12	13	8	9	10
# Down	6	10	6	7	10	10	4	7	6	11	10	9
Total Change	14.60	3.71	16.03	2.77	8.07	4.12	14.70	20.53	19.87	-15.47	-13.27	-1.63
AVG. Change	0.77	0.20	0.84	0.15	0.42	0.22	0.77	1.08	1.05	-0.81	-0.70	-0.09
AVG. Up	1.86	2.36	1.80	1.37	1.56	2.06	1.42	2.25	2.46	0.93	1.13	1.85
AVG. Down	-1.60	-1.76	-1.23	-1.95	-0.60	-1.44	-1.65	-0.93	-2.02	-2.08	-2.34	-2.23

CRUDE OIL WIDELY TRADED CONTRACT PERFORMANCE

PERFORMANCE STATISTICS BASED ON MONTHLY PERFORMANCE AND FOLLOWING-MONTH PERFORMANCE

(Based on monthly trends from **January 1987 – December 2005** using the aforementioned contracts)

Contract	Mar (H)	Apr (J)	Jun (M)	Jun (M)	Sep (U)	Sep (U)	Sep (U)	Dec (Z)	Dec (Z)	Dec (Z)	Jan (F)	Mar (H)
Month	JAN	FEB	MAR	APR	MAY	JUN	JUL	AUG	SEP	OCT	NOV	DEC
Yrs Tested	19	19	19	19	19	19	19	19	19	19	19	19
# Up	13	9	13	12	9	9	15	12	13	8	9	10
# Down	6	10	6	7	10	10	4	7	6	11	10	9
Total Gain (Loss)	14.60	3.71	16.03	2.77	8.07	4.12	14.70	20.53	19.87	-15.47	-13.27	-1.63
Average Gain (Loss)	0.77	0.20	0.84	0.15	0.42	0.22	0.77	1.08	1.05	-0.81	-0.70	-0.09

If Previous Month is Up, then FOLLOWING Month had the following Characteristics

Contract	Mar (H)	Apr (J)	Jun (M)	Jun (M)	Sep (U)	Sep (U)	Sep (U)	Dec (Z)	Dec (Z)	Dec (Z)	Jan (F)	Mar (H)
Month	FEB	MAR	APR	MAY	JUN	JUL	AUG	SEP	OCT	NOV	DEC	JAN
Yrs Tested	13	11	13	13	9	9	13	12	13	8	9	10
# Up	7	6	11	4	5	7	7	7	4	4	7	7
# Down	6	5	2	9	4	2	6	5	9	4	2	3
% Closing Higher	53.8	54.5	84.6	30.8	55.6	77.8	53.8	58.3	30.8	50.0	77.8	70.0
Total Gain (Loss)	6.82	6.52	7.60	1.75	7.36	3.46	12.05	9.79	-9.60	-1.13	8.73	12.18
Average Gain (Loss)	0.52	0.59	0.58	0.13	0.82	0.38	0.93	0.82	-0.74	-0.14	0.97	1.22
# Higher Highs	8	12	9	10	7	8	11	8	11	4	7	9
# Lower Lows	5	3	3	4	3	1	3	4	6	4	2	1

If Previous Month is Down, then FOLLOWING Month had the following Characteristics

Contract	Mar (H)	Apr (J)	Jun (M)	Jun (M)	Sep (U)	Sep (U)	Sep (U)	Dec (Z)	Dec (Z)	Dec (Z)	Jan (F)	Mar (H)
Month	FEB	MAR	APR	MAY	JUN	JUL	AUG	SEP	OCT	NOV	DEC	JAN
Yrs Tested	6	8	6	6	10	10	5	7	6	11	10	9
# Up	2	7	1	5	4	8	4	6	4	5	3	6
# Down	4	1	5	1	6	2	1	1	2	6	7	3
% Closing Lower	66.7	12.5	83.3	16.7	60.0	20.0	20.0	14.3	33.3	54.5	70.0	33.3
Total Gain (Loss)	-3.11	9.51	-4.83	6.32	-3.24	11.24	5.93	10.08	-5.87	-12.14	-10.36	2.42
Average Gain (Loss)	-0.52	1.19	-0.80	1.05	-0.32	1.12	1.19	1.44	-0.98	-1.10	-1.04	0.27
# Higher Highs	2	3	1	4	3	3	2	4	2	2	1	4
# Lower Lows	3	4	4	2	8	7	3	1	4	8	8	4

Key Points Regarding Monthly Performance from 1987 – 2005

- March trends continue through April (16 of 19)
- Crude Oil weakness in June reversed in July (8 of 10)
- Crude Oil rallies in July (15 of 19)
- November trend continues in December (14 of 19)
- December rallies continue through January (7 of 10)

BUY THE RUMOR/SELL THE FACT: ANTICIPATION OF CONSUMER DEMAND DRIVES NATURAL GAS

Natural Gas is a quirky member of the petroleum group. Its pricing shares a lot with Unleaded, as it is purchased on the consumer level like gasoline. However, its peak demand periods share more with Heating Oil, as Natural Gas is used residentially for heating and cooling.

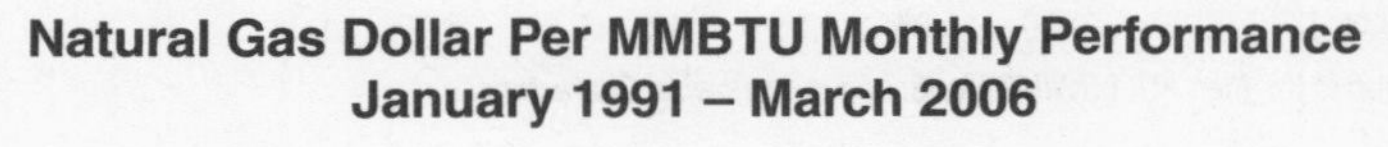

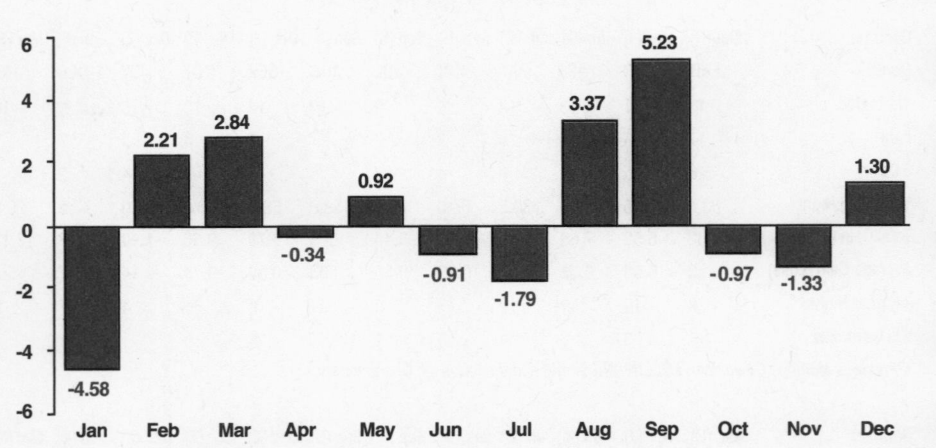

Prices tend to tank after the original onset of either the heating season (October to February) or the cooling season (June through August). However, toward the tail end of these seasons, last-minute purchases to meet demand tend to push prices higher.

Note the strength in March at the end of the Heating Season, as well as strength in September at the end of the cooling season. But just as importantly, note that the trends established near the end of the "dual demand" seasons tend to be reversed — especially with September strength reversed in October in 7 of the last 10 years which saw higher September prices.

Moderate weather during the April-through-June period tends to cause weakness in demand for Natural Gas, and hence prices suffer. However, as air conditioners are run, prices increase as demand increases.

NATURAL GAS FUTURES MARKET PROBABILITY CALENDAR FOR 2007

THE % CHANGE OF THE MARKET RISING ON ANY TRADING DAY OF THE YEAR

(Based on the number of times the widely traded contract rose on a particular trading day during **January 1999 – December 2005**)

Contract	Mar (H)	Jun (M)	Jun (M)	Jun (M)	Oct (V)	Oct (V)	Oct (V)	Jan (F)	Jan (F)	Jan (F)	Mar (H)	Mar (H)
Date	**Jan**	**Feb**	**Mar**	**Apr**	**May**	**Jun**	**Jul**	**Aug**	**Sep**	**Oct**	**Nov**	**Dec**
1	H	44.4	55.6	S	47.4	57.9	S	52.6	S	61.1	44.4	S
2	47.4	55.6	47.4	55.6	47.4	S	73.7	44.4	S	44.4	47.4	S
3	42.1	S	S	47.4	61.1	S	31.6	68.4	H	52.6	S	36.8
4	52.6	S	S	61.1	47.4	57.9	H	S	31.6	52.6	S	47.4
5	55.6	61.1	57.9	57.9	S	33.3	36.8	S	38.9	57.9	36.8	44.4
6	S	36.8	47.4	H	S	47.4	57.9	44.4	47.4	S	55.6	52.6
7	S	73.7	63.2	S	38.9	38.9	S	73.7	68.4	S	31.6	57.9
8	47.4	52.6	52.6	S	47.4	52.6	S	47.4	S	57.9	47.4	S
9	66.7	47.4	57.9	55.6	57.9	S	47.4	57.9	S	63.2	47.4	S
10	47.4	S	S	57.9	63.2	S	52.6	72.2	57.9	55.6	S	44.4
11	38.9	S	S	68.4	57.9	44.4	42.1	S	52.6	36.8	S	55.6
12	42.1	68.4	52.6	55.6	S	44.4	36.8	S	61.1	52.6	52.6	57.9
13	S	38.9	57.9	47.4	S	47.4	47.4	52.6	47.4	S	42.1	52.6
14	S	66.7	38.9	S	63.2	47.4	S	44.4	47.4	S	44.4	47.4
15	H	38.9	38.9	S	52.6	63.2	S	47.4	S	33.3	47.4	S
16	47.4	68.4	52.6	57.9	55.6	S	33.3	47.4	S	52.6	52.6	S
17	73.7	S	S	63.2	63.2	S	47.4	57.9	57.9	33.3	S	66.7
18	55.6	S	S	44.4	42.1	57.9	42.1	S	57.9	52.6	S	36.8
19	42.1	H	55.6	52.6	S	42.1	33.3	S	42.1	52.6	42.1	55.6
20	S	61.1	52.6	77.8	S	44.4	47.4	66.7	44.4	S	44.4	47.4
21	S	36.8	27.8	S	38.9	63.2	S	47.4	66.7	S	47.4	38.9
22	36.8	44.4	63.2	S	47.4	38.9	S	47.4	S	55.6	H	S
23	36.8	47.4	57.9	57.9	31.6	S	31.6	38.9	S	42.1	61.1	S
24	47.4	S	S	44.4	47.4	S	55.6	47.4	47.4	57.9	S	55.6
25	47.4	S	S	42.1	47.4	57.9	42.1	S	47.4	42.1	S	H
26	52.6	55.6	57.9	38.9	S	52.6	36.8	S	47.4	36.8	38.9	42.1
27	S	57.9	52.6	44.4	S	44.4	42.1	44.4	47.4	S	52.6	63.2
28	S	55.6	47.4	S	H	38.9	S	31.6	52.6	S	47.4	47.4
29	47.4		57.9	S	57.9	73.7	S	36.8	S	72.2	42.1	S
30	52.6		44.4	42.1	63.2	S	47.4	63.2	S	52.6	52.6	S
31	44.4		S		57.9		47.4	31.6		52.6		57.9

NATURAL GAS WIDELY TRADED CONTRACT MONTHLY SETTLEMENTS

Contract Month Date	Mar (H) JAN	Jun (M) FEB	Jun (M) MAR	Jun (M) APR	Oct (V) MAY	Oct (V) JUN	Oct (V) JUL	Jan (F) AUG	Jan (F) SEP	Jan (F) OCT	Mar (H) NOV	Mar (H) DEC
1991	1.380	1.430	1.430	1.380	1.420	1.370	1.470	2.150	2.220	2.210	1.500	1.270
1992	1.180	1.180	1.330	1.420	1.720	1.640	1.880	2.270	2.390	2.250	1.620	1.590
1993	1.600	1.770	1.980	2.370	2.280	2.370	2.270	2.560	2.440	2.380	2.060	1.920
1994	2.550	2.150	2.090	2.070	2.110	2.190	1.970	2.100	2.040	2.080	1.750	1.730
1995	1.350	1.550	1.750	1.660	1.850	1.620	1.650	1.920	1.940	1.900	1.830	2.190
1996	2.660	2.010	2.260	2.220	2.390	2.770	2.170	2.220	2.400	2.700	2.700	2.410
1997	2.380	1.900	1.970	2.180	2.230	2.160	2.180	2.920	3.120	3.470	2.340	2.230
1998	2.260	2.350	2.560	2.220	2.290	2.510	1.910	2.380	2.680	2.450	2.000	1.940
1999	1.780	1.700	2.040	2.250	2.410	2.440	2.570	3.090	2.970	2.980	2.290	2.330
2000	2.660	2.780	2.950	3.140	4.340	4.420	3.800	4.850	5.256	4.531	5.836	8.791
2001	5.710	5.330	5.080	4.700	4.050	3.260	3.350	3.190	2.832	3.428	2.799	2.560
2002	2.140	2.480	3.310	3.800	3.350	3.310	2.980	4.029	4.403	4.256	4.048	4.692
2003	5.610	5.770	5.100	5.390	6.300	5.490	4.750	5.401	5.262	5.129	4.882	5.996
2004	5.400	5.490	5.990	5.870	6.490	6.220	6.190	6.637	8.030	9.383	7.560	6.195
2005	6.330	6.870	7.760	6.590	6.560	7.110	7.950	12.147	14.771	12.641	12.481	11.359
2006	9.320	7.075	7.420									

NATURAL GAS WIDELY TRADED CONTRACT MONTHLY CHANGES

Contract Month Date	Mar (H) JAN	Jun (M) FEB	Jun (M) MAR	Jun (M) APR	Oct (V) MAY	Oct (V) JUN	Oct (V) JUL	Jan (F) AUG	Jan (F) SEP	Jan (F) OCT	Mar (H) NOV	Mar (H) DEC
1991	-0.210	-0.140	-0.010	0.000	-0.050	-0.060	-0.050	2.160	2.150	2.220	1.570	1.500
1992	-0.230	0.000	-0.050	0.150	0.030	0.160	-0.080	2.220	2.270	2.390	1.750	1.620
1993	-0.030	0.060	0.140	0.210	0.320	-0.080	0.090	2.540	2.560	2.440	2.150	2.060
1994	-0.140	0.250	-0.010	-0.060	0.020	-0.080	0.080	2.240	2.100	2.040	1.950	1.750
1995	-0.020	-0.220	0.070	0.200	-0.060	0.080	-0.230	1.900	1.920	1.940	1.780	1.830
1996	0.360	0.190	0.060	0.250	0.090	0.220	0.380	2.300	2.220	2.400	2.280	2.700
1997	-0.290	0.020	-0.140	0.070	0.180	0.010	-0.070	2.460	2.920	3.120	2.660	2.340
1998	-0.110	0.140	0.040	0.210	-0.240	-0.070	0.220	2.560	2.380	2.680	2.290	2.000
1999	-0.060	-0.050	-0.170	0.340	0.200	0.080	0.030	2.880	3.090	2.970	2.700	2.290
2000	0.040	0.200	0.220	0.170	0.180	1.170	0.080	4.020	4.850	5.260	4.200	5.840
2001	2.960	-0.220	0.150	-0.250	-0.240	-0.850	-0.790	3.940	3.190	2.840	3.360	2.800
2002	-0.240	-0.360	0.150	0.830	0.440	-0.500	-0.040	3.670	4.030	4.410	4.060	4.050
2003	0.650	0.470	0.870	-0.670	0.420	0.790	-0.810	5.360	5.410	5.270	5.020	4.890
2004	1.110	-0.080	0.450	0.500	-0.020	0.490	-0.270	7.020	6.640	8.030	8.920	7.560
2005	-1.360	0.300	0.440	0.890	-0.940	-0.440	0.550	9.310	12.150	14.780	12.340	12.490
2006	-1.130	-1.983	0.345									
# Up	7	10	11	7	8	7	7	10	11	6	4	5
# Down	9	5	3	8	7	8	8	6	5	9	12	11
Total Change	-4.580	2.210	2.840	-0.340	0.920	-0.910	-1.790	3.370	5.230	-0.970	-1.330	1.300
AVG. Change	-0.286	0.147	0.189	-0.023	0.061	-0.061	-0.119	0.211	0.327	-0.061	-0.083	0.081
AVG. Up	0.359	0.259	0.347	0.267	0.375	0.204	0.207	0.491	0.547	0.442	0.565	1.024
AVG. Down	-0.788	-0.076	-0.327	-0.276	-0.297	-0.293	-0.405	-0.257	-0.158	-0.402	-0.299	-0.347

NATURAL GAS WIDELY TRADED CONTRACT PERFORMANCE

PERFORMANCE STATISTICS BASED ON MONTHLY PERFORMANCE AND FOLLOWING-MONTH PERFORMANCE

(Based on monthly trends from **January 1987 – December 2005** using the aforementioned contracts)

Contract	Mar (H)	Jun (M)	Jun (M)	Jun (M)	Oct (V)	Oct (V)	Oct (V)	Jan (F)	Jan (F)	Jan (F)	Mar (H)	Mar (H)
Month	JAN	FEB	MAR	APR	MAY	JUN	JUL	AUG	SEP	OCT	NOV	DEC
Yrs Tested	16	15	15	15	15	15	15	16	16	16	16	16
# Up	7	10	11	7	8	7	7	10	11	6	4	5
# Down	9	5	3	8	7	8	8	6	5	9	12	11
Total Gain (Loss)	-4.580	2.210	2.840	-0.340	0.920	-0.910	-1.790	3.370	5.230	-0.970	-1.330	1.300
Average Gain (Loss)	-0.286	0.147	0.189	-0.023	0.061	-0.061	-0.119	0.211	0.327	-0.061	-0.083	0.081

If Previous Month is Up, then FOLLOWING Month had the following Characteristics

Contract	Mar (H)	Jun (M)	Jun (M)	Jun (M)	Oct (V)	Oct (V)	Oct (V)	Jan (F)	Jan (F)	Mar (H)	Mar (H)	Mar (H)
Month	FEB	MAR	APR	MAY	JUN	JUL	AUG	SEP	OCT	NOV	DEC	JAN
Yrs Tested	8	10	11	9	8	7	9	10	10	4	5	7
# Up	6	8	6	6	3	2	6	7	3	2	3	4
# Down	2	2	5	3	5	5	3	3	7	2	2	3
% Closing Higher	5.0	80.0	54.5	66.7	37.5	28.6	66.7	70.0	30.0	50.0	60.0	57.17
Total Gain (Loss)	1.620	2.340	-0.180	1.770	-0.970	-1.170	2.510	3.700	-1.410	1.900	-1.980	3.700
Average Gain (Loss)	0.203	0.234	-0.016	0.197	-0.121	-0.167	0.279	0.370	-0.128	0.475	-0.396	0.529
# Higher Highs	7	8	11	7	5	3	7	7	9	4	5	6
# Lower Lows	1	2	2	1	2	6	3	3	3	1	2	0

If Previous Month is Down, then FOLLOWING Month had the following Characteristics

Contract	Mar (H)	Jun (M)	Jun (M)	Jun (M)	Oct (V)	Oct (V)	Oct (V)	Jan (F)	Jan (F)	Mar (H)	Mar (H)	Mar (H)
Month	FEB	MAR	APR	MAY	JUN	JUL	AUG	SEP	OCT	NOV	DEC	JAN
Yrs Tested	6	4	3	6	7	8	7	6	5	12	11	9
# Up	4	3	1	2	4	5	4	4	3	3	4	4
# Down	2	1	2	4	3	3	3	2	2	9	7	5
% Closing Lower	33.3	25.0	66.7	66.7	42.9	37.5	42.9	33.3	40.0	75.0	63.6	55.6
Total Gain (Loss)	0.640	0.500	-0.110	-0.850	0.060	-0.620	0.860	1.530	0.440	-0.600	-2.600	-3.460
Average Gain (Loss)	0.107	0.100	-0.037	-0.142	0.009	-0.078	0.123	0.255	0.088	-0.050	-0.236	-0.384
# Higher Highs	0	2	1	2	4	2	2	4	2	2	2	0
# Lower Lows	2	2	2	4	4	6	4	5	5	9	9	7

Key Points Regarding Monthly Performance from 1987 – 2005

- Natural Gas continues January Strength in February (6 of 8)
- February rallies continue in March (8 of 10)
- Natural Gas rallies in August continue through September (7 of 10)
- September rallies reversed in October (7 of 10)
- October weakness continues through November (9 of 12)

BEAT THE RUSH, BUY GOLD IN AUGUST AHEAD OF THE HOLIDAY SHOPPING SEASON

The most important observation to be made from the performance of Gold futures in the last 19 years is that demand is driven by the jewelry industry.

The lion's share of Gold usage is accounted for by the jewelry industry. The busiest time of the year for jewelry sales is the year-end holiday shopping season. November and December account for almost a third (32.3%) of normal typical jewelry sales. As such, retail jewelers stock up on gold trinkets prior to the holiday shopping season.

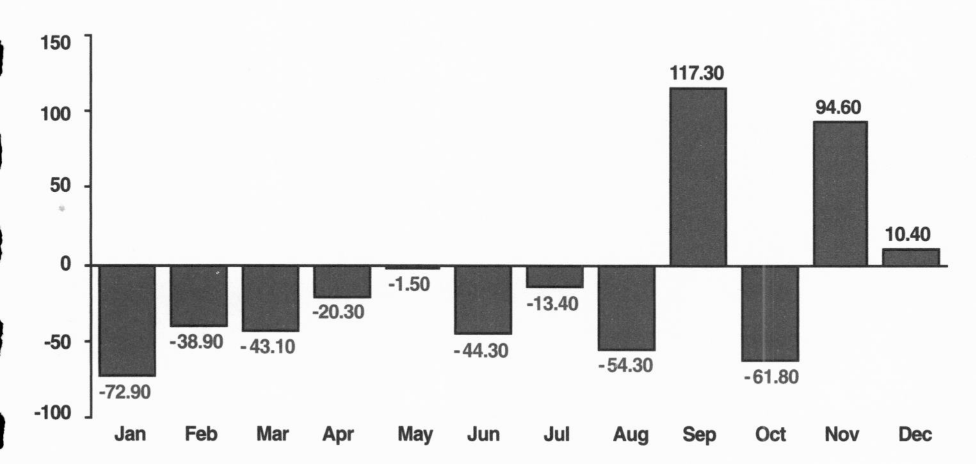

Strength in Gold pricing usually occurs in the September-through-December period when retailers are busily acquiring inventory. As such, the normal yearly low in Gold prices is seen near the beginning of August, before fabricators begin buying bullion ahead of the holiday season.

The adage that price precedes demand is true in the Gold market and is readily evident by the fact that February Gold futures have gained ground in 6 of the last 7 years from September to December on a monthly closing basis. Traders should also watch for August rallies because following each of the last 7 rallies since 1987 April Gold futures have rallied in September.

Following the holiday shopping season, traders should take advantage of New Year strength to establish short positions, as 6 of the last 7 January rallies in April Gold have been followed by February declines, and 5 of the last 7 rallies in February have seen March declines.

GOLD FUTURES MARKET PROBABILITY CALENDAR FOR 2007

THE % CHANGE OF THE MARKET RISING ON ANY TRADING DAY OF THE YEAR

(Based on the number of times the widely traded contract rose on a particular trading day during **January 1987-December 2005**)

Contract	Apr (J)	Apr (J)	Jun (M)	Jun (M)	Aug (Q)	Aug (Q)	Oct (V)	Oct (V)	Dec (Z)	Dec (Z)	Feb (G)	Feb (G)
Date	**Jan**	**Feb**	**Mar**	**Apr**	**May**	**Jun**	**Jul**	**Aug**	**Sep**	**Oct**	**Nov**	**Dec**
1	H	31.6	63.2	S	55.6	26.3	S	57.9	S	52.6	36.8	S
2	78.9	66.7	31.6	63.2	63.2	S	63.2	47.4	S	44.4	47.4	S
3	26.3	S	S	52.6	47.4	S	57.9	47.4	H	57.9	S	47.4
4	31.6	S	S	44.4	63.2	52.6	H	S	61.1	63.2	S	47.4
5	42.1	52.6	38.9	52.6	S	47.4	38.9	S	38.9	47.4	63.2	36.8
6	S	42.1	38.9	H	S	42.1	38.9	52.6	47.4	S	38.9	52.6
7	S	36.8	47.4	S	42.1	61.1	S	33.3	52.6	S	55.6	52.6
8	63.2	21.1	55.6	S	42.1	47.4	S	47.4	S	61.1	52.6	S
9	47.4	72.2	36.8	44.4	31.6	S	61.1	73.7	S	52.6	52.6	S
10	57.9	S	S	63.2	78.9	S	52.6	57.9	63.2	36.8	S	63.2
11	42.1	S	S	44.4	42.1	47.4	27.8	S	42.1	42.1	S	42.1
12	57.9	42.1	73.7	47.4	S	36.8	42.1	S	38.9	42.1	63.2	44.4
13	S	47.4	55.6	57.9	S	44.4	57.9	36.8	42.1	S	63.2	68.4
14	S	21.1	55.6	S	52.6	31.6	S	42.1	42.1	S	57.9	57.9
15	H	47.4	36.8	S	52.6	57.9	S	57.9	S	42.1	38.9	S
16	42.1	42.1	47.4	52.6	68.4	S	73.7	68.4	S	36.8	47.4	S
17	27.8	S	S	38.9	52.6	S	36.8	36.8	47.4	42.1	S	55.6
18	68.4	S	S	47.4	47.4	57.9	36.8	S	42.1	42.1	S	63.2
19	57.9	H	27.8	47.4	S	61.1	73.7	S	36.8	44.4	63.2	68.4
20	S	38.9	57.9	57.9	S	55.6	57.9	57.9	63.2	S	55.6	47.4
21	S	55.6	55.6	S	42.1	27.8	S	47.4	63.2	S	47.4	52.6
22	57.9	55.6	63.2	S	68.4	61.1	S	44.4	S	47.4	H	S
23	63.2	38.9	68.4	57.9	47.4	S	63.2	36.8	S	63.2	52.6	S
24	36.8	S	S	36.8	36.8	S	33.3	47.4	68.4	31.6	S	42.1
25	57.9	S	S	42.1	52.6	47.4	47.4	S	73.7	42.1	S	H
26	61.1	42.1	42.1	36.8	S	47.4	47.4	S	47.4	47.4	47.4	47.4
27	S	44.4	63.2	47.4	S	42.1	36.8	38.9	42.1	S	55.6	73.7
28	S	57.9	21.1	S	H	33.3	S	26.3	31.6	S	57.9	38.9
29	36.8		42.1	S	33.3	63.2	S	42.1	S	38.9	36.8	S
30	33.3		38.9	55.6	57.9	S	66.7	47.4	S	52.6	36.8	S
31	31.6		S		26.3		36.8	61.1		47.4		38.9

GOLD WIDELY TRADED CONTRACT MONTHLY SETTLEMENTS

Contract Month	Apr (J)	Apr (J)	Jun (M)	Jun (M)	Aug (Q)	Aug (Q)	Oct (V)	Oct (V)	Dec (Z)	Dec (Z)	Feb (G)	Feb (G)
Date	**JAN**	**FEB**	**MAR**	**APR**	**MAY**	**JUN**	**JUL**	**AUG**	**SEP**	**OCT**	**NOV**	**DEC**
1987	408.9	407.4	422.7	456.5	461.9	456.0	469.5	453.2	458.8	471.2	497.2	488.9
1988	458.5	431.9	457.9	452.6	457.0	459.8	441.7	434.1	399.2	415.1	429.6	412.3
1989	395.8	390.4	390.0	380.5	384.8	366.5	374.7	361.7	372.0	377.6	417.5	405.2
1990	417.8	408.9	375.0	371.4	376.3	368.6	374.6	384.6	408.1	381.3	385.7	396.2
1991	368.5	369.0	359.4	357.7	360.5	364.8	367.2	349.6	357.3	359.5	371.1	355.2
1992	358.9	354.1	345.5	337.9	339.8	338.4	359.4	343.6	349.4	340.1	335.5	333.3
1993	330.7	329.1	339.3	357.2	358.6	380.3	409.2	373.9	357.1	369.6	371.9	391.9
1994	383.6	382.5	394.3	377.8	380.5	390.0	386.1	387.8	397.6	384.9	384.5	384.4
1995	377.7	378.3	394.3	388.5	391.8	387.6	385.4	384.2	386.5	384.3	388.6	388.1
1996	408.5	401.2	398.4	393.5	395.9	394.4	390.5	388.3	380.5	379.1	375.0	371.2
1997	346.0	365.1	354.0	341.2	343.7	347.5	326.5	325.5	336.9	312.1	298.6	289.9
1998	304.6	300.1	303.3	307.9	310.2	295.1	288.4	276.5	299.0	293.7	295.1	289.2
1999	288.2	288.3	293.8	312.6	289.7	272.0	257.6	256.7	299.5	300.3	293.0	289.6
2000	286.1	294.2	281.4	274.7	277.4	274.8	280.2	279.6	276.9	266.4	273.3	273.6
2001	268.0	267.8	259.2	264.4	265.4	266.9	267.9	275.1	294.0	280.5	274.9	279.0
2002	282.9	297.1	303.7	309.2	310.2	327.5	304.2	312.8	325.2	318.4	317.8	348.2
2003	369.1	350.3	336.9	339.4	340.2	365.6	355.0	375.8	386.1	384.6	398.0	416.1
2004	402.9	396.8	428.3	387.5	388.5	394.9	392.4	410.9	420.4	429.4	453.2	438.4
2005	424.1	437.6	429.5	436.1	438.7	418.9	432.8	435.1	472.3	466.9	498.7	518.9
2006	575.5	565.8	586.7									

GOLD WIDELY TRADED CONTRACT MONTHLY CHANGES

Contract Month	Apr (J)	Apr (J)	Jun (M)	Jun (M)	Aug (Q)	Aug (Q)	Oct (V)	Oct (V)	Dec (Z)	Dec (Z)	Feb (G)	Feb (G)
Date	JAN	FEB	MAR	APR	MAY	JUN	JUL	AUG	SEP	OCT	NOV	DEC
1987	-1.7	-1.5	-1.3	11.3	12.0	34.6	-3.9	11.9	-16.4	0.1	477.2	497.2
1988	-8.3	-36.4	-27.4	22.1	22.3	-5.3	-21.9	-1.2	-7.4	-40.7	420.1	429.6
1989	-17.5	-21.6	-5.3	-5.5	-6.0	-10.4	10.8	-6.6	-13.3	6.6	381.9	417.5
1990	-12.3	7.5	-8.9	-39.5	-40.2	-3.3	-9.3	10.5	10.0	18.9	385.2	385.7
1991	10.8	-31.2	0.6	-13.1	-13.3	-2.0	5.6	-6.3	-17.9	4.4	362.1	371.1
1992	-16.0	1.4	-4.7	-10.8	-10.8	-7.9	6.0	13.2	-16.1	4.1	341.5	335.5
1993	-2.4	-3.7	-1.5	8.9	9.0	17.9	-1.0	28.1	-35.6	-18.6	371.4	371.9
1994	20.1	-10.2	-1.0	9.8	10.1	-16.4	-2.7	-4.3	1.6	6.8	388.4	384.5
1995	-0.1	-10.7	0.1	13.0	12.8	-5.8	-1.7	-3.6	-1.5	-0.4	386.3	388.6
1996	-0.3	18.4	-6.5	-5.6	-5.5	-4.9	-13.3	6.3	-1.8	-10.8	381.1	375.0
1997	-3.6	-27.4	19.1	-13.3	-13.1	-12.9	-12.4	-11.2	-1.2	9.5	313.5	298.6
1998	-8.9	13.0	-4.6	1.4	1.5	4.8	2.9	-11.9	-11.6	20.1	295.7	295.1
1999	-5.9	-3.0	6.8	-7.5	-8.1	5.8	-8.9	-7.5	-1.5	42.2	303.3	293.0
2000	-3.5	-5.6	7.9	-15.2	-15.2	-6.6	16.7	-14.3	-1.1	-5.2	269.0	273.3
2001	0.3	-8.2	-0.3	-10.6	-10.7	4.7	4.6	-4.6	7.3	17.5	281.1	274.9
2002	4.2	3.3	14.3	5.8	6.1	5.6	-13.6	-10.8	8.7	11.3	319.3	317.8
2003	30.4	20.1	-18.9	-14.2	-14.2	2.6	-19.3	8.0	21.0	9.3	385.6	398.0
2004	18.3	-14.3	-6.1	30.5	30.6	-40.8	-2.0	-1.8	18.7	8.0	431.2	453.2
2005	-14.8	-16.4	13.7	-10.6	-9.0	5.0	18.5	-7.3	2.3	34.2	470.7	498.7
2006	20.4	52.1	17.6									
# Up	7	7	8	8	9	7	6	7	14	7	11	7
# Down	12	12	11	11	10	12	13	12	5	12	8	12
Total Change	-72.9	-38.9	-20.3	0.1	-1.5	-44.3	-13.4	-54.3	117.3	-61.8	10.4	-67.7
AVG. Change	-3.8	-2.0	-1.1	0.0005	-0.1	-2.3	-0.7	-2.9	6.2	-3.3	5.0	0.5
AVG. Up	16.5	8.0	11.9	10.0	10.3	9.2	13.0	9.9	13.8	8.3	14.8	16.4
AVG. Down	-15.7	-7.9	-13.3	-10.5	-9.4	-9.1	-7.0	-10.3	-15.1	-10.0	-6.2	-7.8

GOLD WIDELY TRADED CONTRACT PERFORMANCE

PERFORMANCE STATISTICS BASED ON MONTHLY PERFORMANCE AND FOLLOWING-MONTH PERFORMANCE

(Based on monthly trends from **January 1987 – December 2005** using the aforementioned contracts)

Contract	Apr (J)	Apr (J)	Jun (M)	Jun (M)	Aug (Q)	Aug (Q)	Oct (V)	Oct (V)	Dec (Z)	Dec (Z)	Feb (G)	Feb (G)
Month	JAN	FEB	MAR	APR	MAY	JUN	JUL	AUG	SEP	OCT	NOV	DEC
Yrs Tested	19	19	19	19	19	19	19	19	19	19	19	19
# Up	7	7	8	8	9	7	6	7	14	7	11	7
# Down	12	12	11	11	10	12	13	12	5	12	8	12
Total Gain (Loss)	-72.9	-38.9	-43.1	-20.3	-1.5	-44.3	-13.4	-54.3	117.3	-61.8	94.6	10.4
Average Gain (Loss)	-0.2	-0.1	-0.1	0.0	0.0	-0.1	-0.1	-0.1	0.4	-0.2	0.2	0.0

If Previous Month is Up, then FOLLOWING Month had the following Characteristics

Contract	Apr (J)	Apr (J)	Jun (M)	Jun (M)	Aug (Q)	Aug (Q)	Oct (V)	Oct (V)	Dec (Z)	Dec (Z)	Feb (G)	Feb (G)
Month	FEB	MAR	APR	MAY	JUN	JUL	AUG	SEP	OCT	NOV	DEC	JAN
Yrs Tested	7	7	8	8	9	7	6	7	14	7	11	7
# Up	1	2	4	4	2	1	2	7	5	6	5	3
# Down	6	5	4	4	7	6	4	0	9	1	6	4
% Closing Higher	14.3	28.6	50.0	50.0	22.2	14.3	33.3	100.0	35.7	85.7	45.5	42.9
Total Gain (Loss)	-39.8	-40.9	-6.6	7.4	-63.3	-37.8	-38.8	106.0	-76.1	86.3	0.0	11.6
Average Gain (Loss)	-5.7	-5.8	-0.8	0.9	-7.0	-5.4	-6.5	15.1	-5.4	12.3	0.0	1.7
# Higher Highs	3	4	6	5	5	2	5	6	8	5	9	6
# Lower Lows	2	4	2	3	2	2	2	0	7	3	3	3

If Previous Month is Down, then FOLLOWING Month had the following Characteristics

Contract	Apr (J)	Apr (J)	Jun (M)	Jun (M)	Aug (Q)	Aug (Q)	Oct (V)	Oct (V)	Dec (Z)	Dec (Z)	Feb (G)	Feb (G)
Month	FEB	MAR	APR	MAY	JUN	JUL	AUG	SEP	OCT	NOV	DEC	JAN
Yrs Tested	12	12	11	11	10	12	13	12	5	12	8	12
# Up	6	6	4	5	5	5	5	7	2	5	2	4
# Down	6	6	7	6	5	7	8	5	3	7	6	8
% Closing Lower	50.0	50.0	63.6	54.5	50.0	58.3	61.5	41.7	60.0	58.3	75.0	66.7
Total Gain (Loss)	0.9	-2.2	-13.7	-8.9	19.0	24.4	-15.5	11.3	14.3	8.3	10.4	-84.5
Average Gain (Loss)	0.1	-0.2	-1.2	-0.8	1.9	2.0	-1.2	0.9	2.9	0.7	1.3	-7.0
# Higher Highs	1	5	0	0	0	3	3	3	1	4	1	3
# Lower Lows	8	9	10	8	8	6	9	8	3	8	7	10

Key Points Regarding Monthly Performance from 1987 – 2005

- May rallies reversed in June (7 of 9)
- August strength continues through September (7 of 7)
- December Gold rallies in September (14 of 19)
- December weakness continues through January (8 of 12)

SILVER BENEFITS FROM JEWELRY AS WELL AS INDUSTRIAL USAGE

Silver is as much an industrial metal as it is a precious metal. Industrial usage accounts for over 40% of all usage, as Silver is a common element in switches and electrical devices due to its conductivity. Demand from flatware and jewelry accounts for over 28% of normal yearly usage, while photographic usage accounts for 20%. Coins and collectibles make up the rest.

The key factor to understanding Silver is understanding its demand schedule as this commodity is demand-driven. When jewelry, industrial, and photographic demand coincide, prices rise — November to March. However, when demand is weak in multiple sectors — such as April, May, June, and August — prices tend to decline.

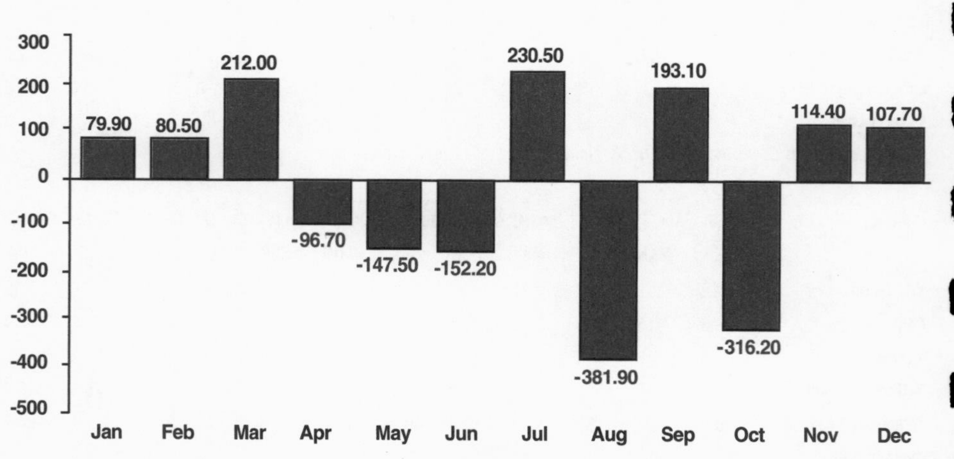

The major bullish months in Silver are March, July, and September when demand from all three sectors begins to increase. It is during these months that wholesale demand increases, pressuring prices higher. However, the late spring/early summer period (April through June) and August and October periods tend to see the worst performance as demand slackens after initial supply builds and normal lower usage prevails.

Just like in the Gold market, price precedes demand; look for rallies before historical weakness as an opportunity to establish short positions, while weakness ahead of usual periods of strength should be used to establish long positions in the Silver market.

SILVER FUTURES MARKET PROBABILITY CALENDAR FOR 2007

THE % CHANGE OF THE MARKET RISING ON ANY TRADING DAY OF THE YEAR

(Based on the number of times the widely traded contract rose on a particular trading day during **January 1987-December 2005**)

Contract	Mar (H)	May (K)	May (K)	Jul (N)	Jul (N)	Sep (U)	Sep (U)	Sep (U)	Dec (Z)	Dec (Z)	Mar (H)	Mar (H)
Date	**Jan**	**Feb**	**Mar**	**Apr**	**May**	**Jun**	**Jul**	**Aug**	**Sep**	**Oct**	**Nov**	**Dec**
1	H	36.8	78.9	S	72.2	47.4	S	68.4	S	55.6	31.6	S
2	63.2	57.9	42.1	52.6	52.6	S	63.2	42.1	S	42.1	42.1	S
3	36.8	S	S	57.9	52.6	S	77.8	42.1	H	44.4	S	57.9
4	42.1	S	S	52.6	66.7	47.4	H	S	57.9	61.1	S	52.6
5	63.2	52.6	44.4	47.4	S	63.2	52.6	S	42.1	47.4	52.6	47.4
6	S	57.9	31.6	H	S	42.1	47.4	57.9	47.4	S	47.4	57.9
7	S	47.4	66.7	S	42.1	66.7	S	42.1	47.4	S	63.2	55.6
8	68.4	26.3	63.2	S	47.4	57.9	S	52.6	S	47.4	63.2	S
9	47.4	68.4	55.6	52.6	52.6	S	52.6	42.1	S	47.4	44.4	S
10	55.6	S	S	47.4	52.6	S	63.2	63.2	57.9	21.1	S	52.6
11	31.6	S	S	47.4	36.8	31.6	55.6	S	33.3	44.4	S	33.3
12	42.1	36.8	68.4	57.9	S	38.9	42.1	S	63.2	42.1	68.4	57.9
13	S	47.4	47.4	61.1	S	55.6	47.4	47.4	38.9	S	63.2	52.6
14	S	57.9	73.7	S	36.8	47.4	S	57.9	42.1	S	57.9	27.8
15	H	47.4	38.9	S	63.2	57.9	S	52.6	S	36.8	52.6	S
16	47.4	36.8	47.4	47.4	55.6	S	63.2	52.6	S	47.4	52.6	S
17	66.7	S	S	63.2	36.8	S	63.2	44.4	52.6	36.8	S	63.2
18	72.2	S	S	47.4	44.4	57.9	36.8	S	42.1	42.1	S	47.4
19	42.1	H	21.1	31.6	S	47.4	63.2	S	63.2	36.8	63.2	66.7
20	S	42.1	63.2	57.9	S	27.8	61.1	77.8	57.9	S	57.9	47.4
21	S	47.4	57.9	S	47.4	47.4	S	38.9	57.9	S	52.6	57.9
22	52.6	42.1	47.4	S	61.1	47.4	S	47.4	S	68.4	H	S
23	52.6	42.1	68.4	73.7	57.9	S	57.9	42.1	S	66.7	38.9	S
24	68.4	S	S	47.4	38.9	S	52.6	47.4	63.2	26.3	S	38.9
25	57.9	S	S	31.6	47.4	47.4	52.6	S	52.6	47.4	S	H
26	63.2	42.1	63.2	52.6	S	52.6	44.4	S	42.1	57.9	42.1	73.7
27	S	26.3	47.4	36.8	S	26.3	38.9	36.8	44.4	S	36.8	68.4
28	S	47.4	42.1	S	H	52.6	S	42.1	47.4	S	61.1	31.6
29	38.9		52.6	S	26.3	63.2	S	44.4	S	33.3	44.4	S
30	44.4		47.4	63.2	44.4	S	73.7	31.6	S	57.9	21.1	S
31	36.8		S		47.4		36.8	57.9		47.4		27.8

SILVER WIDELY TRADED CONTRACT MONTHLY SETTLEMENTS

Contract Month Date	Mar (H) JAN	May (K) FEB	May (K) MAR	Jul (N) APR	Jul (N) MAY	Sep (U) JUN	Sep (U) JUL	Sep (U) AUG	Dec (Z) SEP	Dec (Z) OCT	Mar (H) NOV	Mar (H) DEC
1987	542.8	549.3	622.0	808.0	767.0	741.0	835.0	738.3	761.0	699.0	719.0	677.0
1988	654.5	632.0	678.5	658.5	665.0	677.5	685.5	655.6	622.5	634.8	629.0	613.0
1989	583.5	593.5	582.3	570.5	520.5	524.3	531.3	504.5	531.0	521.8	579.5	527.3
1990	522.8	520.5	498.0	501.5	511.0	496.3	482.2	475.9	483.2	418.0	421.7	424.7
1991	385.1	377.3	386.8	401.5	411.7	447.5	407.8	380.7	417.3	410.8	411.3	391.2
1992	418.0	413.5	414.3	401.5	402.2	405.8	393.7	373.0	376.2	376.2	377.2	368.7
1993	366.0	359.7	389.2	441.7	462.2	458.7	540.8	483.8	408.2	436.7	446.5	511.7
1994	513.5	539.0	578.5	538.3	555.0	542.5	533.2	544.3	565.7	526.2	497.5	491.7
1995	466.3	456.5	531.0	578.3	531.0	506.5	505.2	531.1	548.5	536.0	526.7	520.7
1996	558.8	554.5	554.0	534.0	540.3	503.5	514.8	517.4	487.7	480.8	478.5	481.5
1997	492.0	536.0	507.5	469.3	467.5	464.8	449.0	461.6	523.2	473.7	529.8	598.8
1998	612.5	648.0	646.7	623.0	508.5	553.5	545.8	461.8	536.0	504.3	488.5	502.0
1999	523.5	563.0	497.0	543.0	489.5	528.7	546.5	515.2	561.5	518.0	524.0	545.3
2000	531.7	511.5	504.5	501.5	496.5	508.3	503.8	500.3	494.8	477.8	475.8	463.5
2001	481.5	451.5	429.5	435.8	441.0	432.7	422.8	416.2	467.5	422.5	415.7	458.8
2002	422.3	451.7	465.0	455.5	504.2	485.5	459.8	443.7	454.8	450.5	443.5	481.2
2003	486.0	460.0	446.5	465.2	453.3	456.8	512.0	510.9	514.2	506.5	538.2	596.5
2004	625.0	671.5	794.5	609.0	611.0	579.5	656.0	677.1	693.8	730.5	777.7	683.7
2005	674.7	739.5	714.7	694.0	745.2	707.5	726.2	678.1	751.2	758.0	838.5	889.0
2006	988.5	979.0	1152.0									

SILVER WIDELY TRADED CONTRACT MONTHLY CHANGES

Contract Month	Mar (H)	May (K)	May (K)	Jul (N)	Jul (N)	Sep (U)	Sep (U)	Sep (U)	Dec (Z)	Dec (Z)	Mar (H)	Mar (H)
Date	**JAN**	**FEB**	**MAR**	**APR**	**MAY**	**JUN**	**JUL**	**AUG**	**SEP**	**OCT**	**NOV**	**DEC**
1987	-3.2	6.8	-9.0	73.6	178.9	-41.3	-35.5	94.0	-98.1	8.0	-64.4	5.4
1988	-42.0	-23.6	-30.9	47.2	-28.5	7.2	3.4	8.0	-30.1	-48.5	12.0	-20.3
1989	-16.0	-29.8	0.1	-11.7	-22.8	-51.1	-5.3	7.0	-26.6	14.5	-10.0	46.3
1990	-52.2	-3.9	-10.6	-22.3	-4.7	9.0	-22.9	-14.1	-5.9	-3.6	-66.7	-5.5
1991	3.0	-40.3	-13.0	9.4	10.1	10.3	30.8	-39.7	-27.7	30.3	-7.1	-5.6
1992	-20.1	26.5	-7.6	0.9	-16.1	0.5	0.6	-12.1	-21.1	-0.5	0.2	-2.7
1993	-8.5	-3.0	-8.7	29.6	50.0	20.9	-6.7	82.1	-57.9	-80.3	28.8	5.4
1994	65.2	1.9	22.2	40.0	-44.4	17.2	-17.5	-9.3	10.8	14.5	-39.6	-37.1
1995	-5.8	-26.1	-15.1	74.4	42.0	-47.7	-30.0	-1.3	26.3	9.5	-11.1	-16.4
1996	-6.0	38.3	-9.1	-1.0	-24.6	6.9	-42.4	11.3	2.1	-37.3	-7.6	-9.1
1997	3.0	10.5	39.4	-28.4	-43.2	-2.0	-7.3	-15.8	13.1	54.7	-50.6	50.5
1998	69.0	12.2	35.5	0.0	-23.5	-112.0	41.5	-7.7	-81.2	68.2	-30.7	-20.0
1999	13.5	20.9	36.7	-62.9	43.4	-52.5	36.5	17.8	-26.9	39.5	-43.0	5.3
2000	21.3	-13.2	-21.9	-5.0	-7.0	-5.4	7.9	-4.5	-4.6	-9.7	-16.6	-8.5
2001	-12.3	18.0	-34.3	-22.3	2.5	5.2	-11.7	-9.9	-6.2	46.5	-45.0	-9.3
2002	43.1	-35.0	27.9	13.4	-11.1	48.8	-20.7	-25.7	-15.8	8.0	-4.5	-9.4
2003	37.7	4.8	-27.3	-13.0	17.3	-12.2	2.4	55.2	0.4	1.0	-6.8	30.0
2004	58.3	28.5	45.3	122.8	-186.6	2.5	-33.3	76.5	22.0	12.6	37.1	43.0
2005	-94.0	-8.6	60.9	-21.3	-28.4	51.0	-42.0	18.7	-47.4	65.7	9.6	72.4
2006	50.5	-17.4	173.0									
# Up	10	8	9	7	11	7	9	5	13	4	8	10
# Down	9	11	10	12	8	12	10	14	6	14	11	9
Total Change	79.9	80.5	212.0	79.9	64.6	-152.2	230.5	-381.9	193.1	-316.2	114.4	107.7
AVG. Change	4.2	4.2	11.2	4.2	3.4	-8.0	12.1	-20.1	10.2	-16.6	6.0	5.7
AVG. Up	26.3	33.5	45.5	49.2	16.1	17.6	41.2	14.7	28.7	21.1	32.3	36.5
AVG. Down	-20.4	-17.0	-19.7	-36.7	-40.6	-22.9	-14.0	-32.5	-30.0	-28.6	-13.1	-28.5

SILVER WIDELY TRADED CONTRACT PERFORMANCE

PERFORMANCE STATISTICS BASED ON MONTHLY PERFORMANCE AND FOLLOWING-MONTH PERFORMANCE

(Based on monthly trends from **January 1987 – December 2005** using the aforementioned contracts)

Contract	Mar (H)	May (K)	May (K)	Jul (N)	Jul (N)	Sep (U)	Sep (U)	Sep (U)	Dec (Z)	Dec (Z)	Mar (H)	Mar (H)
Month	JAN	FEB	MAR	APR	MAY	JUN	JUL	AUG	SEP	OCT	NOV	DEC
Yrs Tested	19	19	19	19	19	19	19	19	19	19	19	19
# Up	10	8	9	7	11	7	9	5	13	4	8	10
# Down	9	11	10	12	8	12	10	14	6	14	11	9
Total Gain (Loss)	79.9	80.5	212.0	-96.7	-147.5	-152.2	230.5	-381.9	193.1	-316.2	114.4	107.7
Average Gain (Loss)	4.2	4.2	11.2	-5.1	-7.8	-8.0	12.1	-20.1	10.2	-16.6	6.0	5.7

If Previous Month is Up, then FOLLOWING Month had the following Characteristics

Contract	Mar (H)	May (K)	May (K)	Jul (N)	Jul (N)	Sep (U)	Sep (U)	Dec (Z)	Dec (Z)	Dec (Z)	Mar (H)	Mar (H)
Month	FEB	MAR	APR	MAY	JUN	JUL	AUG	SEP	OCT	NOV	DEC	JAN
Yrs Tested	10	8	9	7	11	7	9	5	13	5	8	10
# Up	5	3	4	3	3	3	2	3	2	3	5	7
# Down	5	5	5	4	8	4	7	2	11	2	3	3
% Closing Higher	50.0	37.5	44.4	42.9	27.3	42.9	22.2	60.0	15.4	60.0	62.5	70.0
Total Gain (Loss)	91.8	44.0	-5.7	-117.8	-162.5	17.0	-267.2	-4.3	-267.9	97.8	76.1	90.6
Average Gain (Loss)	9.2	5.5	-0.6	-16.8	-14.8	2.4	-29.7	-0.9	-20.6	19.6	9.5	9.1
# Higher Highs	7	6	7	6	4	4	6	1	4	5	6	8
# Lower Lows	4	3	4	1	5	2	5	2	5	2	2	2

If Previous Month is Down, then FOLLOWING Month had the following Characteristics

Contract	Mar (H)	May (K)	May (K)	Jul (N)	Jul (N)	Sep (U)	Sep (U)	Dec (Z)	Dec (Z)	Dec (Z)	Mar (H)	Mar (H)
Month	FEB	MAR	APR	MAY	JUN	JUL	AUG	SEP	OCT	NOV	DEC	JAN
Yrs Tested	9	11	9	12	8	12	10	13	5	14	11	9
# Up	3	6	3	8	4	6	3	10	2	5	5	3
# Down	6	5	6	4	4	6	7	3	3	9	6	6
% Closing Lower	66.7	45.5	66.7	33.3	50.0	50.0	70.0	23.1	60.0	64.3	54.5	66.7
Total Gain (Loss)	-11.3	168.0	-67.5	-29.7	13.1	213.5	-114.7	189.5	-48.3	16.6	31.6	-10.7
Average Gain (Loss)	-1.3	15.3	-7.5	-2.5	1.6	17.8	-11.5	13.5	-8.0	1.2	2.9	-1.2
# Higher Highs	4	5	2	3	0	3	3	5	0	4	2	3
# Lower Lows	7	7	6	6	7	7	8	5	3	8	10	7

Key Points Regarding Monthly Performance from 1987 – 2005

- May rallies reversed in June (8 of 11)
- July breaks in September continue through August (7 of 10)
- September Silver breaks in August (14 of 19)
- August breaks reversed in September (10 of 13) basis December Silver
- September rallies reversed in October (11 of 13)

PLANTING, POLLINATION, AND HARVEST! THE THREE DESTRUCTIONS OF SOYBEANS

Planting, pollination, and harvest are all times of great risk for the Soybean crop. As such, the marketplace builds a risk premium into prices due to the uncertainty of future supply. This is readily seen by the fact that in the 3 months prior to planting (Feb/Mar/Apr), the month prior to pollination (Jun), and the harvest months (Oct/Nov), Soybean futures have gained a total of 985 1/2 cents per bushel. The other six months of the year, Soybean futures have lost -853 1/2 cents per bushel in total since January 1987.

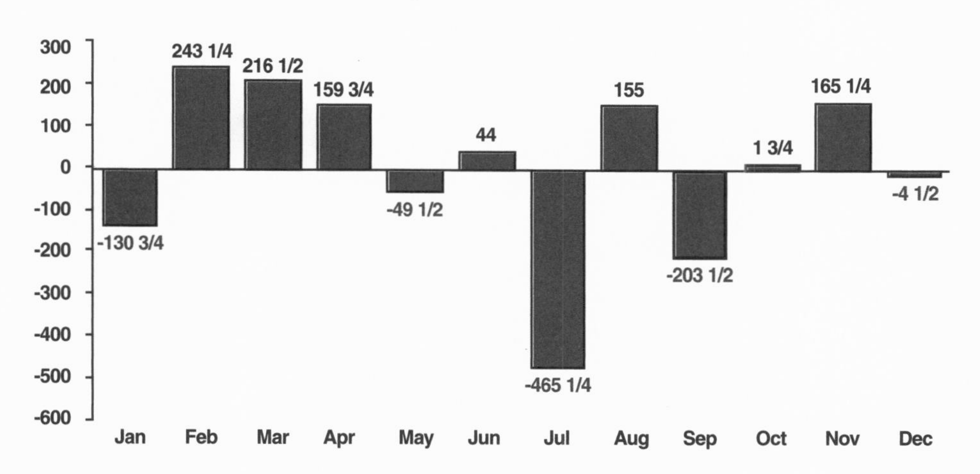

Planting is the foundation of all crops. In anticipation of all that can go wrong during planting — too little or too much rain, or temperature extremes — the marketplace prices in future supply uncertainties through rising prices. In 13 of the last 19 years (and 4 of the last 5), July Soybean futures have rallied from February through May, effectively pricing in crop development problems. In fact, the February-through-May high has exceeded the January settlement in 15 of the last 19 years by 30 cents/bushel or more since 1987.

It is not uncommon for Soybean futures to set their high price in May or June, after the crop is fully sown. With Soybeans pollinating in July, it is not surprising that as future supply becomes more known, July is the worst month on record. Prices tend to fall, with August rallies fairly common after extreme July weakness, into harvest. Post-harvest, Soybeans tend to rally as supply is not readily available in the United States and South America is starting to plant. For the remainder of the year, prices drift lower as the cycle begins anew.

SOYBEANS FUTURES MARKET PROBABILITY CALENDAR FOR 2007

THE % CHANGE OF THE MARKET RISING ON ANY TRADING DAY OF THE YEAR

(Based on the number of times the widely traded contract rose on a particular trading day during **January 1987-December 2005**)

Contract	May (K)	May (K)	Jul (N)	Jul (N)	Jul (N)	Nov (X)	Nov (X)	Nov (X)	Nov (X)	Jan (F)	Jan (F)	Mar (H)
Date	**Jan**	**Feb**	**Mar**	**Apr**	**May**	**Jun**	**Jul**	**Aug**	**Sep**	**Oct**	**Nov**	**Dec**
1	H	47.4	73.7	S	78.9	77.8	S	42.1	S	26.3	63.2	S
2	73.7	38.9	63.2	57.9	63.2	S	52.6	44.4	S	47.4	63.2	S
3	42.1	S	S	57.9	47.4	S	52.6	26.3	H	36.8	S	52.6
4	68.4	S	S	47.4	52.6	47.4	H	S	68.4	47.4	S	52.6
5	57.9	57.9	61.1	47.4	S	47.4	42.1	S	61.1	47.4	52.6	38.9
6	S	44.4	36.8	H	S	44.4	55.6	26.3	73.7	S	61.1	42.1
7	S	47.4	63.2	S	42.1	57.9	S	47.4	73.7	S	52.6	52.6
8	55.6	42.1	55.6	S	63.2	63.2	S	52.6	S	55.6	57.9	S
9	47.4	61.1	55.6	42.1	42.1	S	47.4	66.7	S	63.2	42.1	S
10	52.6	S	S	68.4	68.4	S	36.8	78.9	42.1	68.4	S	42.1
11	36.8	S	S	42.1	26.3	26.3	47.4	S	72.2	52.6	S	57.9
12	47.4	63.2	63.2	42.1	S	63.2	42.1	S	42.1	47.4	52.6	36.8
13	S	55.6	42.1	47.4	S	31.6	47.4	63.2	36.8	S	57.9	68.4
14	S	31.6	57.9	S	52.6	47.4	S	47.4	52.6	S	63.2	31.6
15	H	55.6	52.6	S	31.6	42.1	S	47.4	S	55.6	55.6	S
16	47.4	63.2	38.9	52.6	47.4	S	73.7	63.2	S	33.3	47.4	S
17	61.1	S	S	55.6	52.6	S	47.4	44.4	47.4	55.6	S	57.9
18	57.9	S	S	36.8	63.2	42.1	36.8	S	47.4	47.4	S	36.8
19	47.4	H	66.7	57.9	S	52.6	73.7	S	57.9	63.2	57.9	63.2
20	S	55.6	68.4	33.3	S	47.4	36.8	52.6	63.2	S	47.4	61.1
21	S	47.4	55.6	S	31.6	10.5	S	57.9	61.1	S	42.1	42.1
22	57.9	73.7	61.1	S	47.4	47.4	S	42.1	S	47.4	H	S
23	52.6	36.8	42.1	57.9	42.1	S	36.8	63.2	S	63.2	63.2	S
24	38.9	S	S	72.2	47.4	S	42.1	42.1	31.6	44.4	S	42.1
25	68.4	S	S	36.8	47.4	47.4	47.4	S	44.4	47.4	S	H
26	36.8	47.4	52.6	47.4	S	47.4	31.6	S	47.4	42.1	57.9	72.2
27	S	42.1	33.3	47.4	S	47.4	47.4	61.1	52.6	S	47.4	44.4
28	S	57.9	47.4	S	H	38.9	S	36.8	52.6	S	55.6	15.8
29	47.4		42.1	S	31.6	52.6	S	47.4	S	31.6	72.2	S
30	36.8		33.3	36.8	47.4	S	61.1	36.8	S	38.9	63.2	S
31	31.6		S		77.8		47.4	68.4		31.6		26.3

SOYBEANS WIDELY TRADED CONTRACT MONTHLY SETTLEMENTS

Contract Month Date	Mar (H) JAN	May (K) FEB	Jul (N) MAR	Jul (N) APR	Jul (N) MAY	Nov (X) JUN	Nov (X) JUL	Nov (X) AUG	Nov (X) SEP	Jan (F) OCT	Jan (F) NOV	Mar (H) DEC
1987	500 1/4	483	495 3/4	537	548 3/4	550 1/2	525 3/4	504 1/4	532	541 1/2	605 1/4	614 3/4
1988	609 1/2	642 1/2	660 1/2	698 1/2	798	971 1/2	787 1/2	867 1/2	813	789 1/4	763 3/4	819 1/4
1989	772 3/4	773 1/2	748	729 1/2	714	653 1/2	578 3/4	587 1/2	568	572 1/4	582 3/4	582 1/4
1990	561	580 3/4	608 1/4	648 1/2	607 1/4	650 1/2	610	613 3/4	617 1/2	609 1/4	589 1/2	574 3/4
1991	566 3/4	588	587 1/4	589 1/2	581 3/4	536 3/4	600 1/2	590 1/2	587	567	557	557
1992	572	589 1/4	596 1/2	580 1/4	614	618 3/4	552	541	540 3/4	552 3/4	563 3/4	574 1/4
1993	574	580	593 1/2	591 1/4	608 1/2	658 1/2	688	663 1/2	629 3/4	629 1/2	671 1/2	712 1/2
1994	686 3/4	683 3/4	683 1/2	676 1/2	701	628 3/4	565 3/4	573 3/4	536	554	563 1/2	561 1/2
1995	547 1/2	564 3/4	584 1/4	580	580 3/4	595	614	623	646	684 1/2	686 1/4	744 3/4
1996	738 3/4	745	758 1/4	795	788 1/4	746 1/4	733	794 1/2	758	669	712 3/4	687 3/4
1997	738 1/4	793 1/4	858	887	880 1/2	617 1/2	658	625 1/2	621 1/2	696 1/4	718 1/4	676 1/4
1998	672 3/4	658 1/4	647	638 1/2	618 1/2	616 3/4	560 3/4	511 1/2	520 3/4	568 1/4	593 1/2	541 1/4
1999	506 3/4	458	493 1/4	486 1/2	461 3/4	460 3/4	433 1/4	483	491 1/4	482 3/4	476 1/4	469 3/4
2000	508	511	557 1/2	539 1/4	517 1/2	476 3/4	454	505	490 1/2	470 1/4	506	509 3/4
2001	459 1/2	455 3/4	432 1/2	438	451	464	512 1/2	486	451 1/4	436 3/4	444 1/2	422 1/4
2002	430 1/4	440 1/4	480 1/2	466 3/4	508 3/4	506 3/4	536 1/2	544 3/4	545 3/4	566 1/2	578 3/4	565
2003	564	575	573 1/4	627 1/4	624 1/2	552 1/2	509	589	677 1/4	797 3/4	756 1/4	794
2004	819 1/2	937 1/2	995	1013	814	669	569	627 1/4	527	533 1/2	534 3/4	547 1/4
2005	514 3/4	622	636	626 1/4	680 1/4	666 1/4	686 3/4	598 3/4	573 1/4	576	558	613 1/2
2006	594 1/4	594	585 1/2									

SOYBEANS WIDELY TRADED CONTRACT MONTHLY CHANGES

Contract Month	Mar (H)	May (K)	Jul (N)	Jul (N)	Jul (N)	Nov (X)	Nov (X)	Nov (X)	Nov (X)	Jan (F)	Jan (F)	Mar (H)
Date	JAN	FEB	MAR	APR	MAY	JUN	JUL	AUG	SEP	OCT	NOV	DEC
1987	-12 1/2	1/2	-17 1/2	14 3/4	41 1/4	23	-6	-24 3/4	-21 1/2	28	3 1/4	66 1/4
1988	1 1/2	-5 1/2	23 3/4	11 1/4	38	102 1/2	155 1/2	-184	80	-51	-34 1/4	-25 3/4
1989	43 3/4	-42 3/4	-11 1/2	-33	-18 1/2	-77 1/4	25	-74 3/4	8 3/4	-17 1/4	-8 1/4	10
1990	-13	-22 1/2	7	15 3/4	40 1/4	-37 3/4	28 1/4	-40 1/2	3 3/4	5 1/2	-23 1/2	-20
1991	-29 3/4	-8 1/4	7	-13 1/4	2 1/4	-11 3/4	-57 3/4	63 3/4	-10	-2 3/4	-31	-11 1/4
1992	-6 3/4	14 1/4	12 1/2	-1 3/4	-16 1/4	32 3/4	-8 1/2	-66 3/4	-11	- 3/4	5 1/4	10 1/2
1993	5	-4 3/4	4 3/4	9	-2 1/4	11 1/4	52	29 1/2	-24 1/2	-32 3/4	-7	41 3/4
1994	34 1/2	-25 3/4	-3 1/2	-3 1/4	-7	42 3/4	-45	-63	8	-35 3/4	7 3/4	9
1995	-11 1/2	-14 3/4	12 1/4	9 3/4	-4 1/4	3	-4 1/2	19	9	24	28	1 3/4
1996	50 1/4	-2	3 1/2	4 1/4	36 3/4	-16	-5 1/4	-13 1/4	61 1/2	-34 1/2	-98	34
1997	-19 3/4	51	55 3/4	66	29	-12 3/4	-67 1/4	40 1/2	-32 1/2	-1 3/4	70 1/2	19 1/4
1998	-44 3/4	-8 1/4	-14 1/2	-16 3/4	-8 1/2	-27 1/4	27	-56	-49 1/4	10 3/4	36 3/4	26 1/4
1999	-61 3/4	-35 1/4	-50	27	-6 3/4	-26 1/4	-13 1/4	-27 1/2	49 3/4	8 1/4	-18	-7 1/2
2000	-13 1/2	40	-5 3/4	36 3/4	-18 1/4	-26	-48 3/4	-22 3/4	51	-14	-30 3/4	34 1/4
2001	-3 1/4	-50 3/4	-10 3/4	-30 1/4	5 1/2	-2 1/4	31 3/4	48 1/2	-26 1/2	-31 3/4	-24 1/4	5 1/2
2002	-25	7 3/4	8	35 1/4	-13 3/4	30	19 3/4	29 3/4	8 1/4	4 3/4	15 3/4	11 3/4
2003	-9	2 1/4	16 1/4	-1	54	13 1/4	-7 3/4	-43 1/2	80	89 1/4	118	-30
2004	40	31 3/4	107	75	18	-60 1/4	-15 1/2	-100	58 1/4	-98 1/4	-1 1/4	-4 1/4
2005	11 1/4	-40 3/4	107 1/2	11	-9 3/4	61	-15 3/4	20 1/2	-88	-22 1/2	-7 1/4	-18
2006	47 1/4	-12 3/4	-19 1/4									
# Up	5	11	12	9	9	7	7	11	7	8	13	8
# Down	14	8	7	10	10	12	12	8	12	11	6	11
Total Change	-130 3/4	243 1/4	216 2/4	159 3/4	-49 2/4	44	-465 1/4	155	-203 2/4	1 3/4	165 1/4	-4 2/4
AVG. Change	-7	12 3/4	11 2/4	8 2/4	-2 2/4	2 1/4	-24 2/4	8 1/4	-10 3/4	0	8 3/4	- 1/4
AVG. Up	27 2/4	33 1/4	26 1/4	29 2/4	33	48 2/4	36	38	23	35 3/4	22	29 1/4
AVG. Down	-19 1/4	-15 1/4	-14 1/4	-10 2/4	-34 2/4	-24 2/4	-59 3/4	-33	-30 2/4	-25 3/4	-20 1/4	-21 3/4

SOYBEANS WIDELY TRADED CONTRACT PERFORMANCE

PERFORMANCE STATISTICS BASED ON MONTHLY PERFORMANCE AND FOLLOWING-MONTH PERFORMANCE

(Based on monthly trends from **January 1987 – December 2005** using the aforementioned contracts)

Contract	Mar (H)	May (K)	Jul (N)	Jul (N)	Jul (N)	Nov (X)	Nov (X)	Nov (X)	Nov (X)	Jan (F)	Jan (F)	Mar (H)
Month	JAN	FEB	MAR	APR	MAY	JUN	JUL	AUG	SEP	OCT	NOV	DEC
Yrs Tested	19	19	19	19	19	19	19	19	19	19	19	19
# Up	5	11	12	9	9	7	7	11	7	8	13	8
# Down	14	8	7	10	10	12	12	8	12	11	6	11
Total Gain (Loss)	-130 3/4	243 1/4	216 2/4	159 3/4	-49 2/4	44	-465 1/4	155	-203 2/4	1 3/4	165 1/4	-4 2/4
Average Gain (Loss)	-7	12 3/4	11 2/4	8 2/4	-2 2/4	2 1/4	-24 2/4	8 1/4	-10 3/4	0	8 3/4	- 1/4

If Previous Month is Up, then FOLLOWING Month had the following Characteristics

Contract	Mar (H)	May (K)	Jul (N)	Jul (N)	Jul (N)	Nov (X)	Nov (X)	Nov (X)	Jan (F)	Jan (F)	Jan (F)	Mar (H)
Month	FEB	MAR	APR	MAY	JUN	JUL	AUG	SEP	OCT	NOV	DEC	JAN
Yrs Tested	7	12	12	9	9	7	7	11	7	8	12	8
# Up	5	9	6	3	3	3	2	5	5	7	4	1
# Down	2	3	6	6	6	4	5	6	2	1	8	7
% Closing Higher	71.4	75.0	50.0	33.3	33.3	42.9	28.6	45.5	71.4	87.5	33.3	12.5
Total Gain (Loss)	180	221 1/4	148 1/4	-139 3/4	139 3/4	-247 2/4	-164 1/4	-138 3/4	160 1/4	104	-96 3/4	-110
Average Gain (Loss)	25 3/4	18 2/4	12 1/4	-15 2/4	15 2/4	-35 1/4	-23 2/4	-12 2/4	23	13	-8	-13 3/4
# Higher Highs	4	10	10	6	9	5	3	9	4	8	6	7
# Lower Lows	1	2	1	2	1	4	2	3	3	0	5	2

If Previous Month is Down, then FOLLOWING Month had the following Characteristics

Contract	Mar (H)	May (K)	Jul (N)	Jul (N)	Jul (N)	Nov (X)	Nov (X)	Nov (X)	Jan (F)	Jan (F)	Jan (F)	Mar (H)
Month	FEB	MAR	APR	MAY	JUN	JUL	AUG	SEP	OCT	NOV	DEC	JAN
Yrs Tested	12	7	7	10	10	12	12	8	12	11	7	11
# Up	6	3	3	6	4	4	9	2	3	6	4	4
# Down	6	4	4	4	6	8	3	6	9	5	3	7
% Closing Lower	50.0	57.1	57.1	40.0	60.0	66.7	25.0	75.0	75.0	45.5	42.9	63.6
Total Gain (Loss)	63 1/4	-4 3/4	11 2/4	90 1/4	-95 3/4	-217 3/4	319 1/4	-64 3/4	-158 2/4	61 1/4	92 1/4	-20 3/4
Average Gain (Loss)	5 1/4	- 3/4	1 3/4	9	-9 2/4	-18 1/4	26 2/4	-8	-13 1/4	5 2/4	13 1/4	-2
# Higher Highs	3	3	1	8	2	3	3	2	1	3	2	5
# Lower Lows	10	3	5	6	9	10	7	4	11	7	3	9

Key Points Regarding Monthly Performance from 1987 – 2005

- January down 14 of 19
- February rallies continue through March (9 of 12)
- July breaks reversed in August (9 of 12)
- September breaks continue through October (9 of 12)

WINTER WHEAT'S RISK PREMIUMS

The main variety of Wheat grown throughout the world is winter wheat. This variety of wheat is aptly named because it is planted in the fall, lies dormant during the winter, and is harvested in the late spring or early summer.

Unlike the other grains, the United States is not a major producer of Wheat (ranked 5th worldwide). However, the United States is still a net exporter.

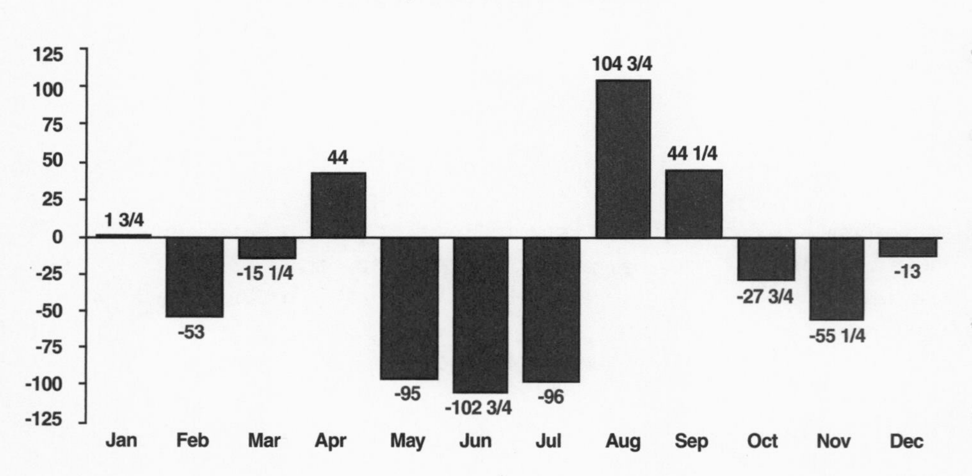

The major periods of risk for the winter wheat crop are planting and harvest. Planting typically begins in October, and as such, the market builds a premium into prices in the months preceding in anticipation. August and September are the two strongest months historically.

Following planting, prices tend to decline as the market is flush with supply from the previous harvest and the crop is dormant. This is accelerated at the beginning of the calendar year, as crop sales (marketings) increase and transportation problems weigh on prices. Fifteen times during the 1987-to-2006 period, March CBOT Wheat futures have declined in February, making it the only member of the grain futures to suffer from the fabled "February Break."

Harvest usually begins in May. Hence, April tends towards strength as supplies are low, the crop is heading, and the market worries about harvest. The height of harvest is June, which by coincidence also happens to be the worst-performing month. As harvest draws to a close, prices begin to recover and start anticipating planting woes and future supply concerns, thus beginning the cycle fresh again.

CBOT WHEAT FUTURES MARKET PROBABILITY CALENDAR FOR 2007

THE % CHANGE OF THE MARKET RISING ON ANY TRADING DAY OF THE YEAR

(Based on the number of times the widely traded contract rose on a particular trading day during **January 1987-December 2005**)

Contract	Mar (H)	May (K)	Jul (N)	Jul (N)	Jul (N)	Sep (U)	Sep (U)	Dec (Z)	Dec (Z)	Dec (Z)	Mar (H)	Mar (H)
Date	**Jan**	**Feb**	**Mar**	**Apr**	**May**	**Jun**	**Jul**	**Aug**	**Sep**	**Oct**	**Nov**	**Dec**
1	H	72.2	44.4	S	72.2	63.2	S	52.6	S	57.9	47.4	S
2	52.6	68.4	61.1	31.6	52.6	S	42.1	63.2	S	42.1	61.1	S
3	63.2	S	S	52.6	52.6	S	42.1	52.6	H	57.9	S	61.1
4	63.2	S	S	66.7	57.9	47.4	H	S	77.8	36.8	S	61.1
5	66.7	61.1	36.8	57.9	S	63.2	44.4	S	47.4	47.4	52.6	31.6
6	S	42.1	16.7	H	S	61.1	52.6	27.8	68.4	S	36.8	57.9
7	S	42.1	78.9	S	63.2	57.9	S	63.2	42.1	S	61.1	57.9
8	68.4	57.9	52.6	S	61.1	52.6	S	57.9	S	73.7	72.2	S
9	61.1	66.7	52.6	47.4	42.1	S	42.1	57.9	S	44.4	57.9	S
10	33.3	S	S	47.4	55.6	S	42.1	57.9	42.1	47.4	S	47.4
11	52.6	S	S	42.1	47.4	42.1	47.4	S	57.9	42.1	S	63.2
12	57.9	57.9	33.3	38.9	S	57.9	47.4	S	44.4	63.2	38.9	36.8
13	S	57.9	42.1	47.4	S	57.9	57.9	57.9	44.4	S	42.1	52.6
14	S	38.9	47.4	S	63.2	42.1	S	52.6	31.6	S	36.8	27.8
15	H	57.9	52.6	S	27.8	27.8	S	52.6	S	42.1	38.9	S
16	57.9	57.9	44.4	57.9	36.8	S	57.9	68.4	S	57.9	47.4	S
17	36.8	S	S	57.9	63.2	S	52.6	47.4	33.3	42.1	S	63.2
18	47.4	S	S	38.9	31.6	21.1	42.1	S	47.4	63.2	S	44.4
19	57.9	H	52.6	68.4	S	61.1	57.9	S	73.7	36.8	42.1	66.7
20	S	44.4	73.7	42.1	S	68.4	68.4	38.9	61.1	S	66.7	61.1
21	S	57.9	52.6	S	42.1	26.3	S	52.6	42.1	S	55.6	36.8
22	66.7	52.6	52.6	S	47.4	47.4	S	42.1	S	57.9	H	S
23	36.8	47.4	55.6	31.6	47.4	S	47.4	72.2	S	47.4	36.8	S
24	42.1	S	S	36.8	36.8	S	57.9	52.6	61.1	42.1	S	47.4
25	55.6	S	S	36.8	44.4	61.1	47.4	S	63.2	42.1	S	H
26	44.4	61.1	22.2	66.7	S	57.9	38.9	S	47.4	42.1	36.8	73.7
27	S	31.6	52.6	36.8	S	42.1	42.1	52.6	57.9	S	47.4	38.9
28	S	44.4	47.4	S	H	31.6	S	26.3	72.2	S	52.6	26.3
29	47.4		52.6	S	42.1	42.1	S	44.4	S	42.1	38.9	S
30	44.4		66.7	33.3	22.2	S	47.4	47.4	S	36.8	36.8	S
31	52.6		S		63.2		47.4	77.8		42.1		42.1

CBOT WHEAT WIDELY TRADED CONTRACT MONTHLY SETTLEMENTS

Contract Month Date	Mar (H) JAN	May (K) FEB	Jul (N) MAR	Jul (N) APR	Jul (N) MAY	Sep (U) JUN	Sep (U) JUL	Dec (Z) AUG	Dec (Z) SEP	Dec (Z) OCT	Mar (H) NOV	Mar (H) DEC
1987	288 1/4	280	269	274	274 1/4	263 1/4	261 1/4	286 3/4	289 1/4	296 1/2	318 1/4	310 3/4
1988	326	323 1/2	307	315 1/2	351 1/2	395 1/2	368 1/4	415 3/4	414 3/4	415 3/4	427 1/2	440
1989	440 1/2	434 3/4	387 1/2	405	387 1/2	404 3/4	384 1/2	399 1/4	407 1/4	394 1/2	407 3/4	409 1/4
1990	375 3/4	362 1/4	337 3/4	345 3/4	333 3/4	331	288 1/4	277 1/2	277 3/4	262	261 3/4	260 1/2
1991	263	269 1/2	296	283 1/4	287	275	294	321	332 1/2	363 1/2	366	404 3/4
1992	440 1/4	400	361	353 1/2	349 1/2	352 1/2	317 1/4	333	350 1/4	354 1/2	371	353 3/4
1993	380	333 1/4	310 1/4	301 1/4	288 1/4	287 1/4	304	315 1/2	318 3/4	335 1/2	350 1/2	378 1/4
1994	371 3/4	345 1/4	323 1/4	330 3/4	327 1/2	322 1/4	330 1/2	379 1/4	403 1/2	384 1/2	384 1/2	401 1/2
1995	373 1/2	347 1/4	339	351	373 1/4	446	464 1/4	462 3/4	492 1/4	497 3/4	495	512 1/4
1996	519 1/2	501 1/2	470 3/4	567	528 3/4	482 1/2	440	453 1/4	436	371 1/4	377 1/2	381 1/4
1997	359 3/4	375 1/4	394	433 1/2	360 1/2	332 1/4	362	394	354 1/4	360 1/2	357 3/4	325 3/4
1998	337 1/4	338 1/4	329 1/2	301 1/4	284 1/4	287 1/2	252 1/2	254	269 1/4	294 1/4	294 1/4	276 1/4
1999	275 1/2	248 1/2	290 3/4	268	252 1/4	264 1/4	263 3/4	282 1/4	275 3/4	255 3/4	249 1/2	248 1/2
2000	256 1/4	259	274 1/4	254 3/4	274 3/4	271 1/4	246 1/4	268 1/4	265	254 3/4	273 3/4	279 1/2
2001	273	276 3/4	266 1/2	283 1/4	267	258	278 1/2	289	270 3/4	293	289 1/2	289
2002	286	276	289	268 3/4	282 1/4	313	334	370	396 1/2	402 1/4	379 3/4	325
2003	320 1/2	310 1/4	289	282 3/4	324 1/4	310 1/2	348 1/2	381	360 1/4	369 1/2	406 3/4	377
2004	389	390 3/4	415 3/4	390	362	345 1/2	312 1/4	322 3/4	306 3/4	316 1/2	301 1/4	307 1/2
2005	291	345 1/4	341	326	331 3/4	331 1/2	327 3/4	317 1/2	346 1/4	317	320 3/4	339 1/4
2006	343 1/4	381	361 1/2									

CBOT WHEAT WIDELY TRADED CONTRACT MONTHLY CHANGES

Contract Month	Mar (H)	May (K)	Jul (N)	Jul (N)	Jul (N)	Sep (U)	Sep (U)	Dec (Z)	Dec (Z)	Dec (Z)	Mar (H)	Mar (H)
Date	**JAN**	**FEB**	**MAR**	**APR**	**MAY**	**JUN**	**JUL**	**AUG**	**SEP**	**OCT**	**NOV**	**DEC**
1987	-11 3/4	10 1/2	4 3/4	11 1/4	5	2 1/4	-15 1/2	4 1/4	11 1/2	2 1/2	11	10
1988	-7 1/2	19 1/2	15 3/4	-21 1/4	8 1/2	37 3/4	34	-25 1/2	35 1/4	-1	2 3/4	3 3/4
1989	12 1/2	9	-8 1/2	-18 3/4	17 1/2	-19 1/2	11 1/2	-20	2 1/2	8	-4	9 1/2
1990	1 1/2	-25	-2 1/2	-7 1/4	8	-12	-8 3/4	-40 1/2	-27 1/2	1/4	-14 3/4	-14 3/4
1991	-1 1/4	4 3/4	0	16	-12 3/4	1 1/2	-19	17 1/2	12 3/4	11 1/2	25 1/2	4 1/4
1992	38 3/4	40 1/2	-2	-24 3/4	-7 1/2	-3 1/4	-1 3/4	-35 3/4	5 1/2	17 1/4	- 1/4	21 1/2
1993	-17 1/4	14 1/2	-14	-4 1/2	-9	-12 1/2	-4	13 3/4	3	3 1/4	9	18 3/4
1994	27 3/4	-6 1/4	-7 1/4	-11 3/4	7 1/2	- 1/2	-11 1/2	10	35	24 1/4	-16	-10 1/2
1995	17	-18	-5 3/4	7 1/2	12	22 1/2	67	21	-8 3/4	29 1/2	5 1/4	-10 1/2
1996	17 1/4	6 1/2	14 3/4	9	96 1/4	-26 1/4	-49 1/4	-47 1/2	8 1/2	-17 1/4	-54	9
1997	3 3/4	-12 1/2	27	29 1/2	39 1/2	-71 1/4	-35 1/4	31 1/4	17 1/2	-39 3/4	5 1/4	-16 1/4
1998	-32	13 3/4	-6 1/4	-18 1/2	-28 1/4	-16 3/4	-7	-35	-14 1/4	15 1/4	24 1/4	-15 1/4
1999	-18	- 3/4	-36	31 3/4	-22 3/4	-15 1/4	1 3/4	1/4	2 1/2	-6 1/2	-20 1/2	-21 1/2
2000	-1	10	-7 1/4	4	-19 1/2	20 1/4	-15 1/2	-24 1/2	4 1/4	-3 1/4	-9 1/4	3/4
2001	5 3/4	-5 1/4	-8	-21 1/4	16 3/4	-16 1/2	-19	19 1/2	-3 1/2	-18 1/4	19	-11 1/4
2002	- 1/2	3 3/4	-10 3/4	6 1/2	-20 1/4	13	24 1/2	20 1/2	26	26 1/2	- 1/4	-20
2003	-54 3/4	-4 1/2	-5 3/4	-15 3/4	-6 1/4	41 3/4	-19 1/2	38 1/2	22	-20 3/4	10 3/4	26 1/2
2004	-29 3/4	16 3/4	3 1/2	23 1/2	-25 3/4	-25 1/2	-24 3/4	-31 3/4	-2 3/4	-16	9 3/4	-27 1/4
2005	6 1/4	-15 1/2	46	-10 1/2	-15	7 3/4	-10 3/4	-1 3/4	-24 3/4	28 3/4	-28 3/4	-12
2006	18 1/2	26 1/2	-32									
# Up	10	4	9	9	8	5	8	13	11	12	9	10
# Down	9	15	10	10	11	14	11	6	8	7	10	9
Total Change	1 3/4	-53	-15 1/4	44	-95	-102 3/4	-96	104 3/4	44 1/4	-27 3/4	-55 1/4	-13
AVG. Change	0	-2 3/4	- 3/4	2 1/4	-5	-5 2/4	-5	5 2/4	2 1/4	-1 2/4	-3	- 3/4
AVG. Up	12 1/4	24 2/4	15 2/4	23 2/4	18	27 3/4	21 2/4	14 1/4	15 1/4	12	11 2/4	15
AVG. Down	-13 2/4	-10	-15 2/4	-16 3/4	-21 3/4	-17 1/4	-24 1/4	-13 2/4	-15 1/4	-24 2/4	-16	-18

CBOT WHEAT WIDELY TRADED CONTRACT PERFORMANCE

PERFORMANCE STATISTICS BASED ON MONTHLY PERFORMANCE AND FOLLOWING-MONTH PERFORMANCE

(Based on monthly trends from **January 1987 – December 2005** using the aforementioned contracts)

Contract	Mar (H)	May (K)	Jul (N)	Jul (N)	Jul (N)	Sep (U)	Sep (U)	Dec (Z)	Dec (Z)	Dec (Z)	Mar (H)	Mar (H)
Month	JAN	FEB	MAR	APR	MAY	JUN	JUL	AUG	SEP	OCT	NOV	DEC
Yrs Tested	19	19	19	19	19	19	19	19	19	19	19	19
# Up	10	4	9	9	8	5	8	13	11	12	9	10
# Down	9	15	10	10	11	14	11	6	8	7	10	9
Total Gain (Loss)	1 3/4	-53	-15 1/4	44	-95	-102 3/4	-96	104 3/4	44 1/4	-27 3/4	-55 1/4	-13
Average Gain (Loss)	0	-2 3/4	- 3/4	2 1/4	-5	-5 2/4	-5	5 2/4	2 1/4	-1 2/4	-3	- 3/4

If Previous Month is Up, then FOLLOWING Month had the following Characteristics

Contract	Mar (H)	May (K)	Jul (N)	Jul (N)	Jul (N)	Sep (U)	Sep (U)	Dec (Z)	Dec (Z)	Dec (Z)	Mar (H)	Mar (H)
Month	FEB	MAR	APR	MAY	JUN	JUL	AUG	SEP	OCT	NOV	DEC	JAN
Yrs Tested	10	6	9	9	8	5	10	13	11	10	9	10
# Up	1	4	4	3	3	2	8	7	7	5	6	4
# Down	9	2	5	6	5	3	2	6	4	5	3	6
% Closing Higher	18.2	66.7	44.4	33.3	37.5	40.0	80.0	53.8	63.6	50.0	66.7	40.0
Total Gain (Loss)	-57 3/4	41 2/4	51 3/4	-101 3/4	45 1/4	-8 3/4	118	4 3/4	18 3/4	-17 1/4	35 2/4	-65 1/4
Average Gain (Loss)	-5 1/4	7	5 3/4	-11 1/4	5 3/4	-1 3/4	11 3/4	1/4	1 3/4	-1 3/4	4	-6 2/4
# Higher Highs	6	5	6	6	5	3	7	7	8	3	7	7
# Lower Lows	4	3	4	4	2	3	1	7	3	5	4	0

If Previous Month is Down, then FOLLOWING Month had the following Characteristics

Contract	Mar (H)	May (K)	Jul (N)	Jul (N)	Jul (N)	Sep (U)	Sep (U)	Dec (Z)	Dec (Z)	Dec (Z)	Mar (H)	Mar (H)
Month	FEB	MAR	APR	MAY	JUN	JUL	AUG	SEP	OCT	NOV	DEC	JAN
Yrs Tested	8	12	10	10	11	14	9	6	8	9	10	9
# Up	2	4	5	5	2	6	5	4	5	4	4	6
# Down	6	8	5	5	9	8	4	2	3	5	6	3
% Closing Lower	75.0	66.7	50.0	50.0	81.8	57.1	44.4	33.3	37.5	55.6	60.0	33.3
Total Gain (Loss)	4 3/4	-72 3/4	-7 3/4	6 3/4	-148	-87 1/4	-13 1/4	39 2/4	-46 2/4	-38	-48 2/4	67
Average Gain (Loss)	2/4	-6	- 3/4	3/4	-13 2/4	-6 1/4	-1 2/4	6 2/4	-5 3/4	-4 1/4	-4 3/4	7 2/4
# Higher Highs	3	5	3	4	1	3	0	3	4	2	3	5
# Lower Lows	6	11	7	7	9	10	6	4	6	5	7	4

Key Points Regarding Monthly Performance from 1987 – 2005

- January rallies reversed in February (9 of 11)
- February down 15 of 19
- May weakness continues through June (9 of 11)
- June down 14 of 19
- July rallies continue through August (8 of 10)

THE THREE DESTRUCTIONS AND CORN PRICING

The United States is the world's largest producer of Corn, accounting for over 40% of world production. Like other annually produced commodities, prices reflect not only current supply and demand, but also future prospects as well. When the crop is at risk, prices tend to rise. The critical stages of development (planting, pollination, and harvest) are the strongest periods for Corn futures.

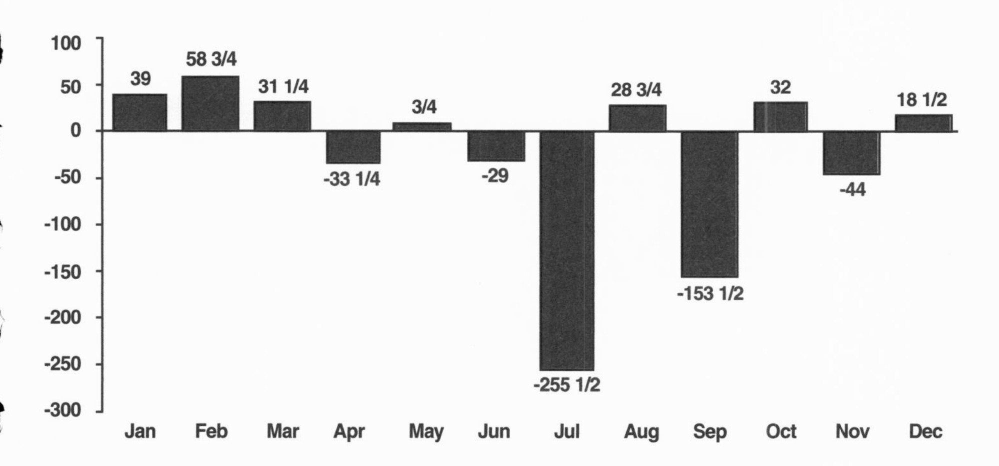

Corn planting typically begins in mid- to late April. The months prior to planting tend towards strength, with prices typically rallying. As planting begins, the market sighs in collective relief about the increasing likelihood of future supply, and prices break. Sixteen times during the 1987 to 2005 period, July Corn futures have declined in April as planting begins.

The formation of silk threads at the end of fledgling ears on the corn stalk indicate the beginning of pollination. Mid- to late June is the critical pollination period. Prior to pollination, future supply is not well-known and the market holds onto its risk premium in the form of high prices. Post-pollination prices usually break as future supply becomes more certain. This is evident by the fact that July is the worst month for Corn futures prices.

Prices usually set their lows in July or early August and then bounce back slightly in August before breaking in September in anticipation of harvest. Corn futures have declined in September 15 times during the 19-year period from 1987 to 2005. Harvest usually begins in October and runs through November; during which time, prices are typically flat.

CORN FUTURES MARKET PROBABILITY CALENDAR FOR 2007

THE % CHANGE OF THE MARKET RISING ON ANY TRADING DAY OF THE YEAR

(Based on the number of times the widely traded contract rose on a particular trading day during **January 1987-December 2005**)

Contract	May (K)	May (K)	Jul (N)	Jul (N)	Jul (N)	Sep (U)	Sep (U)	Dec (Z)	Dec (Z)	Dec (Z)	Mar (H)	Mar (H)
Date	**Jan**	**Feb**	**Mar**	**Apr**	**May**	**Jun**	**Jul**	**Aug**	**Sep**	**Oct**	**Nov**	**Dec**
1	H	33.3	68.4	S	63.2	77.8	S	47.4	S	31.6	42.1	S
2	55.6	55.6	72.2	47.4	68.4	S	61.1	66.7	S	55.6	52.6	S
3	38.9	S	S	68.4	57.9	S	63.2	47.4	H	42.1	S	47.4
4	57.9	S	S	72.2	47.4	44.4	H	S	68.4	44.4	S	52.6
5	89.5	57.9	38.9	38.9	S	68.4	52.6	S	52.6	68.4	44.4	27.8
6	S	31.6	44.4	H	S	36.8	26.3	26.3	57.9	S	31.6	61.1
7	S	52.6	55.6	S	47.4	52.6	S	47.4	52.6	S	52.6	42.1
8	61.1	55.6	44.4	S	55.6	57.9	S	55.6	S	52.6	57.9	S
9	47.4	72.2	68.4	55.6	26.3	S	31.6	73.7	S	44.4	44.4	S
10	47.4	S	S	55.6	66.7	S	31.6	57.9	47.4	61.1	S	38.9
11	38.9	S	S	57.9	47.4	27.8	42.1	S	63.2	63.2	S	61.1
12	47.4	66.7	42.1	47.4	S	52.6	52.6	S	36.8	57.9	47.4	44.4
13	S	61.1	47.4	47.4	S	44.4	42.1	52.6	47.4	S	66.7	61.1
14	S	36.8	61.1	S	55.6	47.4	S	47.4	27.8	S	38.9	52.6
15	H	61.1	36.8	S	47.4	52.6	S	52.6	S	42.1	38.9	S
16	61.1	66.7	44.4	47.4	52.6	S	57.9	52.6	S	38.9	26.3	S
17	68.4	S	S	52.6	55.6	S	36.8	57.9	31.6	42.1	S	63.2
18	52.6	S	S	31.6	47.4	31.6	36.8	S	42.1	57.9	S	42.1
19	47.4	H	47.4	63.2	S	61.1	57.9	S	44.4	27.8	66.7	57.9
20	S	44.4	77.8	31.6	S	55.6	33.3	27.8	57.9	S	52.6	38.9
21	S	52.6	42.1	S	33.3	31.6	S	38.9	63.2	S	26.3	47.4
22	44.4	44.4	47.4	S	44.4	44.4	S	47.4	S	47.4	H	S
23	31.6	47.4	44.4	42.1	42.1	S	27.8	52.6	S	47.4	44.4	S
24	61.1	S	S	61.1	44.4	S	36.8	47.4	27.8	33.3	S	47.4
25	66.7	S	S	31.6	36.8	47.4	63.2	S	44.4	42.1	S	H
26	55.6	66.7	38.9	52.6	S	47.4	31.6	S	47.4	42.1	47.4	66.7
27	S	33.3	33.3	61.1	S	42.1	42.1	52.6	55.6	S	52.6	61.1
28	S	47.4	63.2	S	H	44.4	S	26.3	47.4	S	27.8	38.9
29	44.4		47.4	S	42.1	61.1	S	42.1	S	44.4	33.3	S
30	38.9		38.9	47.4	33.3	S	47.4	38.9	S	27.8	47.4	S
31	33.3		S		77.8		33.3	68.4		38.9		26.3

CORN WIDELY TRADED CONTRACT MONTHLY SETTLEMENTS

Contract Month	May (K)	May (K)	Jul (N)	Jul (N)	Jul (N)	Sep (U)	Sep (U)	Dec (Z)	Dec (Z)	Dec (Z)	Mar (H)	Mar (H)
Date	JAN	FEB	MAR	APR	MAY	JUN	JUL	AUG	SEP	OCT	NOV	DEC
1987	163	153 3/4	165 3/4	184 1/4	188 3/4	186 1/2	163 1/2	166 1/2	179 3/4	179 1/2	196 1/2	184 3/4
1988	202 1/2	209 1/4	215 3/4	211 1/4	224 1/4	337 3/4	275	296 1/2	285 3/4	282 1/4	270 1/2	284 1/2
1989	281 1/2	278 1/2	271	270 1/2	260 3/4	255 1/2	222 1/2	236 3/4	233	237 1/2	241 3/4	239 3/4
1990	243 3/4	253 1/4	263 3/4	283	278	289 1/2	260 1/4	233 1/4	228	229 1/4	237 3/4	231 3/4
1991	252 1/2	251	259 1/2	254	245 3/4	224	258	254 3/4	249 1/4	251	247 1/2	251 1/2
1992	270 1/4	273 1/2	269 1/4	249 1/2	259 1/2	253 1/4	220 1/4	217 1/4	215 1/4	207 1/4	221 1/2	216 1/2
1993	222 1/4	219 1/4	235 3/4	232 1/2	224 1/2	229	235 3/4	237 1/2	244 3/4	257 3/4	285 1/2	306
1994	294 3/4	293 3/4	279 3/4	272	278 3/4	244 1/2	218 3/4	222 3/4	215 3/4	215 3/4	223	231
1995	236 3/4	242	255 3/4	255 1/4	266	278	281 3/4	293 3/4	311 3/4	332 1/2	337 3/4	369 1/4
1996	373	389 1/4	394	452	477 1/4	397 3/4	354 1/4	343 3/4	296 3/4	266	271	258 1/4
1997	268 3/4	295 1/4	310 1/4	293 1/4	270 3/4	238	265 1/2	269 1/4	257 3/4	279 3/4	280 3/4	265
1998	280 1/4	270 1/4	265 3/4	252 1/4	238 1/2	253 1/4	217 1/2	199 1/2	209	219	230	213 1/2
1999	220 1/4	210 1/4	231 1/2	218 3/4	219 1/2	216 1/4	203 1/4	219 1/4	208 1/4	199 1/2	200 1/2	204 1/2
2000	227 3/4	224	244 1/2	232	225	195 3/4	180 1/4	196 1/2	197 3/4	206	220 1/2	231 3/4
2001	217	222 1/2	212	207 1/2	192 3/4	197 1/4	218 3/4	232 1/4	214 1/2	205 1/2	220 1/2	209
2002	213	207 1/2	209	200 1/2	214	233	247 1/4	268	251 1/2	247 1/2	241 1/2	235 3/4
2003	240 1/4	233 1/4	237	231 1/4	244 1/4	223 3/4	206	241 3/4	220 1/4	247 1/4	248 3/4	246
2004	281 1/2	303	325 1/2	320 1/4	304	262 1/2	217 1/4	237 3/4	205 1/2	202 1/2	203 3/4	204 3/4
2005	204 1/2	222 3/4	221	213 1/2	222	222 1/4	236 1/2	216 1/2	205 1/2	196 1/4	201 3/4	215 3/4
2006	229	238 3/4	247 1/4									

CORN WIDELY TRADED CONTRACT MONTHLY CHANGES

Contract Month	May (K)	May (K)	Jul (N)	Jul (N)	Jul (N)	Sep (U)	Sep (U)	Dec (Z)	Dec (Z)	Dec (Z)	Mar (H)	Mar (H)
Date	JAN	FEB	MAR	APR	MAY	JUN	JUL	AUG	SEP	OCT	NOV	DEC
1987	-14 3/4	-4 1/2	-10 3/4	8 1/2	18 1/2	2 3/4	-1 1/2	-18	-7	13 1/4	-3 1/2	11 3/4
1988	-10 3/4	11 1/4	8	2 1/4	-4 1/2	15 1/2	104 1/2	-61 3/4	12 3/4	-10 3/4	-3 3/4	-16 3/4
1989	15 1/4	-8 1/4	-4	-10 3/4	- 1/2	-22 1/2	16	-32 1/4	16 1/4	-3 3/4	1/2	1/2
1990	1	-1 3/4	10	6	19 1/4	-3 3/4	16 3/4	-32 1/4	-22 1/4	-5 1/4	1 3/4	-1 1/2
1991	-5 3/4	13	1/4	3/4	-5 1/2	-6 1/4	-21	37 1/4	-8 1/2	-5 1/2	2	-11 3/4
1992	3 3/4	12 3/4	4 1/2	-10	-19 3/4	16	-10 3/4	-35 3/4	-5 1/2	-2	-6 1/2	3 3/4
1993	-5 1/2	-1 1/2	-4	10	-3 1/4	-7 1/4	- 1/4	3 1/2	-4 1/4	7 1/4	13 1/4	19 3/4
1994	20 3/4	-14 1/4	3/4	-16 3/4	-7 3/4	6 1/2	-28 1/4	-20	3/4	-7	1 1/2	-3 3/4
1995	8 3/4	-1 1/2	6	7 1/2	- 1/2	12 1/2	6 1/2	3/4	12 1/2	18	18 1/4	0
1996	32 3/4	1 1/2	14	12	58	41 1/2	-2 1/4	-41 1/2	24	-47	-31 1/2	-1 1/2
1997	-13 3/4	8 1/4	27 1/4	16 1/4	-17	-23 1/4	-18 1/4	29 1/2	1 1/2	-11 1/2	22 1/2	-8 1/2
1998	-15 1/2	8 1/4	-9	-11	-13 1/2	-15 1/2	10 1/2	-35 3/4	-24 1/4	9 1/2	8 1/2	1/4
1999	-16 3/4	- 1/2	-9 1/4	15 1/2	-12 3/4	1	-8	-11 3/4	4 3/4	-11	-9	-9 3/4
2000	3 3/4	16 1/2	-2 1/4	12 1/4	-12 1/2	-7 1/4	-37 1/4	-15 1/4	4 1/4	1 1/4	8 1/4	3
2001	11	-22 1/2	5 1/2	-18 1/2	-4 1/2	-15	-3 1/4	22	2	-17 3/4	-8 1/4	2 1/2
2002	-12 1/2	-2 1/2	-5 1/2	-5 1/4	-8 1/2	13 1/4	12 1/2	13	11 1/2	-16 1/2	-7	-10 1/2
2003	-3 1/2	1/2	-7 1/2	1 1/2	-5 3/4	11 3/4	-19 1/4	-11 3/4	29 3/4	-21 1/2	23 3/4	-3 3/4
2004	-3 1/4	32 3/4	22	19 3/4	-5 1/4	-19	-37 1/4	-41 1/2	12 1/4	-32 1/4	-3 1/4	-9 1/4
2005	1 3/4	-8 1/2	18	-8 3/4	-7 1/2	9 1/4	-8 1/2	16 1/2	-31 3/4	-11	-7 1/2	-8 1/2
2006	13 1/4	9 3/4	-1									
# Up	9	9	12	3	10	6	7	12	5	9	7	9
# Down	10	10	7	16	9	13	12	7	14	9	11	10
Total Change	39	58 3/4	31 1/4	-33 1/4	3/4	-29	-255 2/4	28 3/4	-153 2/4	32	-44	18 2/4
AVG. Change	2	3	1 3/4	-1 3/4	0	-1 2/4	-13 2/4	1 2/4	-8	1 3/4	-2 1/4	1
AVG. Up	11 3/4	12 2/4	9 1/4	32	10 2/4	27 3/4	17 2/4	11	9 3/4	12	6	12
AVG. Down	-6 2/4	-5 2/4	-11 2/4	-8	-11 3/4	-15	-31 2/4	-14 3/4	-14 2/4	-8 2/4	-7 3/4	-9

CORN WIDELY TRADED CONTRACT PERFORMANCE

PERFORMANCE STATISTICS BASED ON MONTHLY PERFORMANCE AND FOLLOWING-MONTH PERFORMANCE

(Based on monthly trends from **January 1987 – December 2005** using the aforementioned contracts)

Contract	May (K)	May (K)	Jul (N)	Jul (N)	Jul (N)	Sep (U)	Sep (U)	Dec (Z)	Dec (Z)	Dec (Z)	Mar (H)	Mar (H)
Month	JAN	FEB	MAR	APR	MAY	JUN	JUL	AUG	SEP	OCT	NOV	DEC
Yrs Tested	19	19	19	19	19	19	19	19	19	19	19	19
# Up	9	9	12	3	10	6	7	12	5	9	7	9
# Down	10	10	7	16	9	13	12	7	14	9	11	10
Total Gain (Loss)	39	58 3/4	31 1/4	-33 1/4	3/4	-29	-255 2/4	28 3/4	-153 2/4	32	-44	18 2/4
Average Gain (Loss)	2	3	1 3/4	-1 3/4	0	-1 2/4	-13 2/4	1 2/4	-8	1 3/4	-2 1/4	1

If Previous Month is Up, then FOLLOWING Month had the following Characteristics

Contract	May (K)	May (K)	Jul (N)	Jul (N)	Jul (N)	Sep (U)	Sep (U)	Dec (Z)	Dec (Z)	Dec (Z)	Mar (H)	Mar (H)
Month	FEB	MAR	APR	MAY	JUN	JUL	AUG	SEP	OCT	NOV	DEC	JAN
Yrs Tested	9	11	12	3	10	6	7	12	5	9	7	9
# Up	5	7	3	2	3	2	4	2	4	4	2	3
# Down	4	4	9	1	7	4	3	10	1	5	5	6
% Closing Higher	55.6	63.6	25.0	66.7	30.0	33.3	57.1	16.7	80.0	44.4	28.6	33.3
Total Gain (Loss)	52	10 2/4	28 3/4	24 3/4	45	-142 3/4	-17	-159 3/4	51 3/4	-5 3/4	-5 3/4	-26
Average Gain (Loss)	5 3/4	1	2 2/4	8 1/4	4 2/4	-23 3/4	-2 2/4	-13 1/4	10 1/4	- 2/4	-2 1/4	-3
# Higher Highs	5	10	10	3	8	4	3	5	5	4	3	8
# Lower Lows	0	3	1	0	4	3	3	6	0	3	4	2

If Previous Month is Down, then FOLLOWING Month had the following Characteristics

Contract	May (K)	May (K)	Jul (N)	Jul (N)	Jul (N)	Sep (U)	Sep (U)	Dec (Z)	Dec (Z)	Dec (Z)	Mar (H)	Mar (H)
Month	FEB	MAR	APR	MAY	JUN	JUL	AUG	SEP	OCT	NOV	DEC	JAN
Yrs Tested	10	8	7	16	9	13	12	7	13	9	11	10
# Up	4	5	0	8	3	5	8	3	5	3	6	6
# Down	6	3	7	8	6	8	4	4	8	6	5	4
% Closing Lower	60.0	37.5	100.0	50.0	66.7	61.5	33.3	57.1	61.5	66.7	45.5	40.0
Total Gain (Loss)	6 3/4	20 3/4	-62	-24	-74	-112 3/4	45 3/4	6 1/4	-19 3/4	-38 1/4	2	65
Average Gain (Loss)	3/4	2 2/4	-8 3/4	-1 2/4	-8 1/4	-8 3/4	3 3/4	1	-1 2/4	-4 1/4	1/4	6 2/4
# Higher Highs	3	4	0	6	1	6	2	2	3	2	3	5
# Lower Lows	8	4	7	14	9	10	7	5	11	9	8	8

Key Points Regarding Monthly Performance from 1987 – 2005

- March rallies reversed in April (9 of 12)
- April down 16 of 19
- May rallies reversed in June (7 of 10)
- August rallies reversed in September (10 of 12)

UNDERSTANDING PLACEMENTS AND SLAUGHTER PATTERNS IS CRITICAL IN THE CATTLE MARKET

Futures are traded on two types of Cattle: Live and Feeder. Feeder Cattle are younger, lighter Cattle (weighing between 600 and 800 lbs) which will be "placed" on feedlots. For the next 3 to 6 months, the Feeders are fattened up to "Live" weight. Live Cattle are slaughter-weight (900 to 1,400 lbs) animals ready to be processed into various cuts of beef.

Most calves are born in the spring, when weather is mild and grass is plentiful. Usually by summer, they are ready for feedlot placement. As feedlots have limited space, they tend to increase sales (marketings) in anticipation of new placements. The influx of new cattle onto feedlots and the sales of fattened (Live) cattle tends to influence prices.

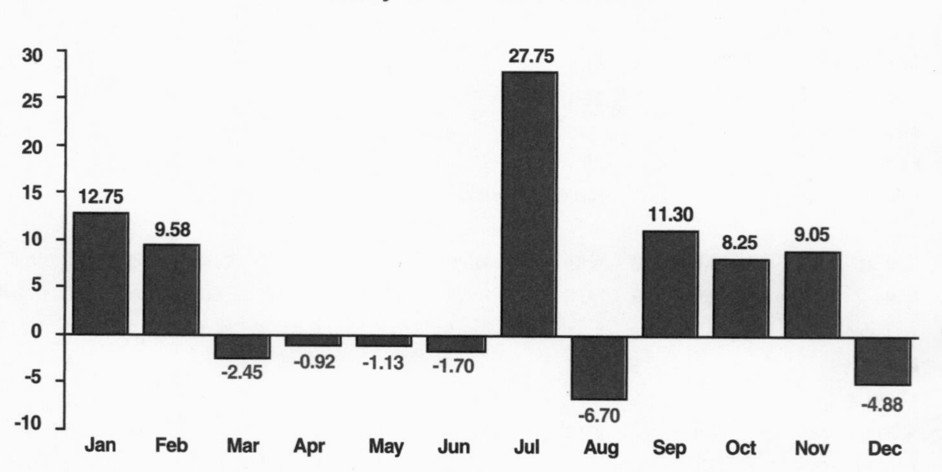

Cattle slaughter tends to increase from February to August and decrease September through January. Placements, on the other hand, tend to increase and decrease in November and December with the rest of the year generally at a flat level. When slaughter rates are low and placements are as well, months like January and February tend towards strength. Transportation is difficult at these times. Spring and summer tend towards increasing slaughter, and normal placements which pressure prices. However, July stands out as the market anticipates decreasing slaughter rates at a time when retail beef demand is high (the height of the BBQ season).

Decreasing slaughter rates and increasing placements work to support prices in the fall and winter as a lack of available supply supports prices.

LIVE CATTLE FUTURES MARKET PROBABILITY CALENDAR FOR 2007

THE % CHANGE OF THE MARKET RISING ON ANY TRADING DAY OF THE YEAR

(Based on the number of times the widely traded contract rose on a particular trading day during **January 1987-December 2005**)

Contract	Apr (J)	Apr (J)	Jun (M)	Jun (M)	Aug (Q)	Aug (Q)	Oct (V)	Oct (V)	Dec (Z)	Dec (Z)	Feb (G)	Feb (G)
Date	Jan	Feb	Mar	Apr	May	Jun	Jul	Aug	Sep	Oct	Nov	Dec
1	H	55.6	44.4	S	61.1	42.1	S	68.4	S	52.6	68.4	S
2	52.6	44.4	61.1	47.4	55.6	S	47.4	42.1	S	63.2	36.8	S
3	38.9	S	S	66.7	63.2	S	57.9	47.4	H	55.6	S	47.4
4	38.9	S	S	57.9	27.8	73.7	H	S	66.7	31.6	S	52.6
5	55.6	52.6	44.4	66.7	S	55.6	55.6	S	42.1	73.7	47.4	26.3
6	S	66.7	61.1	H	S	61.1	47.4	47.4	72.2	S	47.4	52.6
7	S	44.4	42.1	S	47.4	63.2	S	57.9	42.1	S	73.7	55.6
8	68.4	47.4	73.7	S	44.4	47.4	S	68.4	S	52.6	52.6	S
9	55.6	72.2	55.6	31.6	36.8	S	61.1	42.1	S	47.4	61.1	S
10	73.7	S	S	52.6	52.6	S	36.8	47.4	77.8	63.2	S	52.6
11	63.2	S	S	31.6	47.4	47.4	55.6	S	68.4	78.9	S	52.6
12	42.1	42.1	33.3	61.1	S	68.4	52.6	S	44.4	47.4	47.4	66.7
13	S	47.4	36.8	44.4	S	38.9	42.1	47.4	47.4	S	61.1	52.6
14	S	33.3	57.9	S	68.4	38.9	S	66.7	66.7	S	72.2	57.9
15	H	47.4	31.6	S	52.6	27.8	S	38.9	S	31.6	66.7	S
16	61.1	42.1	42.1	52.6	36.8	S	63.2	63.2	S	57.9	44.4	S
17	47.4	S	S	44.4	68.4	S	47.4	47.4	52.6	31.6	S	63.2
18	44.4	S	S	47.4	52.6	33.3	47.4	S	38.9	47.4	S	55.6
19	42.1	H	47.4	55.6	S	42.1	63.2	S	36.8	47.4	61.1	52.6
20	S	47.4	63.2	47.4	S	38.9	47.4	47.4	57.9	S	52.6	38.9
21	S	66.7	57.9	S	52.6	42.1	S	27.8	33.3	S	57.9	84.2
22	26.3	61.1	52.6	S	31.6	52.6	S	31.6	S	66.7	H	S
23	38.9	52.6	63.2	47.4	66.7	S	47.4	42.1	S	36.8	47.4	S
24	47.4	S	S	47.4	57.9	S	47.4	36.8	44.4	66.7	S	66.7
25	63.2	S	S	57.9	38.9	47.4	61.1	S	52.6	63.2	S	H
26	47.4	61.1	38.9	52.6	S	66.7	36.8	S	52.6	47.4	61.1	73.7
27	S	36.8	38.9	72.2	S	47.4	68.4	33.3	44.4	S	57.9	36.8
28	S	42.1	47.4	S	H	63.2	S	63.2	44.4	S	36.8	47.4
29	47.4		57.9	S	55.6	47.4	S	52.6	S	33.3	47.4	S
30	36.8		52.6	47.4	15.8	S	57.9	47.4	S	44.4	47.4	S
31	42.1		S		42.1		47.4	66.7		57.9		61.1

LIVE CATTLE WIDELY TRADED CONTRACT MONTHLY SETTLEMENTS

Contract Month	Apr (J)	Apr (J)	Jun (M)	Jun (M)	Aug (Q)	Aug (Q)	Oct (V)	Oct (V)	Dec (Z)	Dec (Z)	Feb (G)	Feb (G)
Date	**JAN**	**FEB**	**MAR**	**APR**	**MAY**	**JUN**	**JUL**	**AUG**	**SEP**	**OCT**	**NOV**	**DEC**
1987	62.88	64.98	63.43	67.20	62.40	63.30	62.78	66.05	66.60	62.40	61.73	63.13
1988	67.80	71.50	70.88	70.90	67.83	64.60	69.10	71.78	73.78	74.18	72.63	73.95
1989	76.43	78.05	73.03	71.45	66.95	70.15	75.53	73.75	74.33	74.45	74.10	77.38
1990	76.03	75.45	72.93	72.98	73.10	73.08	78.98	76.33	76.45	77.45	75.15	77.20
1991	77.53	80.23	77.13	76.10	73.73	72.23	73.20	70.05	76.78	73.50	74.73	72.40
1992	77.15	77.40	74.78	73.10	69.48	72.43	73.63	73.75	73.65	73.78	74.15	77.13
1993	76.85	80.23	76.25	76.78	73.38	75.05	75.20	75.15	74.13	74.05	72.50	73.45
1994	76.45	77.10	74.28	71.30	65.75	64.15	71.73	70.85	68.50	70.00	67.25	72.68
1995	74.15	74.28	61.70	62.95	59.70	62.80	65.88	63.33	66.65	68.35	67.63	66.43
1996	63.85	63.93	62.48	57.35	64.53	65.83	68.55	72.23	68.15	66.68	63.68	64.98
1997	66.83	69.63	65.08	64.75	64.93	64.45	70.63	67.20	67.10	67.53	68.63	66.45
1998	67.48	64.38	65.78	69.50	66.30	65.03	59.93	59.00	61.75	65.00	62.78	60.53
1999	65.08	68.03	63.60	62.83	62.80	62.63	64.38	66.55	69.30	68.65	70.05	69.60
2000	72.05	71.18	68.98	69.28	67.25	66.73	68.80	66.98	70.68	72.68	74.05	77.93
2001	76.83	81.38	72.68	71.65	74.48	74.00	73.90	73.15	67.33	68.08	70.18	70.70
2002	75.53	74.20	65.80	63.63	60.95	63.55	67.75	67.20	70.63	73.20	78.48	79.63
2003	79.98	75.83	70.38	71.93	69.75	69.88	77.70	82.85	84.95	90.90	93.18	73.53
2004	73.43	76.85	76.23	80.40	88.63	85.75	88.75	84.65	87.28	84.48	89.55	87.83
2005	88.33	86.05	85.25	85.63	84.70	79.30	83.40	82.25	90.00	90.93	95.73	96.38
2006	91.58	87.23	74.75									

LIVE CATTLE WIDELY TRADED CONTRACT MONTHLY CHANGES

Contract Month Date	Apr (J) JAN	Apr (J) FEB	Jun (M) MAR	Jun (M) APR	Aug (Q) MAY	Aug (Q) JUN	Oct (V) JUL	Oct (V) AUG	Dec (Z) SEP	Dec (Z) OCT	Feb (G) NOV	Feb (G) DEC
1987	-2.40	6.72	1.38	1.03	3.15	-0.15	0.50	1.10	2.70	-0.45	-5.45	1.28
1988	1.75	2.38	1.55	2.47	0.67	0.00	-2.07	3.88	0.90	1.28	0.75	-1.68
1989	1.78	0.95	-0.35	-2.02	-2.15	-1.28	4.08	2.43	-0.33	0.70	-0.27	0.13
1990	1.85	0.35	-0.85	1.97	-0.63	1.45	0.05	3.73	-3.00	1.63	0.20	0.25
1991	0.53	1.05	2.18	0.10	0.50	-1.22	-1.25	-1.30	-1.60	3.38	-0.13	0.50
1992	-1.50	4.13	1.33	1.00	0.13	-0.38	3.47	1.25	0.32	1.10	-0.38	2.73
1993	2.25	0.18	1.80	1.93	1.08	-0.50	1.10	0.08	0.02	-1.18	0.33	-2.63
1994	0.88	0.72	0.45	-0.70	-2.85	-3.88	-0.53	3.48	-1.63	-0.58	1.35	-1.80
1995	4.28	1.25	-0.13	-5.70	0.95	-1.40	1.63	2.20	-0.83	1.35	1.82	0.08
1996	-1.23	-2.53	1.63	-0.70	-2.23	4.78	1.73	1.20	1.68	0.10	-1.43	0.20
1997	0.57	1.28	0.52	-0.42	0.85	0.22	-0.48	2.75	-3.75	-1.65	-1.08	-0.15
1998	-3.58	-1.30	-2.08	-0.80	3.15	-3.58	-2.10	-4.28	-0.33	0.77	1.85	-2.13
1999	-1.80	2.05	1.40	-2.00	-0.90	1.25	-0.78	0.42	1.70	1.70	-0.20	0.55
2000	0.22	0.47	-1.25	0.33	-0.08	-2.40	-0.85	-0.38	-1.47	1.65	2.33	-0.03
2001	3.72	-2.30	2.38	-1.28	-0.17	2.70	-1.00	-1.15	-0.02	-7.28	1.38	-1.18
2002	1.38	1.85	-1.10	-3.83	-1.72	-2.83	1.08	2.27	1.35	0.45	3.80	2.53
2003	0.92	1.08	-1.77	-0.03	0.65	1.60	0.32	6.78	3.72	4.00	4.43	6.68
2004	-12.43	1.93	2.32	3.30	7.75	5.77	-1.43	2.45	-2.05	-0.17	-1.70	2.35
2005	-0.10	2.70	-0.27	2.90	2.18	-1.30	-3.90	0.85	0.02	4.50	2.58	1.38
2006	1.80	-3.48	-7.90									
# Up	15	12	9	10	7	8	15	6	13	13	12	12
# Down	4	7	10	9	11	11	4	13	6	6	7	7
Total Change	12.75	9.58	-2.45	-0.92	-1.13	-1.70	27.75	-6.70	11.30	8.25	9.05	-4.88
AVG. Change	0.67	0.50	-0.13	-0.05	-0.06	-0.09	1.46	-0.35	0.59	0.43	0.48	-0.26
AVG. Up	1.50	2.19	1.67	1.58	2.54	1.98	2.32	2.85	1.74	1.59	1.55	2.08
AVG. Down	-2.40	-2.38	-1.75	-1.85	-1.72	-1.60	-1.78	-1.83	-1.88	-2.08	-1.37	-4.25

LIVE CATTLE WIDELY TRADED CONTRACT PERFORMANCE

PERFORMANCE STATISTICS BASED ON MONTHLY PERFORMANCE AND FOLLOWING-MONTH PERFORMANCE

(Based on monthly trends from **January 1987 – December 2005** using the aforementioned contracts)

Contract	Apr (J)	Apr (J)	Jun (M)	Jun (M)	Aug (Q)	Aug (Q)	Oct (V)	Oct (V)	Dec (Z)	Dec (Z)	Feb (G)	Feb (G)
Month	JAN	FEB	MAR	APR	MAY	JUN	JUL	AUG	SEP	OCT	NOV	DEC
Yrs Tested	19	19	19	19	19	19	19	19	19	19	19	19
# Up	15	12	9	10	7	8	15	6	13	13	12	12
# Down	4	7	10	9	11	11	4	13	6	6	7	7
Total Gain (Loss)	12.75	9.58	-2.45	-0.92	-1.13	-1.70	27.75	-6.70	11.30	8.25	9.05	-4.88
Average Gain (Loss)	0.67	0.50	-0.13	-0.05	-0.06	-0.09	1.46	-0.35	0.59	0.43	0.48	-0.26

If Previous Month is Up, then FOLLOWING Month had the following Characteristics

Contract	Apr (J)	Apr (J)	Jun (M)	Jun (M)	Aug (Q)	Aug (Q)	Oct (V)	Oct (V)	Dec (Z)	Dec (Z)	Feb (G)	Feb (G)
Month	FEB	MAR	APR	MAY	JUN	JUL	AUG	SEP	OCT	NOV	DEC	JAN
Yrs Tested	15	11	9	10	7	9	15	9	13	11	12	13
# Up	10	6	7	3	2	9	6	7	10	5	7	11
# Down	5	5	2	7	5	0	9	2	3	6	5	2
% Closing Higher	66.7	54.5	77.8	30.0	28.6	100.0	40.0	77.8	76.9	45.5	58.3	84.6
Total Gain (Loss)	12.40	4.72	6.53	-0.93	-2.60	21.03	-0.05	11.50	12.65	1.48	-12.55	5.78
Average Gain (Loss)	0.83	0.43	0.73	-0.08	-0.37	2.34	0.00	1.28	0.97	0.13	-1.05	0.44
# Higher Highs	9	11	8	9	6	8	11	8	11	9	6	13
# Lower Lows	8	3	3	3	3	2	3	2	2	3	7	2

If Previous Month is Down, then FOLLOWING Month had the following Characteristics

Contract	Apr (J)	Apr (J)	Jun (M)	Jun (M)	Aug (Q)	Aug (Q)	Oct (V)	Oct (V)	Dec (Z)	Dec (Z)	Feb (G)	Feb (G)
Month	FEB	MAR	APR	MAY	JUN	JUL	AUG	SEP	OCT	NOV	DEC	JAN
Yrs Tested	4	8	10	8	11	10	4	10	6	8	7	6
# Up	2	3	3	4	6	6	0	6	3	7	5	4
# Down	2	5	7	4	5	4	4	4	3	1	2	2
% Closing Lower	50.0	62.5	70.0	50.0	45.5	40.0	100.0	40.0	50.0	12.5	28.6	33.3
Total Gain (Loss)	-2.83	-7.18	-7.45	-0.20	4.13	6.73	-6.65	-0.20	-4.40	7.58	7.68	6.98
Average Gain (Loss)	-0.71	-0.90	-0.75	-0.03	0.38	0.67	-1.66	-0.02	-0.73	0.95	1.10	1.16
# Higher Highs	1	1	1	3	6	4	0	4	1	7	4	3
# Lower Lows	2	5	7	5	5	4	7	7	6	1	3	2

Key Points Regarding Monthly Performance from 1987 – 2005

- January up 15 of 19
- March breaks reversed in April (7 of 10)
- April rallies reversed in May (7 of 10)
- June rallies continue in July (9 of 9)
- July up 15 of 19
- September strength continues through October (10 of 13)
- December strength continues through January (11 of 13)

SLAUGHTER PATTERNS SET PRICES IN HOG FUTURES

Lean Hogs are not physically fit, aerobic pork, but the term used to describe hanging carcasses, trimmed of excess fat and other parts. Unlike Cattle which is sold by "Live" weight, Hogs are sold in a post-slaughter environment.

Hog slaughter rates tend to decrease in the first half of the year and increase in the second half of the year. Couple this pattern with major times of pork consumption and the breeding cycle, and the normal behavior of Hog prices becomes very evident.

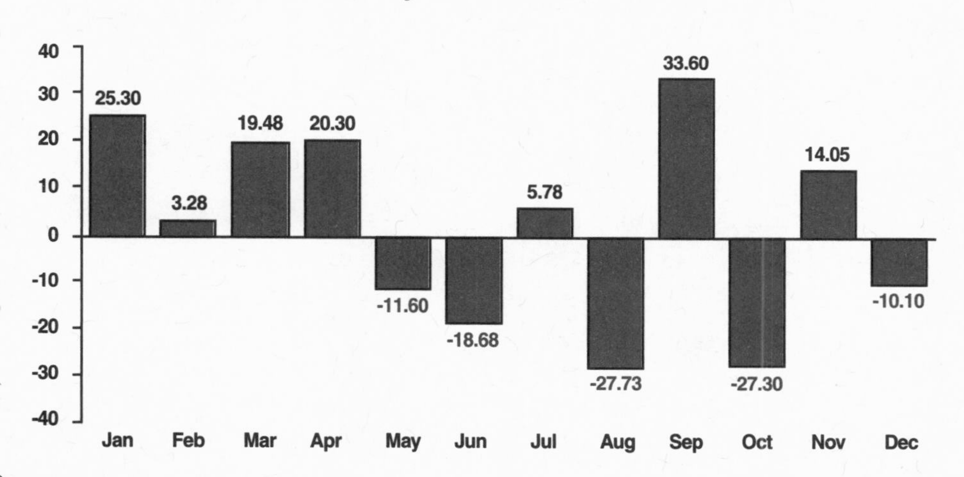

The first half of the year tends to see price increases, especially from January through April when a lack of ready supply is met with inventory-building in anticipation of the summer "cold cut" season as well as the Easter holiday. Supply is lacking this time of the year as Hogs are being farrowed (birthed).

The summer months tend to see increased slaughter rates as well as demand, but usually the increase in slaughter outweighs increased consumption. Excessive summer breaks — especially in June and August — usually see strong rallies shortly afterwards.

September marks the start of the school year and Federal purchases, which support prices. Couple that demand surge with holiday hams, and one can understand how demand pushes prices higher in September and November during a period when slaughter rates are increasing.

The critical factor for hog traders to pay attention to is slaughter rates, as this current supply sets the tone of the market between buyers shopping for price or simply attempting to secure supply.

LEAN HOGS FUTURES MARKET PROBABILITY CALENDAR FOR 2007

THE % CHANGE OF THE MARKET RISING ON ANY TRADING DAY OF THE YEAR

(Based on the number of times the widely traded contract rose on a particular trading day during **January 1987-December 2005**)

Contract	Feb (G)	Apr (J)	Apr (J)	Jun (M)	Jun (M)	Jul (N)	Aug (Q)	Oct (V)	Oct (V)	Dec (Z)	Dec (Z)	Feb (G)
Date	**Jan**	**Feb**	**Mar**	**Apr**	**May**	**Jun**	**Jul**	**Aug**	**Sep**	**Oct**	**Nov**	**Dec**
1	H	52.6	66.7	S	52.6	73.7	S	38.9	S	63.2	57.9	S
2	47.4	52.6	61.1	44.4	68.4	S	47.4	47.4	S	52.6	52.6	S
3	66.7	S	S	63.2	55.6	S	57.9	47.4	H	52.6	S	63.2
4	63.2	S	S	47.4	55.6	63.2	H	S	68.4	44.4	S	68.4
5	66.7	31.6	42.1	52.6	S	52.6	26.3	S	84.2	57.9	68.4	31.6
6	S	52.6	47.4	H	S	47.4	73.7	26.3	78.9	S	52.6	36.8
7	S	42.1	63.2	S	68.4	61.1	S	61.1	57.9	S	68.4	57.9
8	47.4	61.1	78.9	S	55.6	63.2	S	52.6	S	42.1	52.6	S
9	72.2	57.9	52.6	42.1	31.6	S	55.6	36.8	S	42.1	44.4	S
10	47.4	S	S	31.6	52.6	S	22.2	15.8	57.9	47.4	S	47.4
11	57.9	S	S	66.7	47.4	22.2	26.3	S	52.6	52.6	S	36.8
12	47.4	22.2	21.1	61.1	S	57.9	47.4	S	47.4	61.1	47.4	36.8
13	S	57.9	68.4	42.1	S	44.4	52.6	63.2	68.4	S	57.9	52.6
14	S	36.8	57.9	S	52.6	47.4	S	72.2	52.6	S	57.9	61.1
15	H	57.9	52.6	S	44.4	38.9	S	33.3	S	36.8	68.4	S
16	38.9	22.2	63.2	47.4	52.6	S	73.7	33.3	S	42.1	47.4	S
17	47.4	S	S	52.6	52.6	S	55.6	47.4	73.7	36.8	S	63.2
18	66.7	S	S	66.7	38.9	63.2	57.9	S	47.4	61.1	S	36.8
19	47.4	H	47.4	61.1	S	68.4	73.7	S	44.4	57.9	57.9	33.3
20	S	55.6	47.4	47.4	S	57.9	44.4	72.2	44.4	S	52.6	38.9
21	S	22.2	68.4	S	55.6	38.9	S	31.6	47.4	S	42.1	44.4
22	36.8	63.2	52.6	S	36.8	42.1	S	57.9	S	55.6	H	S
23	36.8	61.1	44.4	44.4	38.9	S	44.4	42.1	S	21.1	55.6	S
24	63.2	S	S	77.8	42.1	S	47.4	52.6	47.4	47.4	S	66.7
25	57.9	S	S	72.2	31.6	52.6	31.6	S	47.4	57.9	S	H
26	47.4	42.1	63.2	44.4	S	47.4	78.9	S	27.8	27.8	38.9	47.4
27	S	57.9	63.2	72.2	S	27.8	68.4	36.8	36.8	S	52.6	57.9
28	S	52.6	68.4	S	H	52.6	S	52.6	63.2	S	61.1	42.1
29	47.4		47.4	S	57.9	47.4	S	42.1	S	42.1	52.6	S
30	44.4		31.6	47.4	27.8	S	55.6	36.8	S	42.1	36.8	S
31	47.4		S		73.7		55.6	68.4		38.9		63.2

LEAN HOGS WIDELY TRADED CONTRACT MONTHLY SETTLEMENTS

Contract Month	Apr (J)	Apr (J)	Jun (M)	Jun (M)	Aug (Q)	Aug (Q)	Oct (V)	Oct (V)	Dec (Z)	Dec (Z)	Feb (G)	Feb (G)
Date	JAN	FEB	MAR	APR	MAY	JUN	JUL	AUG	SEP	OCT	NOV	DEC
1987	62.13	58.48	61.63	62.78	67.65	71.75	65.93	68.05	61.18	58.05	57.60	55.50
1988	59.65	58.45	61.58	65.00	71.35	61.18	53.13	52.10	58.13	55.60	59.15	62.85
1989	58.75	59.08	62.10	60.35	60.15	64.08	53.80	54.70	59.95	62.93	67.28	65.80
1990	63.33	68.03	72.98	77.15	81.93	78.78	74.08	65.28	71.20	69.95	65.13	66.03
1991	68.23	70.08	75.93	76.00	69.08	68.33	61.15	59.70	60.43	56.38	57.40	53.10
1992	54.08	53.68	59.25	61.48	57.45	60.40	51.15	54.13	57.93	57.33	58.60	58.95
1993	59.20	61.50	68.10	68.93	64.15	60.68	61.78	63.75	64.05	66.28	62.80	61.28
1994	69.85	66.88	70.80	68.40	62.63	61.28	57.20	52.13	49.20	47.65	46.48	53.18
1995	53.58	53.70	57.35	56.70	59.43	63.00	59.75	60.33	62.98	59.05	65.23	65.63
1996	59.93	65.60	71.15	75.00	73.03	69.63	72.45	70.83	77.43	73.50	78.35	79.23
1997	74.75	74.48	75.65	80.03	79.33	81.95	75.15	70.45	63.43	62.23	60.48	57.70
1998	57.63	49.03	55.25	57.20	57.13	54.93	42.45	37.28	40.40	37.40	36.58	32.65
1999	43.03	43.00	51.30	52.20	55.90	44.58	43.35	45.80	46.63	46.53	56.18	54.50
2000	60.25	58.08	66.55	71.70	67.45	69.03	57.45	52.93	54.20	51.18	56.68	56.83
2001	57.15	62.80	67.15	67.50	63.95	69.05	60.18	58.25	54.83	51.65	55.25	57.05
2002	60.90	60.35	60.27	50.25	46.88	46.73	41.70	30.88	40.55	43.13	54.20	51.60
2003	56.85	54.55	56.88	56.40	68.30	63.98	51.30	54.78	53.60	53.33	55.20	53.43
2004	59.20	62.03	64.70	69.90	73.95	76.70	69.23	65.98	69.13	67.45	77.15	76.40
2005	75.55	74.23	77.50	74.40	70.00	65.03	57.53	63.70	63.35	61.68	67.35	65.28
2006	61.83	61.48	65.28									

LEAN HOGS WIDELY TRADED CONTRACT MONTHLY CHANGES

Contract Month	Apr (J)	Apr (J)	Jun (M)	Jun (M)	Aug (Q)	Aug (Q)	Oct (V)	Oct (V)	Dec (Z)	Dec (Z)	Feb (G)	Feb (G)
Date	JAN	FEB	MAR	APR	MAY	JUN	JUL	AUG	SEP	OCT	NOV	DEC
1987	-4.35	3.28	65.20	66.00	5.48	2.93	0.60	5.87	1.43	-4.62	-2.65	1.33
1988	-0.35	7.70	68.03	69.78	0.77	7.03	-3.75	-5.35	0.00	2.45	-1.20	-2.35
1989	3.85	-3.08	65.78	66.50	0.78	-2.25	2.95	-5.05	1.43	2.55	1.93	4.73
1990	-1.08	2.70	74.45	78.18	7.20	1.03	-0.15	2.80	-5.80	4.28	0.15	-2.38
1991	1.35	4.90	77.55	80.13	0.20	-4.65	-1.65	0.08	-1.65	1.28	-1.93	0.25
1992	-3.95	3.48	63.45	63.20	1.25	-1.70	1.98	-4.13	1.15	3.08	0.55	1.55
1993	1.60	1.90	69.33	77.03	-4.63	-0.85	-3.18	7.33	-0.10	1.35	4.48	-4.78
1994	0.08	6.40	75.68	74.45	-1.85	-3.30	-0.70	-0.58	-3.08	-4.10	1.23	-4.80
1995	6.13	-0.35	62.30	64.93	0.40	1.38	1.68	1.78	-0.55	3.05	-2.80	2.10
1996	-0.58	-4.85	72.70	75.53	4.73	1.05	-1.20	7.18	-2.20	5.08	-3.38	4.20
1997	2.50	-1.48	80.70	82.45	3.85	-3.23	1.65	1.65	-3.83	-3.95	-0.38	-1.65
1998	-1.28	1.38	64.60	60.10	1.43	-0.60	-2.63	-7.13	-5.80	3.45	0.55	-7.28
1999	-2.98	5.83	57.65	56.70	4.88	-4.20	-10.20	-0.30	2.40	3.20	0.75	5.88
2000	-0.95	4.65	69.50	73.75	1.75	-2.80	-1.00	-1.43	-3.05	3.90	-1.22	3.53
2001	1.58	-0.25	67.40	71.80	-0.20	1.50	4.10	1.80	-1.30	0.50	-0.60	1.30
2002	1.58	0.85	68.20	67.15	-5.33	-4.35	-0.80	2.90	-4.75	5.25	2.85	4.33
2003	-1.25	-0.88	63.50	63.40	4.00	5.70	-0.77	-5.75	3.80	-0.33	2.03	-3.30
2004	-3.38	4.30	66.65	75.00	5.02	1.53	5.83	3.13	-1.03	5.40	-0.60	9.95
2005	2.40	-1.25	79.50	82.20	0.60	-5.80	-4.08	0.98	5.90	1.80	0.73	1.45
2006	-1.30	-6.65	-4.68									
# Up	11	8	12	10	8	8	11	8	15	3	12	8
# Down	8	11	7	9	11	11	8	11	4	16	7	11
Total Change	25.30	3.28	19.48	20.30	-11.60	-18.68	5.78	-27.73	33.60	-27.30	14.05	-10.10
AVG. Change	1.33	0.17	1.03	1.07	-0.61	-0.98	0.30	-1.46	1.77	-1.44	0.74	-0.53
AVG. Up	4.01	2.93	3.55	4.30	2.77	3.33	3.23	2.58	3.11	2.59	3.38	1.86
AVG. Down	-2.35	-1.83	-3.31	-2.52	-3.07	-4.12	-3.71	-4.40	-3.25	-2.19	-3.79	-2.27

LEAN HOGS WIDELY TRADED CONTRACT PERFORMANCE

PERFORMANCE STATISTICS BASED ON MONTHLY PERFORMANCE AND FOLLOWING-MONTH PERFORMANCE

(Based on monthly trends from **January 1987 – December 2005** using the aforementioned contracts)

Contract	Apr (J)	Apr (J)	Jun (M)	Jun (M)	Aug (Q)	Aug (Q)	Oct (V)	Oct (V)	Dec (Z)	Dec (Z)	Feb (G)	Feb (G)
Month	JAN	FEB	MAR	APR	MAY	JUN	JUL	AUG	SEP	OCT	NOV	DEC
Yrs Tested	19	19	19	19	19	19	19	19	19	19	19	19
# Up	11	8	12	10	8	8	11	8	15	3	12	8
# Down	8	11	7	9	11	11	8	11	4	16	7	11
Total Gain (Loss)	25.30	3.28	19.48	20.30	-11.60	-18.68	5.78	-27.73	33.60	-27.30	14.05	-10.10
Average Gain (Loss)	1.33	0.17	1.03	1.07	-0.61	-0.98	0.30	-1.46	1.77	-1.44	0.74	-0.53

If Previous Month is Up, then FOLLOWING Month had the following Characteristics

Contract	Apr (J)	Apr (J)	Jun (M)	Jun (M)	Aug (Q)	Aug (Q)	Oct (V)	Oct (V)	Dec (Z)	Dec (Z)	Feb (G)	Feb (G)
Month	FEB	MAR	APR	MAY	JUN	JUL	AUG	SEP	OCT	NOV	DEC	JAN
Yrs Tested	11	11	12	15	8	7	11	6	15	3	12	9
# Up	4	7	7	7	4	5	4	4	3	2	5	4
# Down	7	4	5	8	4	2	7	2	12	1	7	5
% Closing Higher	36.4	63.6	58.3	46.7	50.0	71.4	36.4	66.7	20.0	66.7	41.7	44.4
Total Gain (Loss)	-4.25	16.53	22.28	-4.60	-5.53	5.05	-21.73	5.68	-21.15	3.83	-11.40	7.65
Average Gain (Loss)	-0.39	1.50	1.86	-0.31	-0.69	0.72	-1.98	0.95	-1.41	1.28	-0.95	0.85
# Higher Highs	9	9	10	10	6	5	9	6	11	2	6	8
# Lower Lows	3	3	0	6	3	3	6	3	5	1	4	1

If Previous Month is Down, then FOLLOWING Month had the following Characteristics

Contract	Apr (J)	Apr (J)	Jun (M)	Jun (M)	Aug (Q)	Aug (Q)	Oct (V)	Oct (V)	Dec (Z)	Dec (Z)	Feb (G)	Feb (G)
Month	FEB	MAR	APR	MAY	JUN	JUL	AUG	SEP	OCT	NOV	DEC	JAN
Yrs Tested	8	8	7	4	11	12	8	12	4	16	7	10
# Up	4	5	3	1	4	6	4	10	0	9	3	7
# Down	4	3	4	3	7	6	4	2	4	7	4	3
% Closing Lower	50.0	37.5	57.1	75.0	63.6	50.0	50.0	16.7	100.0	43.8	57.1	30.0
Total Gain (Loss)	7.53	2.95	-1.97	-7.00	-13.15	0.72	-6.00	25.48	-6.15	10.28	1.30	17.65
Average Gain (Loss)	0.94	0.37	-0.28	-1.75	-1.20	0.06	-0.75	2.12	-1.54	0.64	0.19	1.77
# Higher Highs	2	4	1	0	4	3	2	8	1	4	2	6
# Lower Lows	7	6	6	4	8	7	4	3	4	9	5	4

Key Points Regarding Monthly Performance from 1987 – 2005

- August breaks reversed in September (10 of 12)
- September up 15 of 19
- September strength reversed in October (12 of 15)
- October down 16 of 19
- December weakness reversed in January (7 of 10)

COFFEE CONSUMPTION AND PRODUCTION RISKS

Coffee is produced almost exclusively south of the equator. However, most of the world's consumption takes place north of the equator. In other words, the seasons of growing and consumption tend to be the same.

World Coffee consumption is highly correlated to weather. Cold weather means higher coffee consumption, while warm temperatures mean less. From a future supply standpoint the opposite is true — cold weather means crop risk, while warm weather equates to higher future production. Coffee's normal price cycle can be understood as the strongest periods that experience crop risk and increasing demand.

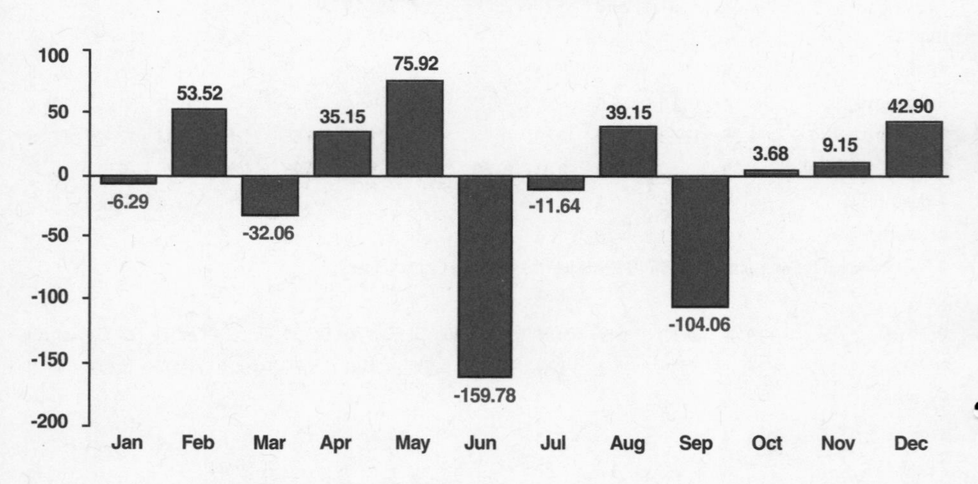

The January-through-May period is typified by some frost-risk to southern hemisphere producers as well as strong demand from northern hemisphere consumers. As such, this period tends to be the strongest. May trends in Coffee futures have broken 16 times during the 19-year period from 1987 to 2005, historically.

The northern hemisphere months of June through September tend to see warmer weather — lower consumption — while the southern hemisphere crops are not at great risk. Prices have usually fallen under the combined weight of weak demand and a lack of risk to future production. September tends to be an especially bearish month as these forces are exaggerated.

October through December tends to see slightly higher prices and a general lack of volatility before the growing and consumption cycle begins again in January.

COFFEE FUTURES MARKET PROBABILITY CALENDAR FOR 2007

THE % CHANGE OF THE MARKET RISING ON ANY TRADING DAY OF THE YEAR

(Based on the number of times the widely traded contract rose on a particular trading day during **January 1987-December 2005**)

Contract	Mar (H)	May (K)	May (K)	Jul (N)	Jul (N)	Sep (U)	Sep (U)	Dec (Z)	Dec (Z)	Dec (Z)	Mar (H)	Mar (H)
Date	**Jan**	**Feb**	**Mar**	**Apr**	**May**	**Jun**	**Jul**	**Aug**	**Sep**	**Oct**	**Nov**	**Dec**
1	H	36.8	47.4	S	52.6	31.6	S	42.1	S	26.3	57.9	S
2	42.1	57.9	47.4	72.2	47.4	S	52.6	61.1	S	36.8	44.4	S
3	66.7	S	S	31.6	47.4	S	63.2	52.6	H	55.6	S	47.4
4	61.1	S	S	55.6	57.9	31.6	H	S	68.4	57.9	S	57.9
5	63.2	47.4	63.2	52.6	S	77.8	42.1	S	63.2	52.6	66.7	36.8
6	S	42.1	57.9	H	S	47.4	31.6	42.1	42.1	S	47.4	57.9
7	S	57.9	63.2	S	31.6	36.8	S	47.4	47.4	S	57.9	42.1
8	57.9	52.6	52.6	S	47.4	52.6	S	47.4	S	61.1	61.1	S
9	52.6	47.4	47.4	47.4	73.7	S	55.6	52.6	S	47.4	57.9	S
10	63.2	S	S	52.6	72.2	S	57.9	31.6	57.9	57.9	S	47.4
11	42.1	S	S	52.6	42.1	63.2	68.4	S	42.1	44.4	S	52.6
12	47.4	57.9	52.6	31.6	S	42.1	42.1	S	47.4	68.4	31.6	52.6
13	S	55.6	52.6	44.4	S	44.4	57.9	42.1	31.6	S	47.4	52.6
14	S	68.4	42.1	S	21.1	42.1	S	42.1	42.1	S	68.4	47.4
15	H	55.6	36.8	S	47.4	31.6	S	36.8	S	47.4	42.1	S
16	52.6	57.9	52.6	63.2	68.4	S	47.4	52.6	S	63.2	47.4	S
17	38.9	S	S	47.4	21.1	S	38.9	52.6	42.1	47.4	S	47.4
18	57.9	S	S	36.8	63.2	61.1	63.2	S	42.1	68.4	S	63.2
19	47.4	H	44.4	77.8	S	36.8	47.4	S	52.6	31.6	47.4	52.6
20	S	52.6	38.9	36.8	S	27.8	52.6	52.6	63.2	S	31.6	55.6
21	S	78.9	42.1	S	47.4	47.4	S	47.4	44.4	S	44.4	55.6
22	44.4	47.4	52.6	S	52.6	31.6	S	57.9	S	47.4	H	S
23	55.6	36.8	55.6	63.2	36.8	S	42.1	78.9	S	47.4	47.4	S
24	57.9	S	S	78.9	31.6	S	33.3	52.6	57.9	68.4	S	31.6
25	31.6	S	S	47.4	36.8	47.4	57.9	S	57.9	57.9	S	H
26	61.1	47.4	63.2	31.6	S	42.1	27.8	S	63.2	52.6	47.4	47.4
27	S	47.4	44.4	33.3	S	52.6	42.1	73.7	26.3	S	26.3	47.4
28	S	36.8	31.6	S	H	36.8	S	47.4	61.1	S	26.3	52.6
29	31.6		47.4	S	42.1	52.6	S	57.9	S	38.9	33.3	S
30	42.1		38.9	42.1	44.4	S	68.4	52.6	S	57.9	68.4	S
31	36.8		S		31.6		47.4	68.4		52.6		44.4

COFFEE WIDELY TRADED CONTRACT MONTHLY SETTLEMENTS

Contract Month	Mar (H)	May (K)	May (K)	Jul (N)	Jul (N)	Sep (U)	Sep (U)	Dec (Z)	Dec (Z)	Dec (Z)	Mar (H)	Mar (H)
Date	JAN	FEB	MAR	APR	MAY	JUN	JUL	AUG	SEP	OCT	NOV	DEC
1987	123.98	129.31	100.04	120.56	119.46	105.75	101.54	118.52	112.77	122.52	129.70	125.96
1988	131.55	135.31	134.51	132.60	133.77	131.43	124.72	123.83	131.93	123.61	123.77	159.34
1989	132.64	127.32	128.13	127.45	130.68	108.06	78.99	85.76	80.60	74.85	77.70	79.57
1990	79.99	93.79	92.14	93.73	94.05	85.60	93.80	102.85	93.00	90.50	86.90	88.65
1991	83.00	92.75	94.70	89.35	86.70	85.90	81.40	89.00	82.90	80.55	83.80	77.70
1992	72.15	70.90	68.50	62.90	63.30	58.10	56.25	54.20	55.70	68.45	73.00	75.80
1993	58.30	64.85	58.60	64.20	63.55	61.35	76.55	77.90	74.50	79.30	77.60	71.55
1994	72.35	76.40	82.20	89.50	126.00	191.60	202.75	210.90	208.85	187.40	160.80	168.85
1995	155.50	181.25	166.30	174.15	153.85	130.30	145.70	147.50	117.25	121.55	104.85	94.90
1996	128.60	115.90	115.45	124.45	116.10	121.45	106.40	118.25	102.95	117.20	107.75	115.95
1997	139.40	176.85	191.15	210.40	276.40	172.40	184.50	179.90	162.50	148.65	155.05	162.45
1998	174.70	162.15	146.25	131.45	132.50	110.20	129.20	116.35	105.15	110.00	110.10	117.75
1999	103.90	102.90	109.70	104.00	121.60	101.40	91.10	89.85	82.45	100.20	134.60	125.90
2000	111.10	100.40	103.70	98.00	93.00	87.45	86.45	79.70	83.00	74.40	71.70	65.55
2001	63.75	65.90	60.30	64.45	57.15	58.50	51.95	54.35	48.30	43.90	46.20	46.20
2002	45.10	46.30	57.20	52.85	51.90	48.85	46.80	53.20	54.50	65.95	70.60	60.20
2003	65.30	59.15	58.65	69.25	58.35	61.10	63.45	63.40	62.90	58.65	60.65	64.95
2004	64.95	76.75	73.75	69.10	85.55	75.30	66.45	72.60	82.35	74.40	97.45	103.75
2005	105.35	121.55	126.40	127.95	118.35	108.05	103.15	101.05	93.45	96.65	97.00	107.10
2006	118.20	113.70	107.00									

COFFEE WIDELY TRADED CONTRACT MONTHLY CHANGES

Contract Month	Mar (H)	May (K)	May (K)	Jul (N)	Jul (N)	Sep (U)	Sep (U)	Dec (Z)	Dec (Z)	Dec (Z)	Mar (H)	Mar (H)
Date	JAN	FEB	MAR	APR	MAY	JUN	JUL	AUG	SEP	OCT	NOV	DEC
1987	-14.02	-11.01	2.32	-28.71	18.40	-1.18	-14.40	-3.48	13.75	-5.75	10.52	2.82
1988	-3.74	5.91	1.02	-0.87	-3.80	1.03	-3.49	-5.74	-1.69	8.10	-6.94	-1.13
1989	35.57	-24.27	-1.27	0.58	3.95	2.11	-16.44	-24.18	4.44	-5.16	-5.79	0.96
1990	1.87	0.14	12.20	-1.22	-0.25	0.41	-10.45	8.95	5.15	-9.85	-2.05	-7.20
1991	1.75	-5.55	7.15	1.65	-7.30	-2.90	-2.90	-4.45	4.20	-6.10	-1.80	-0.80
1992	-6.10	-5.10	-4.45	-2.50	-8.00	0.30	-7.20	-2.15	-4.55	1.50	13.40	2.50
1993	2.80	-16.00	0.60	-6.15	3.90	-0.40	-4.00	15.35	-1.15	-3.40	4.90	-4.35
1994	-6.05	0.90	2.40	5.95	5.75	33.90	67.75	46.80	4.90	-2.05	-20.25	-31.55
1995	8.05	-12.60	23.55	-14.00	6.10	-19.30	-26.50	12.15	3.90	-30.25	4.50	-14.15
1996	-9.95	33.05	-10.90	0.70	9.25	-8.20	6.10	-17.25	17.60	-15.30	6.60	1.65
1997	8.20	21.30	41.90	7.55	36.25	50.25	-65.90	11.65	17.35	-17.40	-11.45	15.10
1998	7.40	11.90	-7.50	-16.15	-8.55	1.85	-19.40	11.10	-6.30	-11.20	3.10	4.15
1999	7.65	-13.35	-2.45	7.05	-7.10	17.60	-21.80	-10.10	-3.35	-7.40	17.80	31.35
2000	-8.70	-14.50	-13.50	3.65	-8.30	-4.75	-8.75	-0.90	-11.05	3.30	-8.50	-7.55
2001	-6.15	-2.05	-0.55	-5.60	1.45	-7.20	-1.70	-7.00	-0.90	-6.05	-4.75	-0.15
2002	0.00	-0.50	-1.35	10.80	-6.35	-1.00	-5.50	-1.85	3.10	1.30	11.50	1.60
2003	-10.40	5.40	-8.85	-0.50	7.95	-10.25	0.60	1.95	-2.40	-0.50	-3.75	-1.00
2004	4.30	10.55	-0.65	-2.70	-6.90	16.20	-12.30	-8.55	2.75	9.75	-8.00	20.10
2005	6.30	1.70	13.85	5.30	-1.30	-9.05	-13.50	-4.25	-6.60	-7.60	3.40	-3.20
2006	10.10	-7.30	-6.70									
# Up	9	9	8	9	9	3	7	10	5	9	9	11
# Down	9	10	11	10	10	16	12	9	14	10	10	7
Total Change	-6.29	53.52	-32.06	35.15	75.92	-159.78	-11.64	39.15	-104.06	3.68	9.15	42.90
AVG. Change	-0.33	2.82	-1.69	1.85	4.00	-8.41	-0.61	2.06	-5.48	0.19	0.48	2.26
AVG. Up	10.45	11.67	6.09	10.33	15.86	24.82	11.91	7.71	4.79	9.23	8.91	8.54
AVG. Down	-11.14	-5.15	-7.34	-5.79	-6.68	-14.64	-7.92	-4.22	-9.14	-7.94	-7.11	-7.30

COFFEE WIDELY TRADED CONTRACT PERFORMANCE

PERFORMANCE STATISTICS BASED ON MONTHLY PERFORMANCE AND FOLLOWING-MONTH PERFORMANCE

(Based on monthly trends from **January 1987 – December 2005** using the aforementioned contracts)

Contract	Mar (H)	May (K)	May (K)	Jul (N)	Jul (N)	Sep (U)	Sep (U)	Dec (Z)	Dec (Z)	Dec (Z)	Mar (H)	Mar (H)
Month	JAN	FEB	MAR	APR	MAY	JUN	JUL	AUG	SEP	OCT	NOV	DEC
Yrs Tested	19	19	19	19	19	19	19	19	19	19	19	19
# Up	9	9	8	9	9	3	7	10	5	9	9	11
# Down	9	10	11	10	10	16	12	9	14	10	10	7
Total Gain (Loss)	-6.29	53.52	-32.06	35.15	75.92	-159.78	-11.64	39.15	-104.06	3.68	9.15	42.90
Average Gain (Loss)	-0.33	2.82	-1.69	1.85	4.00	-8.41	-0.61	2.06	-5.48	0.19	0.48	2.26

If Previous Month is Up, then FOLLOWING Month had the following Characteristics

Contract	Mar (H)	May (K)	May (K)	Jul (N)	Jul (N)	Sep (U)	Sep (U)	Dec (Z)	Dec (Z)	Dec (Z)	Mar (H)	Mar (H)
Month	FEB	MAR	APR	MAY	JUN	JUL	AUG	SEP	OCT	NOV	DEC	JAN
Yrs Tested	9	9	9	9	9	3	7	10	5	9	9	10
# Up	5	4	4	3	1	2	4	2	2	5	6	5
# Down	4	5	5	6	8	1	3	8	3	4	3	5
% Closing Higher	55.6	44.4	44.4	33.3	11.1	66.7	57.1	20.0	40.0	55.6	66.7	50.0
Total Gain (Loss)	43.47	-26.02	24.85	57.13	-112.35	-1.55	5.15	-80.81	-0.67	17.33	11.38	-28.23
Average Gain (Loss)	4.83	-2.89	2.76	6.35	-12.48	-0.52	0.74	-8.08	-0.13	1.93	1.26	-2.57
# Higher Highs	6	6	5	6	2	2	6	8	3	8	8	5
# Lower Lows	1	3	4	3	7	1	1	2	2	1	3	3

If Previous Month is Down, then FOLLOWING Month had the following Characteristics

Contract	Mar (H)	May (K)	May (K)	Jul (N)	Jul (N)	Sep (U)	Sep (U)	Dec (Z)	Dec (Z)	Dec (Z)	Mar (H)	Mar (H)
Month	FEB	MAR	APR	MAY	JUN	JUL	AUG	SEP	OCT	NOV	DEC	JAN
Yrs Tested	10	10	10	10	10	16	12	9	14	10	9	7
# Up	4	4	5	6	2	5	6	3	7	3	5	4
# Down	6	6	5	4	8	11	6	6	7	7	4	3
% Closing Lower	60.0	60.0	50.0	40.0	80.0	68.8	50.0	66.7	50.0	70.0	44.4	42.9
Total Gain (Loss)	10.05	-6.04	10.30	18.79	-61.36	-10.09	27.08	-23.25	4.35	-14.73	31.52	23.04
Average Gain (Loss)	1.01	-0.60	1.03	1.88	-6.14	-0.63	2.26	-2.58	0.31	-1.47	3.15	3.29
# Higher Highs	2	4	1	2	0	3	2	3	4	2	4	2
# Lower Lows	10	5	9	7	9	15	10	7	10	7	7	6

Key Points Regarding Monthly Performance from 1987 – 2005

- 8 of 10 May breaks continue through June
- June down 16 of 19
- August rallies reversed in September (8 of 10)
- October breaks continue in November (7 of 10)

SUGAR IS ESPECIALLY SWEET AT THE END OF THE YEAR

There are two types of Sugar grown in the world: beet and cane. In its finished and refined form, they are indistinguishable. But by risk to crop, the two are very different.

Cane sugar is grown in moderate climates, with the biggest risk occurring at harvest from insects. Beet sugar, however, is more susceptible to frost and drought than cane sugar due to the climates it is grown in. Risk to crops is centered around specific times of the year, most notably late spring and end of year.

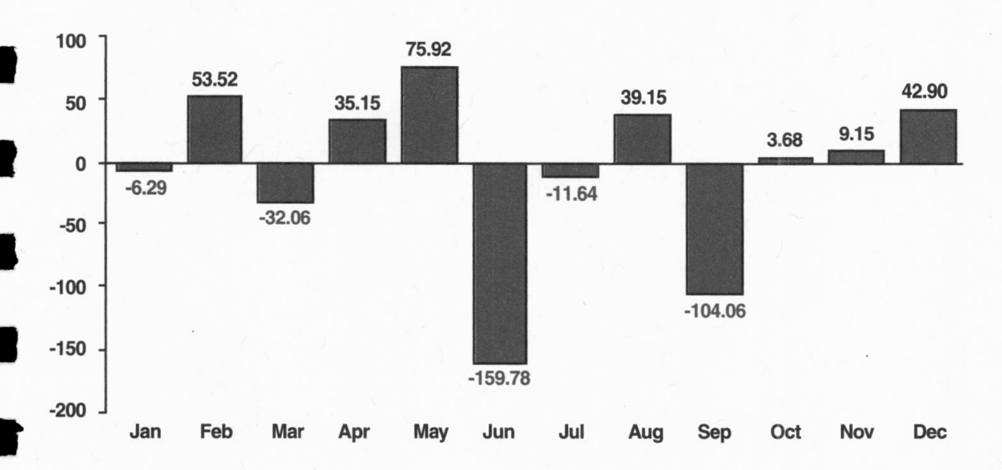

During much of the year, the Sugar market tends to go generally sideways, driven by major supply and demand trends. However, in the late spring/early summer (April/May), future supply becomes much more uncertain.

The April/May period is when sugar cane in many locales is harvested, and sugar beets are planted. Both of these stages are wrought with potential hazards, ranging from insects to weather. Future supply is uncertain, and prices tend to rally to compensate.

The end-of-year period from October to December is another period of rising prices, but this is mainly demand-driven. The beet crop is freshly harvested, but processing often lags demand. Demand tends to be strong with the holiday season, and consumers must pay up for available supply until harvested supply is processed for use.

SUGAR FUTURES MARKET PROBABILITY CALENDAR FOR 2007

THE % CHANGE OF THE MARKET RISING ON ANY TRADING DAY OF THE YEAR

(Based on the number of times the widely traded contract rose on a particular trading day during **January 1987-December 2005**)

Contract	Mar (H)	May (K)	May (K)	Jul (N)	Jul (N)	Oct (V)	Oct (V)	Oct (V)	Mar (H)	Mar (H)	Mar (H)	Mar (H)
Date	**Jan**	**Feb**	**Mar**	**Apr**	**May**	**Jun**	**Jul**	**Aug**	**Sep**	**Oct**	**Nov**	**Dec**
1	H	47.4	66.7	S	22.2	63.2	S	44.4	S	47.4	44.4	S
2	73.7	26.3	66.7	57.9	38.9	S	57.9	63.2	S	36.8	47.4	S
3	47.4	S	S	36.8	52.6	S	57.9	42.1	H	52.6	S	47.4
4	31.6	S	S	72.2	47.4	57.9	H	S	57.9	72.2	S	73.7
5	68.4	55.6	36.8	52.6	S	42.1	47.4	S	52.6	38.9	33.3	47.4
6	S	47.4	44.4	H	S	36.8	55.6	63.2	47.4	S	52.6	63.2
7	S	55.6	33.3	S	78.9	52.6	S	47.4	33.3	S	47.4	33.3
8	83.3	31.6	63.2	S	36.8	61.1	S	47.4	S	52.6	66.7	S
9	42.1	44.4	47.4	36.8	73.7	S	36.8	31.6	S	52.6	57.9	S
10	47.4	S	S	42.1	57.9	S	47.4	63.2	55.6	42.1	S	47.4
11	52.6	S	S	31.6	72.2	38.9	47.4	S	44.4	84.2	S	27.8
12	36.8	66.7	78.9	57.9	S	42.1	57.9	S	38.9	31.6	47.4	55.6
13	S	63.2	36.8	47.4	S	47.4	66.7	31.6	55.6	S	44.4	47.4
14	S	33.3	61.1	S	55.6	44.4	S	47.4	55.6	S	52.6	42.1
15	H	63.2	61.1	S	63.2	47.4	S	52.6	S	55.6	36.8	S
16	22.2	66.7	55.6	44.4	42.1	S	68.4	42.1	S	47.4	42.1	S
17	66.7	S	S	31.6	55.6	S	47.4	47.4	42.1	55.6	S	47.4
18	36.8	S	S	78.9	63.2	52.6	63.2	S	47.4	31.6	S	36.8
19	36.8	H	63.2	47.4	S	77.8	68.4	S	38.9	44.4	44.4	42.1
20	S	55.6	42.1	52.6	S	57.9	63.2	42.1	33.3	S	47.4	66.7
21	S	61.1	47.4	S	36.8	38.9	S	68.4	55.6	S	55.6	26.3
22	61.1	31.6	57.9	S	55.6	36.8	S	36.8	S	52.6	H	S
23	42.1	33.3	42.1	63.2	63.2	S	57.9	57.9	S	36.8	52.6	S
24	55.6	S	S	57.9	47.4	S	44.4	44.4	61.1	72.2	S	26.3
25	47.4	S	S	63.2	31.6	57.9	36.8	S	38.9	47.4	S	H
26	31.6	47.4	47.4	38.9	S	63.2	52.6	S	38.9	38.9	36.8	66.7
27	S	36.8	47.4	21.1	S	68.4	77.8	38.9	52.6	S	57.9	73.7
28	S	52.6	66.7	S	H	52.6	S	47.4	47.4	S	63.2	47.4
29	44.4		42.1	S	44.4	57.9	S	47.4	S	66.7	47.4	S
30	33.3		52.6	57.9	16.7	S	57.9	47.4	S	33.3	73.7	S
31	47.4		S		63.2		47.4	57.9		36.8		47.4

SUGAR WIDELY TRADED CONTRACT MONTHLY SETTLEMENTS

Contract Month	Mar (H)	May (K)	May (K)	Jul (N)	Jul (N)	Oct (V)	Oct (V)	Oct (V)	Mar (H)	Mar (H)	Mar (H)	Mar (H)
Date	JAN	FEB	MAR	APR	MAY	JUN	JUL	AUG	SEP	OCT	NOV	DEC
1987	7.74	8.24	6.72	7.31	6.72	6.97	5.94	5.63	6.96	7.59	8.01	9.49
1988	9.64	7.91	8.88	8.51	9.47	12.63	11.54	10.25	9.64	10.59	11.07	11.15
1989	10.49	11.63	12.62	11.54	10.86	14.43	14.65	13.39	14.16	13.97	14.15	13.16
1990	14.73	14.46	15.69	16.02	13.68	12.77	11.09	10.33	10.11	9.42	9.82	9.37
1991	8.79	8.78	8.90	7.73	8.05	8.52	9.68	8.83	9.01	8.98	8.92	9.00
1992	8.18	8.02	8.68	9.36	10.03	9.76	9.51	9.23	8.71	8.77	8.41	8.39
1993	8.30	9.96	11.89	12.82	10.76	10.45	9.36	9.07	10.45	10.62	10.36	10.77
1994	10.59	11.80	11.96	11.67	12.04	11.68	11.68	12.14	12.40	12.80	14.71	15.17
1995	14.12	14.42	14.28	11.56	11.72	10.79	10.50	10.86	10.18	10.56	10.97	11.60
1996	12.15	11.60	11.79	10.39	11.21	11.15	11.70	11.78	10.89	10.30	10.66	10.99
1997	10.45	10.97	10.79	10.96	11.17	11.19	11.68	11.60	11.56	12.39	12.24	12.22
1998	11.23	9.85	10.19	8.46	8.28	8.58	8.76	7.55	7.65	7.71	8.23	7.86
1999	7.11	6.26	5.91	4.33	5.00	6.22	5.98	6.82	6.93	6.88	5.78	6.12
2000	5.42	4.99	5.90	6.64	7.55	8.48	10.40	10.56	9.45	9.90	9.75	10.20
2001	9.95	8.99	7.75	8.50	8.55	9.36	7.93	7.91	6.63	6.74	7.68	7.39
2002	6.38	5.69	5.93	5.36	5.90	4.96	5.80	5.98	6.44	7.36	7.41	7.61
2003	8.64	8.45	7.68	7.20	7.08	6.22	7.21	6.29	6.44	5.93	6.25	5.67
2004	5.86	6.12	6.40	6.95	7.06	7.69	8.28	7.99	9.06	8.60	8.84	9.04
2005	9.22	9.17	8.70	8.66	8.76	9.33	9.83	10.07	11.23	11.33	12.43	14.68
2006	18.02	17.12	17.90									

SUGAR WIDELY TRADED CONTRACT MONTHLY CHANGES

Contract Month Date	Mar (H) JAN	May (K) FEB	May (K) MAR	Jul (N) APR	Jul (N) MAY	Oct (V) JUN	Oct (V) JUL	Oct (V) AUG	Mar (H) SEP	Mar (H) OCT	Mar (H) NOV	Mar (H) DEC
1987	-0.44	1.50	0.41	-1.46	0.44	-0.35	-0.13	-1.03	-0.15	0.40	0.63	0.42
1988	1.48	0.04	-1.54	0.95	-0.29	0.74	3.18	-1.09	-0.40	-0.63	0.95	0.48
1989	0.08	-0.58	1.26	1.08	-1.15	-0.65	3.58	0.22	-0.84	1.42	-0.19	0.18
1990	-0.99	1.45	-0.20	1.39	0.31	-2.31	-0.84	-1.68	-0.49	-0.19	-0.69	0.40
1991	-0.45	-0.64	-0.08	0.14	-0.95	-0.21	1.00	1.16	-0.41	0.66	-0.03	-0.06
1992	0.08	-0.68	-0.14	0.46	0.72	0.41	0.40	-0.25	-0.30	-0.24	0.06	-0.36
1993	-0.02	0.07	1.39	2.47	0.29	-1.10	-0.57	-1.09	-0.27	1.04	0.17	-0.26
1994	0.41	0.02	0.83	0.24	-0.55	0.66	-0.47	0.00	0.51	0.22	0.40	1.91
1995	0.46	-1.17	0.34	-0.20	-1.58	-0.54	0.50	-0.29	0.04	-0.07	0.38	0.41
1996	0.63	0.12	0.26	0.14	-0.57	0.24	0.51	0.55	0.01	-0.54	-0.59	0.36
1997	0.33	-0.58	0.56	-0.14	0.38	0.18	0.19	0.49	0.13	-0.45	0.83	-0.15
1998	-0.02	-1.06	-1.08	-0.03	-1.29	-0.36	0.16	0.18	-1.18	-0.29	0.06	0.52
1999	-0.37	-0.96	-0.61	-0.38	-1.34	0.48	0.95	-0.24	0.83	-0.19	-0.05	-1.10
2000	0.34	-0.79	-0.53	0.54	0.86	0.74	0.85	1.92	0.21	-0.87	0.45	-0.15
2001	0.45	-0.14	-0.64	-1.00	1.08	0.21	1.04	-1.43	-0.18	-1.00	0.11	0.94
2002	-0.29	-1.04	-0.07	0.13	0.11	0.49	-0.82	0.84	0.11	0.48	0.92	0.05
2003	0.20	1.21	0.33	-0.59	-0.07	-0.18	-0.75	0.99	-0.80	0.03	-0.51	0.32
2004	-0.58	0.16	0.10	0.55	0.37	0.12	0.37	0.59	-0.15	0.49	-0.46	0.24
2005	0.20	0.29	-0.37	-0.32	-0.24	0.24	0.46	0.50	0.76	0.66	0.10	1.10
2006	2.25	-0.84	0.78									
# Up	7	9	12	9	13	13	10	7	9	12	13	12
# Down	12	10	7	10	6	6	8	12	10	7	6	7
Total Change	-0.61	0.22	3.35	-3.47	-0.08	9.61	0.34	-5.24	0.93	2.54	5.25	4.19
AVG. Change	-0.03	0.01	0.18	-0.18	0.00	0.51	0.02	-0.28	0.05	0.13	0.28	0.22
AVG. Up	1.00	0.61	0.67	0.51	0.45	1.01	0.74	0.33	0.60	0.42	0.56	0.58
AVG. Down	-0.64	-0.53	-0.67	-0.80	-1.00	-0.60	-0.89	-0.63	-0.45	-0.36	-0.35	-0.39

SUGAR WIDELY TRADED CONTRACT PERFORMANCE

PERFORMANCE STATISTICS BASED ON MONTHLY PERFORMANCE AND FOLLOWING-MONTH PERFORMANCE

(Based on monthly trends from **January 1987 – December 2005** using the aforementioned contracts)

Contract	Mar (H)	May (K)	May (K)	Jul (N)	Jul (N)	Oct (V)	Oct (V)	Oct (V)	Mar (H)	Mar (H)	Mar (H)	Mar (H)
Month	JAN	FEB	MAR	APR	MAY	JUN	JUL	AUG	SEP	OCT	NOV	DEC
Yrs Tested	19	19	19	19	19	19	19	19	19	19	19	19
# Up	7	9	12	9	13	13	10	7	9	12	13	12
# Down	12	10	7	10	6	6	8	12	10	7	6	7
Total Gain (Loss)	-0.61	0.22	3.35	-3.47	-0.08	9.61	0.34	-5.24	0.93	2.54	5.25	4.19
Average Gain (Loss)	-0.03	0.01	0.18	-0.18	0.00	0.51	0.02	-0.28	0.05	0.13	0.28	0.22

If Previous Month is Up, then FOLLOWING Month had the following Characteristics

Contract	Mar (H)	May (K)	May (K)	Jul (N)	Jul (N)	Oct (V)	Oct (V)	Oct (V)	Mar (H)	Mar (H)	Mar (H)	Mar (H)
Month	FEB	MAR	APR	MAY	JUN	JUL	AUG	SEP	OCT	NOV	DEC	JAN
Yrs Tested	9	9	11	9	11	13	10	8	9	12	13	12
# Up	6	5	6	6	9	8	4	3	5	8	8	5
# Down	3	4	5	3	2	5	6	5	4	4	5	7
% Closing Higher	6.7	55.6	54.5	66.7	81.8	61.5	40.0	37.5	55.6	66.7	61.5	41.7
Total Gain (Loss)	1.21	0.94	-0.85	-2.50	6.66	2.31	-3.95	-0.76	1.03	4.91	2.95	1.05
Average Gain (Loss)	0.13	0.10	-0.08	-0.28	0.61	0.18	-0.40	-0.09	0.11	0.41	0.23	0.09
# Higher Highs	5	7	8	6	10	9	8	6	8	8	8	9
# Lower Lows	2	2	4	4	1	4	3	0	1	3	3	1

If Previous Month is Down, then FOLLOWING Month had the following Characteristics

Contract	Mar (H)	May (K)	May (K)	Jul (N)	Jul (N)	Oct (V)	Oct (V)	Oct (V)	Mar (H)	Mar (H)	Mar (H)	Mar (H)
Month	FEB	MAR	APR	MAY	JUN	JUL	AUG	SEP	OCT	NOV	DEC	JAN
Yrs Tested	10	10	8	10	8	5	8	11	10	7	6	7
# Up	3	7	3	7	4	2	2	6	7	5	4	2
# Down	7	3	5	3	4	3	6	5	3	2	2	5
% Closing Lower	70.0	30.0	62.5	30.0	50.0	60.0	75.0	45.5	30.0	28.6	33.3	71.4
Total Gain (Loss)	-0.99	2.41	-2.62	2.42	2.95	-1.97	-1.75	1.69	1.51	0.34	1.24	-1.66
Average Gain (Loss)	-0.10	0.24	-0.33	0.24	0.37	-0.33	-0.22	0.15	0.15	0.05	0.21	-0.24
# Higher Highs	3	4	1	4	3	2	2	3	2	2	1	3
# Lower Lows	8	4	6	6	6	4	6	9	8	4	5	6

Key Points Regarding Monthly Performance from 1987 – 2005

- January breaks continue through February (7 of 10)
- February breaks reversed in March (7 of 10)
- April weakness reversed in May (7 of 10)
- May rallies continue in June (9 of 11)
- September breaks reversed in October (7 of 10)

DUAL CROPS WEIGH ON PRICES MOST OF THE YEAR

The Cocoa tree thrives in the lower growth of the evergreen rainforest where the climate meets the following conditions: Temperature is relatively high (average temperature between 66 F to 92 F), rainfall plentiful and well-distributed with average monthly rainfalls in excess of 1500 mm (rainfall below 100 mm per month for three months will damage Cocoa trees), and shade and humidity are abundant.

The Cocoa tree typically produces two crops each year. In the Ivory Coast, the largest Cocoa-producing nation in the world, the main Cocoa harvest runs from October to March, which is roughly five to six months after the wet season. The mid-crop harvest runs from May through August. The main crop accounts for roughly 75 to 80% of the total Cocoa produced in Africa, while the mid-crop accounts for roughly 15 to 20% of production. Cocoa prices tend towards weakness in anticipation of the harvest and rally when the harvest is at risk.

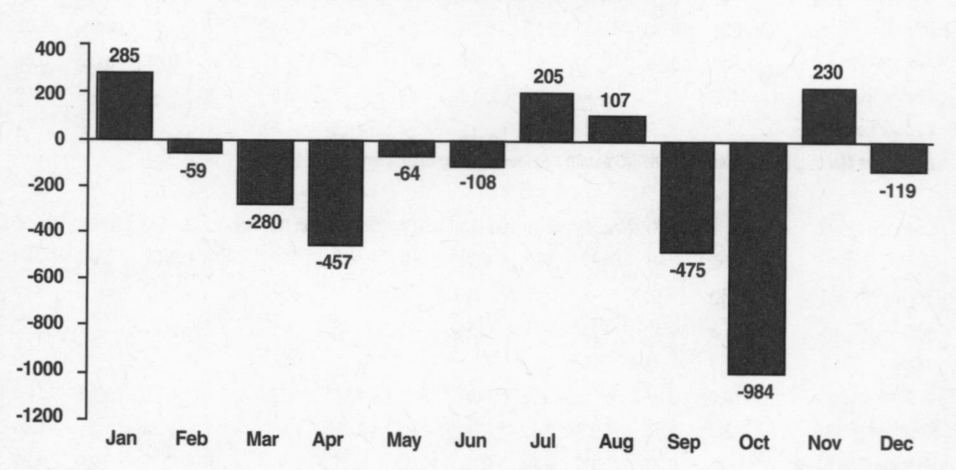

The main crop harvest begins in October, but in November prices tend to bounce back as the market begins factoring in harvest problems or political strife, as Cocoa is grown in generally unstable political regions. July tends towards strength as this period is between mid-crop and main-crop harvests as well. The rest of the year tends towards weakness as Cocoa production becomes more efficient and supply is almost constant.

COCOA FUTURES MARKET PROBABILITY CALENDAR FOR 2007

THE % CHANGE OF THE MARKET RISING ON ANY TRADING DAY OF THE YEAR

(Based on the number of times the widely traded contract rose on a particular trading day during **January 1987-December 2005**)

Contract	Mar (H)	May (K)	May (K)	Jul (N)	Jul (N)	Sep (U)	Sep (U)	Dec (Z)	Dec (Z)	Dec (Z)	Mar (H)	Mar (H)
Date	**Jan**	**Feb**	**Mar**	**Apr**	**May**	**Jun**	**Jul**	**Aug**	**Sep**	**Oct**	**Nov**	**Dec**
1	H	21.1	33.3	S	55.6	57.9	S	31.6	S	44.4	38.9	S
2	44.4	47.4	42.1	68.4	47.4	S	57.9	33.3	S	38.9	47.4	S
3	52.6	S	S	21.1	61.1	S	66.7	57.9	H	57.9	S	61.1
4	42.1	S	S	55.6	55.6	31.6	H	S	57.9	61.1	S	36.8
5	61.1	61.1	47.4	52.6	S	47.4	47.4	S	42.1	52.6	38.9	52.6
6	S	44.4	36.8	H	S	36.8	55.6	38.9	42.1	S	42.1	72.2
7	S	47.4	52.6	S	44.4	36.8	S	47.4	52.6	S	47.4	47.4
8	42.1	42.1	57.9	S	42.1	26.3	S	47.4	S	42.1	63.2	S
9	36.8	57.9	57.9	42.1	52.6	S	42.1	47.4	S	55.6	52.6	S
10	42.1	S	S	26.3	36.8	S	42.1	47.4	47.4	31.6	S	38.9
11	57.9	S	S	52.6	61.1	57.9	38.9	S	42.1	42.1	S	42.1
12	57.9	52.6	27.8	47.4	S	36.8	57.9	S	42.1	42.1	68.4	47.4
13	S	52.6	42.1	52.6	S	47.4	57.9	55.6	52.6	S	36.8	36.8
14	S	36.8	73.7	S	42.1	47.4	S	31.6	57.9	S	42.1	36.8
15	H	52.6	52.6	S	63.2	47.4	S	63.2	S	47.4	52.6	S
16	47.4	52.6	47.4	63.2	42.1	S	63.2	36.8	S	52.6	44.4	S
17	42.1	S	S	42.1	42.1	S	57.9	52.6	52.6	47.4	S	73.7
18	63.2	S	S	42.1	55.6	73.7	27.8	S	38.9	42.1	S	47.4
19	57.9	H	63.2	57.9	S	42.1	63.2	S	47.4	47.4	36.8	47.4
20	S	38.9	26.3	57.9	S	61.1	66.7	26.3	57.9	S	47.4	47.4
21	S	52.6	52.6	S	61.1	52.6	S	57.9	47.4	S	63.2	47.4
22	63.2	55.6	33.3	S	57.9	47.4	S	63.2	S	57.9	H	S
23	52.6	47.4	57.9	52.6	42.1	S	52.6	68.4	S	47.4	38.9	S
24	44.4	S	S	55.6	57.9	S	44.4	55.6	42.1	63.2	S	31.6
25	42.1	S	S	47.4	21.1	42.1	42.1	S	57.9	42.1	S	H
26	55.6	68.4	52.6	47.4	S	47.4	47.4	S	57.9	22.2	57.9	55.6
27	S	63.2	47.4	27.8	S	68.4	36.8	42.1	31.6	S	36.8	77.8
28	S	38.9	31.6	S	H	52.6	S	68.4	66.7	S	42.1	22.2
29	36.8		47.4	S	47.4	57.9	S	52.6	S	52.6	36.8	S
30	57.9		57.9	52.6	47.4	S	36.8	52.6	S	52.6	47.4	S
31	21.1		S		57.9		57.9	57.9		42.1		31.6

COCOA WIDELY TRADED CONTRACT MONTHLY SETTLEMENTS

Contract Month	Mar (H)	May (K)	May (K)	Jul (N)	Jul (N)	Sep (U)	Sep (U)	Dec (Z)	Dec (Z)	Dec (Z)	Mar (H)	Mar (H)
Date	JAN	FEB	MAR	APR	MAY	JUN	JUL	AUG	SEP	OCT	NOV	DEC
1987	1935	1888	1928	1977	1881	1997	1962	1988	1823	1807	1866	1814
1988	1814	1621	1570	1622	1619	1580	1468	1256	1132	1309	1476	1500
1989	1500	1485	1431	1211	1128	1229	1267	1149	1040	977	939	925
1990	925	1055	1183	1297	1415	1246	1248	1319	1281	1153	1283	1150
1991	1150	1138	1105	1035	1030	908	1036	1091	1220	1208	1231	1245
1992	1245	1116	986	933	864	954	1013	1092	1009	932	1150	1068
1993	1068	936	919	936	894	903	939	1079	1151	1120	1263	1144
1994	1144	1139	1148	1128	1388	1305	1490	1357	1320	1327	1228	1280
1995	1280	1427	1308	1408	1362	1289	1236	1336	1293	1311	1308	1258
1996	1258	1268	1306	1368	1376	1384	1333	1352	1377	1353	1416	1354
1997	1354	1286	1453	1400	1469	1713	1513	1717	1679	1603	1582	1630
1998	1630	1614	1652	1686	1674	1575	1552	1614	1512	1506	1441	1379
1999	1379	1278	1192	1019	874	1039	1001	951	1029	874	899	837
2000	837	778	800	774	842	835	826	795	797	755	730	758
2001	758	1137	1073	987	936	964	957	949	1077	1017	1339	1310
2002	1310	1450	1494	1510	1598	1647	1787	2002	2191	1927	1703	2021
2003	2021	2034	1960	1991	1493	1651	1465	1761	1626	1440	1438	1515
2004	1515	1570	1549	1413	1465	1341	1645	1686	1453	1469	1651	1547
2005	1547	1730	1613	1492	1422	1452	1479	1404	1413	1351	1415	1504
2006	1504	1461	1489									

COCOA WIDELY TRADED CONTRACT MONTHLY CHANGES

Contract Month	Mar (H)	May (K)	May (K)	Jul (N)	Jul (N)	Sep (U)	Sep (U)	Dec (Z)	Dec (Z)	Dec (Z)	Mar (H)	Mar (H)
Date	JAN	FEB	MAR	APR	MAY	JUN	JUL	AUG	SEP	OCT	NOV	DEC
1987	-41	-102	26	42	21	-89	83	-19	0	-165	6	16
1988	16	-52	-169	-73	42	0	-58	-92	-231	-124	151	179
1989	179	-95	84	-88	-148	-59	73	32	-145	-109	-58	-56
1990	-56	24	98	140	98	126	-193	12	29	-38	-109	70
1991	70	-28	-27	-34	-103	-8	-148	129	0	129	-4	-38
1992	-38	-70	-99	-129	-91	-68	45	64	19	-83	-83	7
1993	7	-15	-5	-11	-13	-36	-25	48	100	72	-27	104
1994	104	-53	16	14	-51	259	-109	188	-175	-37	-1	-144
1995	-144	96	34	-114	76	-48	-92	-55	70	-43	18	-38
1996	-38	-16	0	32	44	19	-9	-41	-20	25	-13	24
1997	24	-39	-55	166	-82	72	212	-196	157	-38	-73	-56
1998	-56	-71	24	26	17	-3	-126	-24	24	-102	-5	-105
1999	-105	-37	-85	-83	-200	-148	135	-37	-88	78	-152	-14
2000	-14	-35	-50	32	-57	67	-36	-7	-69	2	-41	-57
2001	-57	256	108	-57	-99	-60	26	-15	5	128	-60	321
2002	321	45	108	42	28	104	69	167	196	189	-296	-202
2003	-202	348	-320	-98	90	-447	171	-185	318	-135	-197	29
2004	29	-4	55	-21	-136	54	-131	308	26	-233	15	167
2005	167	-20	198	-107	-141	-68	5	33	-109	9	1392	1415
2006	23	-51	28									
# Up	6	10	8	8	7	9	9	10	8	4	10	8
# Down	13	8	11	11	12	10	10	7	11	15	9	11
Total Change	285	-59	-280	-705	-457	-108	205	107	-475	-984	230	-119
AVG. Change	15	-3	-15	-37	-24	-6	11	6	-25	-52	12	-6
AVG. Up	135	75	61	52	95	91	102	94	79	55	94	81
AVG. Down	-40	-101	-70	-102	-93	-93	-71	-120	-101	-80	-79	-70

COCOA WIDELY TRADED CONTRACT PERFORMANCE

PERFORMANCE STATISTICS BASED ON MONTHLY PERFORMANCE AND FOLLOWING-MONTH PERFORMANCE

(Based on monthly trends from **January 1987 – December 2005** using the aforementioned contracts)

Contract	Mar (H)	May (K)	May (K)	Jul (N)	Jul (N)	Sep (U)	Sep (U)	Dec (Z)	Dec (Z)	Dec (Z)	Mar (H)	Mar (H)
Month	JAN	FEB	MAR	APR	MAY	JUN	JUL	AUG	SEP	OCT	NOV	DEC
Yrs Tested	19	19	19	19	19	19	19	19	19	19	19	19
# Up	6	10	8	8	7	9	9	10	8	4	10	8
# Down	13	8	11	11	12	10	10	7	11	15	9	11
Total Gain (Loss)	285	-59	-280	-705	-457	-108	205	107	-475	-984	230	-119
Average Gain (Loss)	15	-3	-15	-37	-24	-6	11	6	-25	-52	12	-6

If Previous Month is Up, then FOLLOWING Month had the following Characteristics

Contract	Mar (H)	May (K)	May (K)	Jul (N)	Jul (N)	Sep (U)	Sep (U)	Dec (Z)	Dec (Z)	Dec (Z)	Mar (H)	Mar (H)
Month	FEB	MAR	APR	MAY	JUN	JUL	AUG	SEP	OCT	NOV	DEC	JAN
Yrs Tested	5	10	8	8	7	9	8	10	8	4	10	8
# Up	4	5	5	3	2	4	5	3	0	3	3	4
# Down	1	5	3	5	5	5	3	7	8	1	7	4
% Closing Higher	80.0	50.0	62.5	37.5	28.6	44.4	62.5	30.0	0.0	75.0	30.0	50.0
Total Gain (Loss)	28	-116	18	-441	-197	-202	-59	-283	-650	324	-391	522
Average Gain (Loss)	6	-12	2	-55	-28	-22	-7	-28	-81	81	-39	65
# Higher Highs	5	6	6	5	4	6	8	3	6	4	4	5
# Lower Lows	1	4	4	3	1	1	3	5	3	1	3	4

If Previous Month is Down, then FOLLOWING Month had the following Characteristics

Contract	Mar (H)	May (K)	May (K)	Jul (N)	Jul (N)	Sep (U)	Sep (U)	Dec (Z)	Dec (Z)	Dec (Z)	Mar (H)	Mar (H)
Month	FEB	MAR	APR	MAY	JUN	JUL	AUG	SEP	OCT	NOV	DEC	JAN
Yrs Tested	13	8	11	11	11	10	9	7	11	15	9	11
# Up	6	2	3	4	7	5	5	4	4	7	5	2
# Down	7	6	8	7	4	5	4	3	7	8	4	9
% Closing Lower	53.8	75.0	72.7	63.6	36.4	50.0	44.4	42.9	63.6	53.3	44.4	81.8
Total Gain (Loss)	-87	-202	-723	-16	147	407	166	-156	-334	-94	272	-237
Average Gain (Loss)	-6	-25	-66	-1	13	41	17	-22	-30	-6	30	-22
# Higher Highs	3	2	2	2	2	4	3	2	3	3	3	3
# Lower Lows	10	6	10	9	9	6	6	6	11	11	6	8

Key Points Regarding Monthly Performance from 1987 – 2005

- February breaks continue in March (6 of 8)
- March breaks continue in April (8 of 11)
- September rallies reversed in October (8 of 8)
- November rallies reversed in December (7 of 10)
- December weakness continued through January (9 of 11)

WIDELY TRADED COMMODITY FUTURES CONTRACT SPECIFICATIONS

	Trading Hours	Symbol	Contract Size	Units Quoted	Point Value	Min Change	Daily Trade Limit
METALS							
COMEX GOLD	8:20-1:30	GC	100 TROY OZ	$/OZ	1¢=$1	$0.10 = $10.00	NONE
COMEX SILVER	8:25-1:25	SI	5000 TROY OZ	¢/OZ	1¢=$50	0.5¢=$25.00	NONE
GRAINS							
WHEAT	10:30-2:15	W	5000 BU	¢/BU	1¢=$50	1/4¢=$12.50	30¢=$1500
CORN	10:30-2:15	C	5000 BU	¢/BU	1¢=$50	1/4¢=$12.50	20¢=$1000
SOYBEANS	10:30-2:15	S	5000 BU	¢/BU	1¢=$50	1/4¢=$12.50	50¢=$2500
FOOD & FIBER (SOFTS)							
COCOA	8:00-11:50	CO	10 TONS	$/TON	$1=$10	$1=$10.00	$88=$880
COFFEE	8:15-12:30	KC	37,500 LBS	¢/LB	1¢=$375	0.05¢=$18.75	NONE
SUGAR	9:00-12:00	SB	112,000 LBS	¢/LB	1¢=$1,120	0.01¢=$11.20	50¢=$560
MEATS							
LIVE CATTLE	10:05-2:00	LC	40,000 LBS	¢/LB	1¢=$400	0.025¢=$10.00	3¢=$1200
LEAN HOGS	10:10-2:00	LH	40,000 LBS	¢/LB	1¢=$400	0.025¢=$10.00	2¢=$800
ENERGIES							
CRUDE OIL	10:00-2:30	CL	1000 BBL	$/BBL	$1=$1,000	$0.01=$10.00	NONE
NATURAL GAS	10:00-2:30	NG	10000MM BTU	$1MMBTU	0.01¢=$100	0.001¢=$10.00	NONE

OZ = Troy Ounces, BU = Bushels, LB = Pounds, BBL = Barrel, BTU = British Thermal Units

UNDERSTANDING CONTRACT SPECIFICATIONS

A commodity futures contract is a legally binding agreement between a buyer and a seller to accept or make delivery of a predetermined amount of a commodity at a specified location and time. All aspects of the contract are standardized so the only aspect left to be negotiated — on an exchange — is price.

Because futures contracts are standardized to size, quantity, quality, and time of delivery, each contract is interchangeable. For example, if you bought (long) a contract of Gold, he/she would not have to accept delivery of Gold if you "offset" the contract by selling the contract on the exchange before first notice day of the contract — the date upon which all commodity contracts are subject to delivery (*see pages 10-11 and 116 for a list of 1st Notice Days and Options Expirations*).

Commodities are traded on a base unit basis. For example, if Gold is quoted at $630.00, it means that 1 ounce (the unit) of Gold is worth $630/ounce. The minimum fluctuation — or the smallest price change allowed by the exchange — is set at $0.10/ounce. With a contract size of 100 ounces per futures contract, each minimum move is worth $0.10/ounce × 100, or $10 per contract.

The **Units Quoted** in the table above show the normal pricing of the abovementioned commodities. For example, Soybeans are quoted in cents/bushel (bu), so when you see a price of 589 1/2, that would read as 589 1/2 cents/bu — $5.89 1/2 per bushel.

Futures contracts are standardized in size as well. The **Contract Size** represents how much of the commodity is controlled by a futures contract and also how much a move is worth. For example, Gold futures represent 100 ounces of Gold; as such, each $1/ounce move is worth $100 before trading costs (commissions and fees). For a listing of what each contract is worth per unit move, see the **Point Value** column in the table above.

The futures exchanges also designate a minimum and sometimes maximum amount of movement allowed. The **Minimum Change** is also known as a "tick" in trading lingo. The value of a "tick" is derived by multiplying the minimum change amount by the contract size. For example, with a tick in Crude Oil being $0.01/bbl, a minimum move is worth $10/bbl, given the 1,000-barrel contract size. The maximum amount of movement is also known as **Daily Trade Limit**, meaning prices cannot move more than this amount in a single session. When they reach this threshold, trading beyond this price is halted.

G.M. LOEB'S "BATTLE PLAN" FOR SPECULATIVE SURVIVAL

LIFE IS CHANGE: Nothing can ever be the same a minute from now as it was a minute ago. Everything you own is changing in price and value. You can find the last price of an active security, but you cannot find the next price anywhere. The value of your money is changing. Even the value of your home is changing, though no one walks in front of it with a sandwich board consistently posting the changes.

RECOGNIZE CHANGE: Your basic objective should be to profit from change. The art of speculating is being able to recognize change and to adjust goals accordingly.

WRITE THINGS DOWN: You will score more investment success and avoid more investment failures if you write things down. Very few traders have the drive and inclination to do this, and therefore most speculators fail.

KEEP A CHECKLIST: If you aim to improve your investment results, get into the habit of keeping a checklist on every issue you consider buying. Before making a commitment, it will pay to write down the answers to at least some of the basic questions —How much am I investing in this position? How much do I think I can make? How much do I have to risk? How long do I expect to take to reach my goal?

HAVE A SINGLE RULING REASON: Above all, writing things down is the best way to find "the ruling reason." When all is said and done, there is invariably a single reason that stands out above all others why a particular security transaction can be expected to show a profit. All too often many relatively unimportant statistics are allowed to obscure this single important point.

Any one of a dozen factors may be the point of a particular purchase or sale. It could be a fundamental reason — an increase in supply or demand in the market price — a change of weather — a promising new use — an expected problem with production — or many others. But in any given case, one of these factors will almost certainly be more important than all the rest put together.

CLOSING OUT A COMMITMENT: If you have a loss, the solution is automatic, provided you decide what to do at the time you buy/sell. Otherwise, the question divides itself into two parts. Are we in a bull or bear market? Few of us really know until it is too late. For the sake of the record, if you think it is a bull/bear market, just put that consideration first and buy/sell as much as your conviction suggests and your account allows with prudent money management.

If you think it is a bull/bear market, or at least a market where the commodity moves up/down, do not sell/buy unless:

1) You see a bear/bull market ahead.

2) You see trouble for the particular market which you purchased.

3) Time and circumstances have turned up a new and seemingly far better trade than the the contract you like least on your list.

4) Your contracts stop going up/down and starts going down/up.

A subsidiary question is, which position to sell first? Two further observations may help:

1) Do not exit solely because you think a market is "overvalued" or "undervalued."

2) If you want to exit some of your positions and not all, in most cases it is better to go against your emotional inclinations and exit first the issues with losses, small profits or none at all, the laggards, the most disappointing, etc.

Mr. Loeb is the author of ***The Battle for Investment Survival****, John Wiley & Sons. The above list was originally put together for the stock market, and has been adapted by the author for futures — hence some paraphrasing and reorganization was done which hopefully does not diminish the work of the original author.*

G.M. LOEB'S INVESTMENT SURVIVAL CHECKLIST

OBJECTIVES AND RISKS

Position and Commodity	Entry Price	# of Contracts	Date

Ruling Reason For Position Entry:

Price Objective	Est. Time to Achieve	I Will Risk $	Which Will Be % of Account

TECHNICAL POSITION

Price Action:			Market Sentiment
New Highs	Y N	Consolidation Pattern	Commercial COT Trending Up / Trend Down
New Lows	Y N	Reversal Pattern	Non-Commercial COT Trending Up / Trend Down
Relative Strength vs Similar	Y N	Continuation Pattern	Non-Reportable COT Trending Up / Trend Down

FUNDAMENTAL YARDSTICK

	Current	Projected	Trend
Supply			Up / Down / Flat
Demand			Up / Down / Flat
Class	Tight / Neutral / Excessive	Tight / Neutral / Excessive	

Comments in Futures Supply/Demand Situation:

PERIODIC RECHECK

Date	Price	Stop Loss	Action Taken (If Any)

COMPLETED TRANSACTIONS

Entry Date	Entry Price	Exit Date	Exit Price	P & L
				$

Reason for Profit (Loss):

SHORT–TERM TRANSACTIONS

Pages 186 – 190 can accompany next year's income tax return (Schedule D). Enter transactions as completed to avoid last-minute pressures.

ENTRY DATE	LONG/ SHORT	CONTRACT	# OF CONTRACTS	EXIT DATE	P & L (in POINTS)	P & L (in $'s)	COMMISSIONS & FEES	NET P & L IN $'s
TOTALS:								

SHORT–TERM TRANSACTIONS

Pages 186 – 190 can accompany next year's income tax return (Schedule D). Enter transactions as completed to avoid last-minute pressures.

ENTRY DATE	LONG/ SHORT	CONTRACT	# OF CONTRACTS	EXIT DATE	P & L (in POINTS)	P & L (in $'s)	COMMISSIONS & FEES	NET P & L IN $'s
						TOTALS:		

SHORT–TERM TRANSACTIONS

Pages 186 – 190 can accompany next year's income tax return (Schedule D). Enter transactions as completed to avoid last-minute pressures.

ENTRY DATE	LONG/ SHORT	CONTRACT	# OF CONTRACTS	EXIT DATE	P & L (in POINTS)	P & L (in $'s)	COMMISSIONS & FEES	NET P & L IN $'s
					TOTALS:			

SHORT–TERM TRANSACTIONS

Pages 186 – 190 can accompany next year's income tax return (Schedule D). Enter transactions as completed to avoid last-minute pressures.

ENTRY DATE	LONG/ SHORT	CONTRACT	# OF CONTRACTS	EXIT DATE	P & L (in POINTS)	P & L (in $'s)	COMMISSIONS & FEES	NET P & L IN $'s
						TOTALS:		

SHORT–TERM TRANSACTIONS

Pages 186 – 190 can accompany next year's income tax return (Schedule D). Enter transactions as completed to avoid last-minute pressures.

ENTRY DATE	LONG/ SHORT	CONTRACT	# OF CONTRACTS	EXIT DATE	P & L (in POINTS)	P & L (in $'s)	COMMISSIONS & FEES	NET P & L IN $'s
						TOTALS:		

TOP COMMODITY WEB SITES

COMMODITY RESEARCH AND NEWS WEB SITES

PITNEWS: **http://www.PITNEWS.com**

Up-to-date research articles presented by a variety of industry analysts are available on Pitnews. More than a news site, Pitnews also offers a discussion board — "the Wall" — where traders of all stripes post questions and opinions. An excellent source of information.

DAILY FUTURES: **http://www.DAILYFUTURES.com**

A collection of brokerage industry reports and opinions covering all the major futures markets. An excellent source of information about the latest changes in supply and demand, as well as analysts' opinions on various markets.

COMMODITY FUTURES EXCHANGE WEB SITES

The exchanges post a lot of valuable information for futures traders. Contract specifications, expiration tables, time and sales data as well as news are all available on the various exchange sites.

CHICAGO BOARD OF TRADE (CBOT)	**http://www.CBOT.com**
CHICAGO MERCANTILE (CME)	**http://www.CME.com**
KANSAS CITY BOARD OF TRADE (KCBT)	**http://www.KCBT.com**
MINNEAPOLIS GRAIN EXCHANGE (MGEX)	**http://www.MGEX.com**
NEW YORK BOARD OF TRADE (NYBOT)	**http://www.NYBOT.com**
NEW YORK MERCANTILE (NYMEX)	**http://www.NYMEX.com**

COMMODITY FUTURES QUOTES AND CHARTS

Access to prices and charts are important for futures traders. The following list presents some of my own personal favorite charting and price Web sites. All offer free 20-minute delayed futures/options quotes, with some offering historical charting capabilities, data conversions, or news and current weather information.

CHARTBOOK *(historical charting)*	**http://www.CHARTBOOK.com**
FUTURES SOURCE *(news & weather)*	**http://www.FUTURESOURCE.com**
TFC TRADING CHARTS *(news & weather)*	**http://FUTURES.TRADINGCHARTS.com**

CSI DATA **http://www.CSIDATA.com**

A great source for long-term data with the ability to splice and dice the data into weekly/monthly data files.

PINNACLE DATA **http://www.PINNACLEDATA.com**

An excellent source for historical data. Pinnacle provides data sets not readily available from other vendors, such as cash prices, money supply figures, as well as a host of other esoteric data often not found from other providers. Their depth and accuracy of data is also extremely impressive.

COMMODITY FUTURES REGULATORY BODIES

The futures industry is regulated by the National Futures Association (NFA) and the Commodity Futures Trading Commission (CFTC), in a fashion similar to the way the Stock Market is regulated by the Securities and Exchange Commission (SEC) and the National Association of Securities Dealers (NASD). The regulatory entities have a tremendous amount of information available for traders, including informational brochures as well as background information on registered firms and their representatives (brokers).

COMMODITY FUTURES TRADING COMMISSION (CFTC)	**http://www.CFTC.gov**
COMMITMENT OF TRADERS	**http://www.cftc.gov/cftc/cftccotreports.htm**
NATIONAL FUTURES ASSOCIATION (NFA)	**http://www.NFA.FUTURES.org**
INVESTOR LEARNING CENTER	**http://www.nfa.futures.org/investor/investorLearningCenter.asp**
BACKGROUND AFFILIATION SERVICE	**http://www.NFA.FUTURES.org/BASICNET/**

IMPORTANT CONTACTS

NAME	TELEPHONE		E-MAIL